# Inventing Elvis

# Inventing Elvis

## An American Icon in a Cold War World

*Mathias Haeussler*

BLOOMSBURY ACADEMIC
LONDON · NEW YORK · OXFORD · NEW DELHI · SYDNEY

BLOOMSBURY ACADEMIC
Bloomsbury Publishing Plc
50 Bedford Square, London, WC1B 3DP, UK
1385 Broadway, New York, NY 10018, USA

BLOOMSBURY, BLOOMSBURY ACADEMIC and the Diana logo
are trademarks of Bloomsbury Publishing Plc

First published in Great Britain 2021

Cover Design: Terry Woodley
Cover image: Elvis backstage before his second appearance on the
Ed Sullivan show © CBS Photo Archive / Getty Images

A catalogue record for this book is available from the British Library.

Library of Congress Cataloging-in-Publication Data

Names: Haeussler, Mathias, 1988- author.
Title: Inventing Elvis : an American icon in a cold war world / Mathias Haeussler.
Description: New York : Bloomsbury Academic, 2020. | Includes bibliographical
references and index.
Identifiers: LCCN 2020032064 (print) | LCCN 2020032065 (ebook) | ISBN 9781350107663
(hardback) | ISBN 9781350107656 (paperback) | ISBN 9781350107670 (epub) |
ISBN 9781350107687 (ebook)
Subjects: LCSH: Presley, Elvis, 1935–1977–Criticism and interpretation. | Popular culture–United
States–History–20th century. | Popular culture–Europe–History–20th century. |
Music and race–United States–History–20th century.
Classification: LCC ML420.P96 H2 2020 (print) | LCC ML420.P96 (ebook) |
DDC 782.4216092 [B]–dc23
LC record available at https://lccn.loc.gov/2020032064
LC ebook record available at https://lccn.loc.gov/2020032065

ISBN:     HB:      978-1-3501-0766-3
          PB:      978-1-3501-0765-6
          ePDF:    978-1-3501-0768-7
          eBook:   978-1-3501-0767-0

Typeset by Integra Software Services Pvt. Ltd.,

To find out more about our authors and books visit www.bloomsbury.com and
sign up for our newsletters.

# CONTENTS

# ILLUSTRATIONS

# ACKNOWLEDGMENTS

On a hot summer evening in August 2010, I boarded the City of New Orleans overnight train in Chicago and traveled down the Mississippi to see Memphis for the very first time. The visit to Graceland, of course, was the highlight of the trip. Passing through the mansion's Trophy Room and staring at all the flashy jumpsuits, golden records, and other awards on display, I noticed a small, rather unpretentious certificate in one corner of the room. It was issued by Secretary of Defense Donald Rumsfeld, and it thanked Elvis for his service during the Cold War. It immediately got me thinking: what on earth might somebody like Elvis Presley have to do with the Cold War? While I have since learned that the so-called Cold War Recognition Certificate can be obtained by any person who had served the armed forces or federal government during the period, the question stuck in my mind, and the vague idea to write something about Elvis and the Cold War has not left me since. Ten years later, here we are.

That such a fairly exotic idea could eventually turn into reality has been made possible by the strong support of a large number of people and institutions. First and foremost, I would like to thank my colleagues at the Chair of European History at the University of Regensburg, particularly Thomas Götz, Christin Hansen, Cornelius Merz, Bernadette Mischka, and Alexandra Prem, for all their support and encouragement. Rainer Liedtke has been an outstanding mentor over the past few years, and I am glad that he took over the responsibility of patiently reintegrating me into the German academic system after my sixteen-year hiatus. I am also grateful to the German Historical Institute in Washington DC for providing me with a Postdoctoral Research Fellowship to conduct research in the United States, as well as to my "alma mater" the John W. Kluge Center at the Library of Congress for administrative assistance during my stays—and for welcoming me back with open arms! The project first took shape during my time as Lumley Research Fellow at Magdalene College of the University of Cambridge, and I still feel immeasurably privileged that I have been able to spend three years in such a vibrant and intellectually stimulating community.

Many archivists have aided my research over the past few years, and they often went out of their way to identify some of the rather peculiar materials I was looking for. I would particularly like to thank Ned Comstock at the Cinematic Arts Library at the University of Southern California who uncovered some amazing sources for Elvis's Hollywood years, Valoise

Armstrong at the Eisenhower Presidential Library, Jim Cole at the University of Memphis, and Grace Hall at Tupelo's Lee County Library. I would also like to thank the staff at the Margaret Herrick Library in Los Angeles, the Kultur- und Militärmuseum Grafenwöhr, the Roosevelt Institute for American Studies in Middelburg (Netherlands) and the U.S. National Archives in College Park, MD.

Many friends and colleagues have graciously devoted their time and energy to read all or parts of the manuscript. I am indebted to Christiane Bauer, Tobias Becker, Florian Greiner, and Mechthild Roos for their thorough and incredibly useful feedback. As renowned Elvis experts as well as brilliant academics in their own right, Mark Duffett and Bertel Nygaard have both offered invaluable comments on large parts of the manuscript, as well as numerous other tips and advice over the years. Thank you! Finally, Jasmin Lörchner and Matthias Scherer have read the manuscript with the eyes of the general reader: I am lucky to count them among my closest friends, and I am so happy that they have approved of it.

The project has benefited enormously from the input and encouragement of many others who have all offered encouragement and help in big or small ways at various stages of the project. They include Michael Bertrand, Mark Fenemore, Peter Guralnick, Douglas Harrison, Kyle Longley, Brian McAllister Linn, Landon Palmer, Helmut Rademacher, David Reynolds, Paul Vickers, James Woodall, and Tom Zeiler. The support of the editorial team at Bloomsbury has also been outstanding—thank you, Maddie Holder, Dan Hutchins, and Abigail Lane!

Many friends have generously tolerated my ramblings on Elvis over the years, while at the same time never failing to demonstrate that there are some things in life even bigger than the King of Rock 'n' Roll. For all the fun and friendship, I am grateful to Phillip Brandl, Florian Bruns, Phillip Feier (Sinatra is in Chapter 3!), Anja Fricke, Alexa Kornau, Therese Herrmann (Elvis The Concert 2003!), Martin Huber, Paul Langfermann, Jenny Leetsch, Wanda Martini, Kati and Maximilian Meckes, Frank Michel, Lizzie Norton (Elvis The Concert 2011!), Manuel Wagner, Sina Weidner, Maximilian Westphal, and Katharina Zech.

I am extremely blessed that I can always rely on the unquestioning support of my family, and I am grateful to everybody for having endured my frequent physical (and non-physical) absences so patiently over the past few years. As always, my parents, Astrid and Gerhard Häußler, have been unwavering in their help and encouragement, as has my "other" family: Karin Grundler and, on the other side of the pond, Karin Grundler-Whitacre, Matthew Withacre, and all the McLaughlins! The biggest thanks, however, are due to Maria-Theresa, whose energy, sparkle, and good humor have brightened up even the most challenging of writing days. This book would never have happened without her love and support—and her willingness to sit through countless hours of Elvis movies.

# Introduction

Elvis Presley defined American culture to billions of adoring fans around the world. Elvis fused gospel, country, and rhythm and blues to create a sound all his own, selling more than a billion records. Elvis also served nearly 2 years in the United States Army, humbly accepting the call to serve despite his fame. He later starred in 31 films, drew record-breaking audiences to his shows, sent television ratings soaring, and earned 14 GRAMMY Award nominations. He ultimately won 3 GRAMMY Awards for his gospel music. Elvis Presley remains an enduring American icon 4 decades after his death.—*Statement by the White House, 'Presidential Medal of Freedom', 16 November 2018.*[1]

In November 2018, US President Donald Trump awarded Elvis Presley the Presidential Medal of Freedom, the country's highest civilian honor, to commemorate the singer's cultural and historical importance. But he was by no means the first American President trying to bask in the glory of the King of Rock 'n' Roll. In 2006, for example, George W. Bush took the Japanese Prime Minister Junichiro Koizumi on a much-publicized tour of Elvis's former mansion Graceland, where the lifelong Elvis fan Koizumi astounded journalists with karate kicks and an impromptu rendition of "Love Me Tender."[2] In 1992, Bill Clinton's election campaign received a much-needed boost by the presidential candidate's saxophone performance of "Heartbreak Hotel" on live television.[3] And Richard Nixon's famous 1970 photograph with Elvis Presley in the Oval Office remains the most

---

[1]The White House, "Medal of Freedom," www.whitehouse.gov/medaloffreedom/ [last accessed February 12, 2019].
[2]*Los Angeles Times*, July 1, 2006.
[3]Daniel Marcus, *Happy Days and Wonder Years: The Fifties and the Sixties in Contemporary Cultural Politics* (Piscataway, NJ: Rutgers University Press, 2004), 155–60.

requested item in the history of the US National Archives, more popular even than the Declaration of Independence.[4]

The associations of Elvis Presley with American culture run deep, and they stretch far beyond such narrow political appropriations. As early as 1975, the music writer Greil Marcus used Elvis as a case study to investigate the role of rock 'n' roll in constructing US cultural identities after 1945, depicting him as "a supreme figure in American life, one whose presence, no matter how banal or predictable, brooks no real comparisons ... Presley's career almost has the scope to take America in."[5] Already at the time, however, such equations of Elvis with notions of American identity could evoke negative as well as positive associations. "Nowhere is the adage that America seeks heroes not for their qualities but for their marketability more brutally illustrated than in the case of Elvis," the journalist and later Elvis biographer Peter Guralnick wrote around the same time, depicting him as an artist "whom success first gutted, then abandoned to a twenty-years state of suspended animation."[6] When Elvis died on August 16, 1977, President Jimmy Carter issued a statement that transfigured the singer into the very embodiment of US popular culture. "Elvis Presley's death deprives our country of a part of itself," he declared. "His music and his personality, fusing the styles of white country and black rhythm and blues, permanently changed the face of American popular culture. His following was immense and he was a symbol to people the world over, of the vitality, rebelliousness, and good humor of his country."[7]

And yet, Elvis Presley was an unlikely American hero at first. Growing up as a marginalized poor white in the postwar South, Elvis belonged to a socioeconomic group that seemed excluded even from the allegedly all-encompassing American Dream of capitalist advancement and social mobility. As Elvis then gained national popularity against all odds, his controversial fusion of African American rhythm 'n' blues with hillbilly country, as well as his sexually charged live performances, sent shockwaves through Eisenhower's deeply conservative 1950s America, and in so doing exposed the country's profound divisions along the lines of class, gender, and race. And although Elvis achieved unprecedented levels of popularity all around the globe, he was frequently denounced in East and West as part of an

[4]*Daily Telegraph*, June 20, 2016.

[5]Greil Marcus, *Mystery Train: Images of America in Rock 'n' Roll Music* (New York: E.P. Dutton & Co., 1975), 137–8.

[6]"Elvis Presley and the American Dream," as reprinted in Peter Guralnick, *Lost Highway: Journeys & Arrivals of American Musicians* (Edinburgh: Canongate, 1979 [2002]), 4; 118–40. Guralnick states that the essay was written approximately 18 months before Elvis died, i.e. around February 1976.

[7]"Death of Elvis Presley: Statement by the President," August 17, 1977, in Jimmy Carter, *Public Papers of the Presidents of the United States: Jimmy Carter, 1977* (Washington, DC: United States Government Printing Office, 1978), 1478.

unwanted American cultural infiltration; a symbol of the alleged decadence and corruption of US mass culture amid the ideological competition of the Cold War. So, why the apotheosis? What changed?

This book is not a biography. Rather, it seeks to explore the complex transformation of Elvis Presley from a seeming outsider position into one of the US' major pop-cultural icons of the twentieth century, as well as the rich political and cultural meanings that were attributed to him between his rise to fame in the mid-1950s and his tragic death in August 1977. Setting Elvis firmly against the rapidly changing sociocultural background of his times, it asks which factors facilitated Elvis's rise in the first place, why he came to embody such manifold and diverse meanings to so many people, and what bigger questions of American identity became articulated through his public image. The book's perspective is both multilayered and transnational: it integrates voices of politicians, diplomats, and soldiers as well as fans, journalists, and the wider public, and it looks not only at Elvis's reception in the United States but all around the world, particularly in Eastern and Western Europe. In so doing, the book not only offers a fresh take on Elvis Presley's unique career from a historical perspective but also sheds light on the powerful, yet ambivalent, role of popular culture in shaping internal and external perceptions of the United States after 1945.

# The Rise of Elvis and Youth Culture after 1945

Elvis Presley was, of course, by no means the first celebrity that ever existed on this earth. He was not even the first celebrity of modern times. Although some have traced the concepts of fame and celebrity back to ancient history, modern-day celebrity culture had its origins in the eighteenth century, a time in which the wider public first became fascinated by *living* artists, performers, or writers, as opposed to religious icons or mythical figures from the past.[8] It was only in the mid-nineteenth century, however, that an almost industrialized production of celebrities came into being, largely as the result of new opportunities for the mass replication of sounds and images through technological advances like photography, film, or phonographic recordings. By the end of the century, personalities from theater to opera were routinely marketed as "stars" in illustrated fan magazines or popular newspapers, a practice eventually adapted and popularized by Hollywood's studio system in the 1920s.[9] Major companies like Metro-Goldwyn-Mayer (MGM) or Warner Bros. Pictures, Inc. consciously centered their marketing efforts on their in-house actresses and actors, who at the time received up to 32 million

---

[8]Sharon Marcus, *The Drama of Celebrity* (Princeton, NJ: Princeton University Press, 2019), 9.
[9]Ibid., 10–13.

items of fan mail every year.[10] Popular singers like Bing Crosby or Frank Sinatra too had by the 1940s come to amass hordes of admirers.[11]

Elvis, however, signaled a new and arguably even more profound phenomenon: the arrival and eventual dominance of an altogether new type of popular culture in the late 1950s and 1960s.[12] Although the roots of mass entertainment can be traced back as far as the nineteenth century, it was only after 1945 that popular culture became a truly dominant historical force, and that it acquired some new features that distinguished it from previous modes of mass entertainment.[13] This was due to a complex combination of cultural and socioeconomic transformations, technological advances, and the resulting changes in the media landscape in the postwar years.[14] During the late 1940s and early 1950s, high economic growth and rising prosperity, as well as the expansion of secondary and tertiary education, had triggered the emergence of a new demographic group: the so-called teenagers, young adolescents somewhere between childhood and full adulthood who suddenly found themselves with a lot more time and money on their hands than previous generations.[15] Trying to carve themselves new and distinct generational identities, they relied heavily on mass media and other cultural products, as well as on more abstract generational denominators like clothing styles, haircuts, and day-to-day leisure activities. In marked contrast to nineteenth-century mass culture, the *active* and *creative* adaptation of mass-produced cultural products was therefore an integral part of the postwar popular culture, which was intrinsically connected to a new generation's attempt to create its own distinct cultural niche.

Elvis Presley was not the first teenage hero of the 1950s, but he quickly became the new generation's major embodiment and most prominent cultural icon. Part of the reason was that Elvis managed to appeal on several levels, rather than being confined to a particular genre or media outlet. While Hollywood stars like James Dean or Marlon Brando had already popularized images of juvenile rebellion during the early 1950s, just as Alan Freed and Bill Haley had demonstrated youths' appetite for rock 'n' roll.

---

[10]Mark Duffett, *Understanding Fandom: An Introduction to the Study of Media Fan Culture* (London: Bloomsbury, 2013), 7.

[11]Ibid., 8.

[12]Bodo Mrozek, *Jugend—Pop—Kultur: Eine transnationale Geschichte* (Berlin: Suhrkamp, 2019), 14–28.

[13]Lawrence W. Levine, *Highbrow/Lowbrow: The Emergence of Cultural Hierarchy in America* (Cambridge, MA: Harvard University Press, 1990); Jon Savage, *Teenage: The Creation of Youth 1875–1945* (London: Pimlico, 2008); Kaspar Maase, *Grenzenloses Vergnügen: Der Aufstieg der Massenkultur 1850–1970* (Frankfurt a. Main: Fischer Taschenbuch Verlag, 1997).

[14]The classic work is Richard A. Peterson, "Why 1955? Explaining the Advent of Rock Music," *Poplar Music* 9/1 (1990), 97–116. More generally Deena Weinstein, *Rock'n America: A Social and Cultural History* (Toronto: University of Toronto Press, 2015), 23–71.

[15]Leerom Medovoi, *Rebels: Youth and the Cold War Origins of Identity* (Durham, NC and London: Duke University Press, 2005), 24–30.

Elvis was the first celebrity to fuse these two major trends, and in so doing became the focal point for his generation's emerging self-consciousness.[16] It also helped that such cross-platform appeal was accentuated by a highly innovative marketing strategy that made full use of the new opportunities provided by the changing media landscape, turning the singer into a new type of mass media phenomenon.[17]

What further differentiated Elvis from previous-day celebrities was that he became politicized almost in an instant. In the mid-1950, Elvis's public image was immersed in much bigger debates over questions of taste and appropriate public behavior, as well as underlying issues of class, gender, and race. Indeed, his rise offers a supreme example of how 1950s youth culture constituted a struggle over cultural hegemony and generational control: as traditional authorities denounced Elvis as a morally dangerous threat, his hordes of (usually young) supporters embraced him precisely because he was seen to challenge the established social and moral orders of the day.[18] Yet, while Elvis might well be seen as a case study for the emancipatory potential of postwar popular culture,[19] his political meaning became reversed as time went on. Elvis's two years of military service between 1958 and 1960 reframed the erstwhile rebel into a patriotic all-American boy; while his subsequent careers as Hollywood movie star and Las Vegas entertainer were often, if somewhat misleadingly, seen as his ultimate commodification by the American establishment.[20] Although neither Elvis's 1950s rebel persona nor his more conservative image in the 1960s and 1970s were entirely accurate characterizations of his multifaceted personality, they both still resonate heavily with Elvis's legacy today.

Finally, Elvis was novel in that his popularity constituted an almost global phenomenon from the very beginning of his career. To some extent, of course, the singer's international exposure was simply the result of the US' unprecedented political and economic expansion after 1945, which

---

[16]J. Ronald Oakley, *God's Country: America in the Fifties* (New York: W. W. Norton, 1986), 276.

[17]David Shumway, *Rock Star: The Making of Musical Icons from Elvis to Springsteen* (Baltimore, MD: Johns Hopkins University Press, 2014), 24–45; Landon Palmer, "'And Introducing Elvis Presley': Industrial Convergence and Transmedia Stardom in the Rock 'n' Roll Movie," *Music, Sound & the Moving Image* 9/2 (2015), 177–90; Marc Weingarten, *Station to Station: The Secret History of Rock 'n' Roll on Television* (New York, NY: Pocket Books, 2000), 18–39.

[18]James Gilbert, *A Cycle of Outrage: America's Reaction to the Juvenile Delinquent in the 1950s* (New York and Oxford: Oxford University Press, 1986), 10.

[19]For the emancipatory potentials of popular culture during the 1960s, see also Detlef Siegfried, *Time Is On My Side: Konsum und Politik in der westdeutschen Jugendkultur der 60er Jahre* (Göttingen: Wallstein, 2006); Julia Sneeringer, *A Social History of Early Rock 'n' Roll in Germany: Hamburg from Burlesque to The Beatles, 1956–69* (London: Bloomsbury, 2018), 39–40.

[20]Mark Duffett, *Elvis: Roots, Image, Comeback, Phenomenon* (Sheffield: Equinox, 2020), 13.

also opened up lucrative new markets for American popular culture abroad.[21] Yet, Elvis's international popularity was not merely a question of cultural export; at its heart were much more complex dynamics, not least the emergence of a highly transnational youth culture that was intimately interconnected and shared structural similarities that transcended national borders.[22] Nonetheless, the meaning of Elvis at home could at times differ substantially from his reception abroad: like all cultural exports, Elvis was often understood, modified, and appropriated to particular national or local circumstances.[23]

At first sight, then, Elvis Presley might seem to simply have been in the right place at the right time; the first major beneficiary of the wider political, socioeconomic, and cultural transformations after 1945. Yet, while all of these bigger dynamics undoubtedly constituted important preconditions for his rise to fame, they are not in themselves sufficient to explain his enormous cultural significance. For this, we have to zoom in further and look at the particularities of his life and career.

## Why Elvis? An American Icon in a Cold War World

"Icons are stars who have acquired their own myths and mythologies," Mark Duffett writes in his major study of media fan culture; they "represent points of intervention in the broadest moral discourses that define society."[24] Much like historical or religious icons, modern-day celebrities often serve as articulation points for bigger questions; and many of the discourses and images we associate with them reflect bigger cultural meanings.[25] Elvis's

---

[21]Emily S. Rosenberg, *Spreading the American Dream: American Economic and Cultural Expansion, 1890–1945* (New York, NY: Hill and Wang, 1982); Victoria de Grazia, *Irresistible Empire. America's Advance Through Twentieth-Century Europe* (Cambridge, MA: Belknap Press, 2005); Mary Nolan, *The Transatlantic Century: Europe and America, 1890–2010* (Cambridge: Cambridge University Press, 2012).

[22]Mrozek, *Jugend—Pop—Kultur*, 28–33.

[23]Reinhold Wagnleitner and Elaine Tyler May (eds.), *"Here, There and Everywhere": The Foreign Politics of American Popular Culture* (Hanover, NH: University Press of New England, 2000); Richard Pells, *Not Like Us: How Europeans Have Loved, Hated, and Transformed American Culture Since World War II* (New York, NY: BasicBooks, 1997); Sabrina P. Ramet and Gordana P. Crnković (eds.), *Kazaaam! Splat! Ploof! The American Impact on European Popular Culture since 1945* (Lanham, MD: Rowman & Littlefield, 2003).

[24]Duffett, *Understanding Fandom*, 213–14.

[25]Russell Meeuf and Raphael Raphael, "Introduction," in Russell Meeuf and Raphael Raphael (eds.), *Transnational Stardom: International Celebrity in Film and Popular Culture* (New York, NY: Palgrave Macmillan, 2013), 2; For Elvis as a cultural articulation point, see Gilbert B. Rodman, *Elvis after Elvis: The posthumous career of a living legend* (London and New York: Routledge, 1996), 24; also Harry Sewall, "'Image, Music, Text': Elvis Presley as a Postmodern, Semiotic Construct," *Journal of Literary Studies* 26/2 (2010), 44–57.

popularity was not only the result of his unquestionable musical talent; it was also due to the fact that his public image was inextricably intertwined with some of the most heavily contested issues in the postwar United States. Indeed, Elvis's image has been seen to reflect, as well as to challenge, some of the most central myths at the heart of American identity constructions after 1945.[26]

Elvis's relationship with key themes of US postwar history has always been complicated and often contradictory, and even some of the most central aspects of his legacy continue to be hotly contested even today.[27] Did Elvis emancipate Southern culture on the national stage, for example, or did he never quite manage to shake off the class contempt and cultural snobbism that was often directed against him?[28] Did his creative adaptation of rhythm 'n' blues music pave the way for the eventual acceptance of African American styles in mainstream US popular culture, or did the singer appropriate and exploit its cultural heritage for personal gain?[29] And did his sexualized on-stage performances liberate 1950s America from the stiffness and conservatism of the Eisenhower years, perhaps even paving the way for the 1960s sexual revolution, or did the Elvis phenomenon ultimately reinforce traditional and patriarchal gender roles? Many of these debates already emerged during the earliest days of his career, and, while their parameters often changed massively over time, they continue to be associated with Elvis Presley to this day.

During the 1950s, such debates resonated particularly powerfully because they played out at a crucial historical moment: the early Cold War.[30] The all-out competition between the United States and the Soviet Union not only encompassed the two superpowers' global rivalry, but it also penetrated domestic societies. In the United States, it manifested itself in deep-seated fears of communist infiltration, triggering a period of particularly acute self-reflection that resulted in various attempts to create a seemingly homogenous US identity based on mass consumption and the suburbanized nuclear family.[31] In reality, however, such identity constructions were never

---

[26]Rodman, *Elvis after Elvis*, 82; Duffett, *Elvis*, 2–3.

[27]Rodman, *Elvis after Elvis*, 40.

[28]Linda Ray Pratt, "Elvis, or the Ironies of a Southern Identity," in Kevin Quain (ed.), *The Elvis Reader* (New York: St. Martin's Press, 1992), 93–103; Susan Doll, *Understanding Elvis: Southern Roots Vs. Star Image* (London and New York: Routledge, 1998 [2016]).

[29]Michael Bertrand, *Race, Rock, and Elvis* (Chicago, IL: University of Illinois Press, 2004).

[30]For an earlier stimulating interpretive take on Elvis's relationship with the Cold War, inspired by the author's visit of an Elvis exhibit at the General George Patton Museum, see Jon Wiener, *How We Forgot the Cold War: A Historical Journey across America* (Berkeley, CA: University of California Press, 2012), 166–82.

[31]Elaine Tyler May, *Homeward Bound: American Families in the Cold War Era* (New York, NY: Basic Books, 1988 [1999]); Douglas Field (ed.), *American Cold War Culture* (Edinburgh: University Press, 2005), 1–16.

accepted completely, particularly in light of the country's strong social and racial divisions breeding underneath the surface of the so-called Cold War consensus.[32] Set against this background, Elvis not only reflected some of the major tensions of the 1950s United States; he also constituted a formidable challenge to some of the prevailing societal norms of the day.

Outside the United States, the Cold War politicized Elvis in rather different ways. Although the generational dynamics underlying the singer's rise in many parts of the world constituted a highly transnational phenomenon, the burgeoning East–West conflict infused Elvis with a powerful additional connotation: the idea of Elvis as the major example of an alleged American infiltration of external societies. In Europe in particular, Elvis came to serve as focal point to negotiate much more general attitudes toward the postwar United States: in West Germany, for example, the singer's opponents depicted him as a prime example of the US' alleged cultural imperialism and primitivism of its mass culture, whereas his supporters embraced him as the prime symbol of American-style modernity and coolness.[33] Elvis's intimate association with bigger notions of American culture and lifestyles thus meant that much bigger questions of social and cultural change in the age of modernity were negotiated through his public image.

There were also more direct attempts to utilize Elvis for political purposes. To be sure, the US State Department stayed well clear of recruiting Elvis for its extensive cultural diplomacy efforts during the 1950s.[34] Given the singer's class background, as well as his widespread association with juvenile delinquency and African American culture, most US officials seem to have regarded Elvis as a danger, rather than as an opportunity, to the

---

[32]Joanne Meyerowitz, "The Liberal 1950s? Reinterpreting Postwar U.S. Sexual Culture," in Karen Hagemann and Sonya Michel (eds.), *Gender and the Long Postwar: Reconsiderations of the United States and the Two Germanys, 1945–1989* (Baltimore, MD: Johns Hopkins University Press, 2014), 297–319; Medovoi, *Rebels*, 23.

[33]Uta G. Poiger, *Jazz, Rock, And Rebels: Cold War Politics and American Culture in a Divided Germany* (Berkeley and Los Angeles, CA: University of California Press, 2000), 167–205; Kaspar Maase, *BRAVO Amerika: Erkunden zur Jugendkultur der Bundesrepublik in den fünfziger Jahren* (Hamburg: Junius, 1992); for longer-term continuities, Alf Lüdtke, Inge Marßolek and Adelheid von Saldern, "Amerikanisierung: Traum und Alptraum im Deutschland des 20. Jahrhunderts," in Alf Lüdtke, Inge Marßolek, Adelheid von Saldern (eds.), *Amerikanisierung: Traum und Alptraum im Deutschland des 20. Jahrhunderts* (Stuttgart: Steiner Verlag, 1996), 7–36; Jessica Gienow-Hecht, *Transmission Impossible: American Journalism as Cultural Diplomacy in Postwar Germany 1945–1955* (Baton Rouge, LA: Louisiana State University Press, 1999), 10–11.

[34]For general background, see David Caute, *The Dancer Defects: The Struggle for Cultural Supremacy during the Cold War* (Oxford: Oxford University Press, 2003); Michael L. Krenn, *The History of United States Cultural Diplomacy: 1770 to the Present Day* (London: Bloomsbury Academic, 2017).

bigger messages the United States hoped to project at the time.[35] In due course, however, many realized Elvis's propagandistic value not as a singer, but as a pop-cultural symbol for American ideals of social mobility and mass consumerism. During his much-publicized stint in the army, for example, Elvis also acted as a sort of informal ambassador for the so-called American Way of Life in West Germany; many of his 1960s Hollywood movies too projected highly positive, if somewhat blunt, images of capitalist life in the postwar United States.

None of the bigger images and narratives associated with Elvis remained constant or static over time. Like all other cultural artefacts, Elvis's image and the cultural constructions surrounding him constantly and continuously changed their meanings throughout his lifetime. In so doing, they often reflected their exponents' changing needs and agendas, as well as a rapidly changing sociocultural background. Elvis's stint as G.I. soldier, for example, almost single-handedly eradicated his rebel image and turned him into an all-American patriotic boy in the eyes of the wider American public; just as his subsequent Hollywood movies showcased him as a one-dimensional happy-go-lucky chap in ways that completely ignored the racial and sexual dimensions that had been at the heart of his earlier appeal. In the 1970s, Elvis was then re-constructed and canonized as the seeming embodiment of an imagined American past, even though the highly sanitized images of his 1950s legacy frequently ignored the historical tensions that had facilitated his rise in the first place. And today, the countless cultural fragments of Elvis continue to resonate in highly ambivalent and often contradictory ways. It is part of the reason why, more than forty years after his passing, Elvis still "evokes like crazy."[36]

# Inventing Elvis: The Making of a Pop-Cultural Icon

This book does not seek to offer yet another impressionistic interpretation of Elvis Presley's complex relationship with the United States; nor does it provide an in-depth investigation of his contemporary cultural relevance or posthumous popularity. Rather, it takes a step back to offer a historically grounded study of Elvis that is firmly embedded in its wider political, social, and cultural background. As a result, the book focuses primarily on

---

[35]Danielle Fosler-Lussier, *Music in America's Cold War Diplomacy* (Oakland, CA: University of California Press, 2015), 143–5; Laura A. Belmonte, *Selling the American Way: US. Propaganda and the Cold War* (Philadelphia: University of Pennsylvania Press, 2008), 179.
[36]Marcus, *Mystery Train*, 147.

Elvis's active career from the mid-1950s to his death in August 1977, rather than on his curious cultural afterlife on which most academic studies have concentrated to date.[37] By contrast, the comparatively few historical works on Elvis's actual life and career have largely been confined to a plethora of biographies,[38] or they have tended to investigate only particular aspects of his life and career.[39] With a few very notable exceptions, most of these works have also adapted largely US-centric perspectives.[40] This book thus breaks

---

[37]Apart from the above-mentioned excellent *Elvis after Elvis* by Gilbert Rodman, there are Greil Marcus, *Dead Elvis: A Chronicle of a Cultural Obsession* (New York, NY: Doubleday, 1991); Ted Harrison, *The Death and Resurrection of Elvis Presley* (London: Reaktion Books, 2016); Erika Lee Doss, *Elvis Culture: Fans, Faith & Image* (Lawrence, KA: University Press of Kansas, 1999); Vernon Chadwick (ed.), *In Search of Elvis: Music, Race, Art, Religion* (New York, NY and London: Routledge, 1997).

[38]There have been countless biographies written on Elvis Presley. The gold standard is Peter Guralnick's two-volume magnum opus: Peter Guralnick, *Last Train to Memphis: The Rise of Elvis Presley* (London: Abacus, 1995); Peter Guralnick, *Careless Love: The Unmaking of Elvis Presley* (London: Abacus, 2000). For the first serious biography of Elvis published during his lifetime, see Jerry Hopkins, *Elvis* (New York: Simon & Schuster, 1971). It still contains a lot of useful information, as does Dave Marsh's more interpretative *Elvis* (New York, NY: Times Books, 1982). The singer's earliest years are covered particularly well in Elaine Dundy, *Elvis and Gladys* (New York: Macmillan, 1985). Mark Duffett's recent *Elvis: Roots, Image, Comeback, Phenomenon* (Sheffield: Equinox, 2020) provides a brilliant cultural-studies perspective on some of the major interpretations surrounding the singer. A handy little introductory guide written by one of the foremost Elvis specialists is Paul Simpson, *The Rough Guide to Elvis* (London: Rough Guides, 2002). For recent attempts to add something new to the vast canon of biographies, see Spencer Leigh, *Elvis Presley: Caught in a Trap* (Carmarthen: McNidder & Grace, 2017); Ray Connolly, *Being Elvis: A Lonely Life* (London: Weidenfeld & Nicholson, 2016); Joel Williamson, *Elvis Presley: A Southern Life* (Oxford: Oxford University Press, 2014); Glen Jeansonne, David Luhrssen, and Dan Sokolovic, *Elvis Presley, Reluctant Rebel: His Life and Our Times* (Santa Barbara, CA: Praeger, 2011).

[39]There are various general histories of 1950s rock 'n' roll, which are included in the first chapter. As regards historical studies that focus on particular aspects of Elvis's life, career, and image, see Bertrand, *Race, Rock, and Elvis*; Richard Zoglin, *Elvis in Vegas: How the King Reinvented the Las Vegas Show* (London: Simon & Schuster, 2019); Doll, *Understanding Elvis*; Mark Duffett, *Counting Down Elvis: His 100 Finest Songs* (Lanham, MD: Rowman & Littlefield, 2018); James L. Neibaur, *The Elvis Movies* (London: Rowman & Littlefield, 2014); Paul Simpson, *Elvis Films FAQ: All That's Left to Know about the King of Rock 'n' Roll in Hollywood* (New York, NY: Applause, 2014); Douglas Brode, *Elvis Cinema and Popular Culture* (Jefferson, NC: McFarland & Company, 2006); Allen J. Wiener, *Channeling Elvis: How Television Saved the King of Rock 'n' Roll* (Potomac, MD: Beats & Measures Press, 2014).

[40]Poiger, *Jazz, Rock, And Rebels*, 167–205; Christian Peters and Jürgen Reiche, *Elvis in Deutschland* (Bonn: Haus der Geschichte, 2004); Bertel Nygaard, "The High Priest of Rock and Roll: The Reception of Elvis Presley in Denmark, 1956–1960," *Popular Music and Society* 42/3 (2019), 330–47; Timo Toivonen and Antero Laiho, "'You Don't Like Crazy Music': The Reception of Elvis Presley in Finland," *Popular Music and Society* 13 (1989), 1–22; Harry Sewlall, "Elvis Presley in the South African Musical Imaginary," *Acta Academica* 47/2 (2015), 54–71. There are also several general studies of rock 'n' roll with an international dimension, discussed in Chapter 2.

new ground not only by setting Elvis firmly within the historical context of his life and times, but also by putting his career in a wider transnational and international setting.

Celebrities like Elvis Presley, of course, do not simply pop up out of nowhere: they are products of complex interplays between their own art and personality, the mediation of their images by management, press, and media, as well as by the meanings that are endowed on them by fans and the wider public.[41] In trying to investigate Elvis's historical importance and cultural meanings, the book thus explores a broad range of perspectives and actors, who continuously influenced but quite often also competed with each other.

The by far most important inventor of "Elvis," of course, was Elvis himself. In light of some of the broader structural reasons behind his success, it is necessary to first stress the originality and brilliance of Elvis as a vocalist and performer. Although he never wrote his own songs, his almost encyclopedical knowledge of music—gospel, rhythm 'n' blues, country, pop ballads, schmaltz—not only enabled him to indiscriminately select and interpret a great variety of different material but also helped him fuse many different and highly diverse musical styles in a highly creative and original manner. In so doing, Elvis used his voice almost like an instrument in its own right, displaying a remarkable breadth and drawing heavily on the vocal techniques he had copied from the countless singers he had autodidactically studied during his childhood and youth.[42] And Elvis's personal creativity stretched far beyond his music. With his gyrating moves on stage, for example, Elvis created a unique style of performance and expression, again something that came to be at the very heart of his appeal. Finally, Elvis was also a highly innovative maker of his off-stage persona. Long before he became famous, for example, Elvis had already acquired notoriety for his long hair, sideburns, and flashy clothes; and he continued to re-invent himself as an eccentric and cross-cultural personality throughout his life.[43] Elvis Presley was not a helpless pawn in the bigger game of mass entertainment; he was a highly original creator of his own art and personality.

At the same time, however, Elvis's artistic output was not shaped exclusively, at times not even primarily, by himself. His recordings, for example, were often influenced by congenial musicians like Scotty Moore, or by occasionally dominant producers like Sam Phillips or Chips Moman. Even his selection of recording material was at times determined by commercial considerations, particularly during his early years when his publishers

---

[41]Marcus, *Drama of Celebrity*, 1–9; Shumway, *The Making of Musical Icons*, 1–23.

[42]For excellent takes on Presley's singing voice, see Dick Bradley, *Understanding Rock 'n' Roll: Popular Music in Britain, 1955–1964* (Buckingham: Open University Press, 1992), 65–9; Henry Pleasants, *The Great American Popular Singers* (London: Simon & Schuster, 1974), 274–8.

[43]Zoey Goto, *Elvis Style: From Zoot Suits to Jump Suits* (Faringdon: Redshank Books, 2016).

tended to choose songs with the sole objective of claiming copyright and thus receiving additional royalties for Elvis's two publishing companies.[44] In 1960s Hollywood, producers like Hal Wallis frequently utilized Elvis for their commercial pursuits with little regard to the singer's acting ambitions; and the machinery behind the extensive range of Elvis merchandise and memorabilia was orchestrated largely by the advertising professional Hank Saperstein. Above all, however, there is the towering figure of Colonel Tom Parker, Elvis's lifelong personal manager who took charge and responsibility of almost every aspect of the singer's career from 1956 onward. Indeed, Parker has since turned into almost as much of a mythical figure as Elvis himself: he is either praised as the genius mastermind behind Elvis's meteoric rise, or he is denounced as an unscrupulous money-maker who sacrificed his protégée's artistic brilliance on the altar of commercialism.[45]

Elvis's dissemination to the wider public was inextricably tied to the profound changes in the postwar media landscape. Independent radio stations, for example, were of paramount importance in facilitating Elvis's initial rise; and the singer's controversial television appearances in 1956 transformed him from a local phenomenon into a nationwide celebrity literally within minutes. The bigger public debates over Elvis, however, were still waged largely in print publications: national magazines like *Life, Time*, or *Cosmopolitan*, as well as major newspapers such as the *Washington Post* and *The New York Times*. The extensive media coverage from the very beginning of his career not only endowed Elvis with political and social significance, but it also transmitted the debates surrounding Elvis far beyond the United States. European newspapers in particular frequently copied their coverage of Elvis almost word-by-word from US publications, and in many instances started reporting on the phenomenon even before his music could be received or bought there. Indeed, Elvis might well be considered a new type of mass media phenomenon, and one that played out on a scale that would have been impossible only a few years earlier.

The media, however, could only offer its own particular interpretations of Elvis; but it could not determine his actual reception by fans or the wider public. As the book shows, public attitudes toward Elvis often differed substantially from the published opinion in magazines and newspapers: after all, many of Elvis's earliest fans embraced him precisely as a sign of nonverbal rebellion against the values and worldviews of the establishment. It is thus vital not to lose sight of the voices that arguably matter the most: the voices of fans and supporters, who were the ones that endowed Elvis with popularity and meaning in the first place.

---

[44]Simpson, *Rough Guide to Elvis,* 86–7; Duffett, *Elvis,* 42–3.
[45]For a somewhat sensationalist biography that tends to side with the latter view, see Alanna Nash, *The Colonel: The Extraordinary Story of Colonel Tom Parker and Elvis Presley* (London: Aurum Press, 2004).

# Writing Elvis: Structure

Looking at the period of Elvis's active career from the mid-1950s to his death in 1977, it is striking how much the debates surrounding Elvis tend to reflect the more general historical transformations of his times. While the book's five main chapters are structured loosely chronologically, each of them therefore has its own distinct theme, and in so doing also sheds light on some of the bigger issues at the time.

The first chapter centers on Elvis's meteoric, yet highly contested, rise in the mid-1950s United States, which reveals some of the major social tensions breeding underneath the surface of Eisenhower's Cold War America. As Elvis was initially rejected and denounced by vast amounts of the US establishment, an emerging new generation of teenage fans endorsed him precisely to rebel against the conformity and sterility of their conscripted postwar lives. Yet Elvis was also seen as a major challenge to the political and social order at the time, particularly as regards racial segregation and sexuality. These tensions surrounding Elvis's rise were eventually mediated and partially resolved by the powerful forces of the emerging teenage market, which transfigured Elvis's image into a popular American Dream narrative that focused on the singer's rags-to-riches life story while sidelining or completely ignoring the bigger tensions at the heart of his appeal. Elvis thus ended up both challenging and reinforcing the fragile 1950s Cold War consensus, offering a platform for generational rebellion while ultimately remaining within the traditional confines of American society.

The hype surrounding Elvis Presley was not confined to the United States; it was transmitted around the world in almost an instant. The second chapter looks at Elvis's global impact during the 1950s, concentrating primarily, but by no means exclusively, on the European continent. While the generational dynamics underlying Elvis's reception often mirrored developments in the United States, there was an important difference: at the height of the early Cold War, the debates over Elvis also offered an opportunity to negotiate bigger questions concerning American influences in postwar Europe. Major controversies over the role of US-style consumerism and postwar modernity were thus fought through Elvis's public image, often drawing on the language of "Americanization." Behind and beyond the Iron Curtain too, the Cold War heavily conditioned Elvis's reception. While his records and films were freely available and highly popular in Western-oriented countries like Japan, for example, Communist countries like China or the Soviet Union rigorously prohibited them throughout the singer's lifetime. A particularly interesting case study is Eastern Europe, where the initial reception of Elvis closely mirrored West European patterns, but where the governments' eventual crackdown on rock 'n' roll often turned him into a symbol of political resistance and subversion.

If Elvis was seen as a highly contentious entertainer for much of the 1950s, his time in the army between March 1958 and March 1960 triggered a profound reconfiguration of his image. As the third chapter shows, the fact that Elvis was drafted like anybody else and did not ask for any special favors turned the erstwhile juvenile rebel into a deeply patriotic figure almost overnight; a process that was consciously staged by Elvis's management and would eventually pave the ground for his transformation into a mainstream entertainer. Yet, Elvis's military service also served as an articulation point for many bigger issues. Within the United States, the controversies surrounding the singer's military service tied neatly into ongoing debates over the inequity of the draft and the army's more general egalitarian principles; whereas the eighteen months Elvis was stationed in West Germany offer a fascinating glimpse into the day-to-day interactions between American soldiers and ordinary German citizens. It also highlights the transnational nature of the Elvis phenomenon, as well as the increasing blurring of transatlantic celebrity cultures at the time.

After his return from the army, Elvis's attention turned firmly on Hollywood, which is the focus of the fourth chapter. During the 1960s, Elvis starred in roughly three movies a year, ranging from serious efforts like *Blue Hawaii* or *Viva Las Vegas* to eminently forgettable B-movie embarrassments like *Kissin' Cousins* or *Tickle Me*. Although highly formulaic and often with little artistic value, these so-called Elvis movies offer a fascinating window into popular self-understandings of the early 1960s United States as a country of natural beauty, technological advancement, and consumerist abundance. The Elvis movies were also highly successful outside the United States, where they injected concrete images into abstract notions like the American Way of Life to millions of audiences all around the world. Such mainstream success triggered a certain professionalization of his fan scene, which resulted in countless transnational exchanges that occasionally even transcended the Iron Curtain. As the 1960s went on, however, the Elvis movies suffered a marked decline in popularity, not least because their idealized and cliché-laden images increasingly contrasted with the harsh realities of the decade. Amid a rapidly changing political landscape, Elvis increasingly came to be seen as an anachronistic relic of a bygone age that was far removed from the cultural rejuvenation and social upheavals of the 1960s.

Things did not stay that way, as the fifth chapter shows. In December 1968, Elvis reclaimed his legacy through a sixty-minute NBC television special, followed by his return to live performances and reinvention as an eclectic and contemporary artist. The highly successful comeback not only manifested Elvis's iconic status and triggered the first serious evaluations of his wider cultural impact, but it also resurrected the singer as a major generational reference point precisely at a time when the 1950s came to occupy a central place in public memory. As part of such nostalgic reconstructions of the 1950s in popular culture, as well as the wider canonization of rock music at the time, Elvis became transfigured into a larger-than-life American icon, whose legacy eventually came to overshadow his actual music and performances. As Elvis's personal problems increasingly took center stage, however, he eventually turned into a pop-cultural symbol of the general confusion and solipsism of the mid-1970s United States, as well as of the darker sides of capitalist society and mass consumerism—perceptions that were seemingly vindicated by his tragic death.

# Finding Elvis: Sources

A book on a major historical figure like Elvis Presley inevitably constitutes a work of synthesis. As regards Elvis's actual life and career, much use has been made of the excellent studies by Peter Guralnick and Ernst Jorgensen, which remain the gold standard for all works on Elvis.[46] I have supplemented their findings with extensive research in numerous national and regional US newspapers, occasionally with the help of dedicated clippings on Elvis in archives and fan collections. The collections preserved at the Margaret Herrick Library and the University of Southern California Cinematic Arts Library in Los Angeles, California, have been incredibly valuable in uncovering the behind-the-scenes dynamics behind Elvis's Hollywood career. I have also made extensive—if highly cautious—use of the countless memoirs by Elvis's real and imagined partners, friends, colleagues, collaborators, business associates, bodyguards, relatives, and army buddies.[47]

Given the book's international scope, it was of paramount importance to trace the impact of Elvis beyond the United States. The files of the United States Information Agency (USIA) at the United States National Archives (NARA) in College Park, Maryland, have been useful in that regard, although they naturally tend to focus on more general subjects like rock

---

[46]Apart from Guralnick's two-volume biography already mentioned above, two excellent reference works are Peter Guralnick and Ernst Jorgensen, *Elvis Day by Day: The Definitive Record of His Life and Music* (New York: Ballantine Books, 1999), and Ernst Jorgensen, *Elvis Presley: A Life in Music: The Complete Recording Sessions* (New York, NY: St. Martin's Press, 1998).

[47]To name just a few: Priscilla Presley, *Elvis and Me* (New York: Putnam, 1985); Joe Esposito, *Good rockin' Tonight: Twenty Years on the Road and on the Town with Elvis* (New York: Simon & Schuster, 1994); Charlie Hodge, *Me 'n Elvis* (Memphis: Castle Books, 1984); Jerry Schilling, *Me and A Guy Named Elvis: My Lifelong Friendship with Elvis Presley* (London: Gotham Books, 2006 [2007]); Larry Geller and Joel Spector, *If I Can Dream* (New York: Simon And Schuster, 1989); Alanna Nash, *Elvis Aaron Presley: Revelations from the Memphis Mafia* (New York: HarperCollins, 1995); George Klein, *Elvis: My Best Man* (New York, NY: Three Rivers Press, 2011); June Juanico, *Elvis: In the Twilight of Memory* (New York, NY: Arcade, 1997); Linda Thompson, *A Little Thing Called Life: On Loving Elvis Presley, Bruce Jenner, and Songs in Between* (New York, NY: Dey St., 2016); Ginger Alden, *Elvis and Ginger: Elvis Presley's Fiancée and Last Love Finally Tells Her Story* (New York, NY: Ace Books, 2014).

'n' roll or Hollywood movies rather than on Elvis Presley as an individual. Files by the Department of Defense brought up some fascinating findings about Elvis's time in the army. Again, these findings have been completed by extensive research in European newspapers, as well as by more general secondary literature and fan collections.

As with any such study of popular culture, there is a danger of relying too heavily on elite discourses at the expense of those voices that arguably mattered the most: the everyday perceptions of fans and the wider public. Throughout this study, I have therefore tried to integrate the perspectives of Elvis's followers and supporters as fully as possible. A particularly helpful resource in that regard has been the UK periodical *Elvis Monthly,* which started in 1960 and soon developed into the major news hub and discussion forum for Elvis fans around the globe. Luckily, it is preserved in all UK copyright libraries. I have also tried to make everyday spectators speak as much as possible through their own voices by including readers' letters printed in newspapers, as well as correspondence preserved in other archives.

Although many of these sources offer new and fascinating insights, the book obviously cannot hope to provide a definitive take on Elvis's historical impact. What it does offer is a fresh perspective on how Elvis became such a prominent pop-cultural icon in the first place, how and why his diverse cultural meanings changed over time, and what his story can tell us about the wider impact of popular culture in shaping perceptions of the United States at home and abroad. In so doing, the book also hopes to make a sizable contribution to the burgeoning literature on postwar popular culture in its wider transnational and transatlantic contexts.

# 1

# Rebellious Elvis: An (un)American Dream

On April 22, 1954, millions of Americans gazed at their television sets as they watched the Army–McCarthy congressional hearings unfold. It turned out to be the sad climax of the Red Scare that had kept the United States holding its breath since the early 1950s. Driven by the deceiving and brutish demagogue Senator Joseph McCarthy, the previous few years had seen an all-out witch-hunt against the perpetrators of an allegedly widespread communist subversion of US society. In the 1950s, communism was perceived not only as an external, but also as an internal, threat, and McCarthy's binary rhetoric was only one of many attempts to create a conformist, homogenous American identity against the wider Cold War background.[1]

The fact that millions of Americans were watching the McCarthy trials unfold on their own television sets—probably comfortably tucked away on a couch in some newly built, standardized suburban unit—was not coincidental: it was key to the prevalent Cold War mind-set at the time. As part of a wider civic ideology of consumerism and mass consumption, the act of purchasing goods and spending money not only served individual advancement; it was also seen as an almost patriotic act in demonstrating the alleged superiority of the American system of free enterprise and capitalism over the state-controlled Soviet economy.[2] The domesticity and conformity associated with such lifestyles constituted another puzzle-piece

---

[1]William I. Hitchcock, *The Age of Eisenhower: America and the World in the 1950s* (New York and London: Simon & Schuster, 2018), 115–47; Stephen J. Whitfield, *The Culture of the Cold War* (Baltimore, MD: Johns Hopkins University Press, 1991); Field, *American Cold War Culture*, 5.

[2]Lizabeth Cohen, *A Consumers' Republic: The Politics of Mass Consumption in Postwar America* (New York, NY: Vintage Books, 2004).

in the construction of postwar American identities: the nuclear family, and its ingrained social containment, was seen as a crucial safeguard against a potential moral deprivation or communist subversion of American society.[3]

The popular image of the 1950s as a decade of conservatism and conformity, however, is only part of the story, as bigger societal transformations took place behind the façade of such constructed American identities. The alleged domesticity of the nuclear family, for example, stood increasingly at odds with the growing sexual liberalism of the decade, which found its most famous expression in the Kinsey report on "Sexual Behavior in the Human Female" in 1953 and the founding of *Playboy* magazine that same year.[4] The alleged Cold War consensus also turned a blind eye to the major social inequalities still deeply ingrained in postwar American society, often reaffirming patriarchal hierarchies and the racial segregation of many African Americans. Here too, things were changing: in 1954, the Supreme Court's *Brown v. Board of Education* ruling put an end to racial segregation in schools and colleges, and the Montgomery bus boycott marked a watershed in the burgeoning civil rights movement and the slow erosion of Jim Crow legislation in the South. The 1950s United States was not the monolithic entity as which it was often depicted; it was a deeply divided society with major tensions multiplying underneath the surface of Cold War conformity.

The rise of Elvis Presley illustrates the deeply ingrained conflicts and complex transformations of the mid-1950s United States like few others. As the most important icon of a burgeoning youth culture that challenged traditional norms and conventions, Elvis's public image became intrinsically intertwined with much bigger debates over class, race, and sexuality in the mid-1950s United States, as well as over the role of censorship and the power of the marketplace at a new age of mass media. The public controversies surrounding Elvis's rise thus offer a unique window into a rapidly changing postwar society, and show how bigger questions of American Cold War identities became negotiated through Elvis's public image.

## The Southern Origins of Elvis

Elvis Presley's Southern background is crucial to understand not only the person, but also the wider forces that shaped his life, music, and reception.[5] It is a story that is inextricably intertwined with the American South's complex transformations during the second half of the twentieth century; a history that few places exemplify better than Tupelo, a small city with

---

[3]May, *Homeward Bound.*
[4]Meyerowitz, "The Liberal 1950s?" 297–319.
[5]For much broader investigations, see Pratt, "Ironies of Southern Identity," and Doll, *Understanding Elvis.*

approximately 6,500 citizens in the North of Mississippi.[6] One of the last key battlefields in the Civil War, it had based its reconstruction efforts largely on the cotton industry, and retained its cotton city character and the almost feudal community structures that came with it well into the 1930s. It also remained an almost completely segregated city: a major rail line separated the Western side of the city's white landowners and businessmen from the city's 40 percent African American population, who lived in the so-called "Shake Rag" neighborhood on the Eastern side of the rail tracks. Even further East, however, there was a small community of poor marginalized whites, who worked in unskilled manual labor jobs and often lived in abject poverty. This is where Elvis Aaron Presley was born on January 8, 1935.[7] His father Vernon could not even pay the doctor for the baby's delivery and had to receive money from welfare; Elvis's stillborn twin brother Jesse Garon was unceremoniously buried in a shoe box.

Growing up in the poorest part of Tupelo "on the wrong side of the tracks," Elvis's earliest years were characterized by poverty and hardship.[8] Elvis's father Vernon had worked on-and-off as a milk delivery driver and in various other manual jobs; his mother Gladys took shifts at the ironing section of the Tupelo Garment Company six days a week, which required her to operate a heavy steam iron and stand up for twelve hours straight well into her pregnancy. They lived in a so-called "shotgun" house, a provisionally constructed two-room hut with old newspapers functioning as wallpaper and no electricity or running water.[9] The young Elvis found escape from such hardship in the colorful and extravagant dream worlds of comic books, a popular commodity among youngsters at the time. At the age of eight, he signed up for membership at Tupelo's Lee County Library and spent much of his free time borrowing and trading comics with friends. He was particularly drawn to *Captain Marvel's Adventures,* the story of a rough-sleeping homeless newsboy in New York City who becomes transformed into a superhero: some commentators have noted the uncanny resemblance of some of Elvis's 1970s jumpsuits with Captain Marvel's red body suit and white cape outfit.[10]

---

[6]For an Elvis-infused history of Tupelo on which a lot of information in this section is based, see Michael T. Bertrand, "'A Tradition-Conscious Cotton City': (East) Tupelo, Mississippi, Birthplace of Elvis Presley," in Karen L. Cox (ed.), *Destination Dixie: Tourism & Southern History* (Gainesville, FL: University Press of Florida, 2012), 87–112.

[7]Although Elvis's birth certificate read "Elvis Aron Presley," he later adopted the correct spelling Aaron. For a comprehensive investigation, see Elvis Australia, "'Elvis Aaron Presley—Elvis' middle name, is it Aron or Aaron?" January 25, 2008, www.elvis.com.au/presley/news/article-aron-or-aaron.shtml [last accessed November 7, 2019].

[8]For the most detailed reconstruction of Elvis's earliest years in Tupelo, see Dundy, *Elvis and Gladys*; for a slightly more compact overview, Guralnick, *Last Train*, 11–30.

[9]Bertrand, "Tradition-Conscious Cotton City," 96–7.

[10]Simpson, *Rough Guide to Elvis*, 389–90.

Elvis's earliest years in Tupelo were also shaped by the rich cultural heritage of Southern music that surrounded him, as well as by a certain transcendence of racial boundaries in every-day life. At the First Assembly of God Pentecostal church, which Elvis attended regularly with his parents, he was exposed to gospel-style communal singing, a music that became his earliest and perhaps biggest musical love.[11] He also developed a taste for the country music of the white working-class community, following the local country performer Mississippi Slim around the neighborhoods at every opportunity. In 1945, Elvis even won the fifth prize at the local Mississippi-Alabama Fair and Dairy show for his performance of Mississippi Slim's country standard "Old Shep."[12] Two years later, Elvis was thrown into an altogether different world when the Presley family moved to a "colored" neighborhood that only had a few houses designated for whites. Here, Elvis observed how black musicians jammed on the streets, jukeboxes blasted rhythm 'n' blues music, and black churches offered eclectic gospel performances filled with singing and dancing.[13] Elvis displayed no hesitation getting in touch with his new environment, and eagerly sucked up all such influences. He had also started to take his newly bought guitar everywhere he went. As Mississippi Slim's brother later recalled, Elvis always walked to school with the guitar over his shoulder, making some of the girls leave home early to avoid passing the "goofy" kid.[14]

In November 1948, the Presley family's move to Memphis, Tennessee, exposed Elvis to yet another different environment. If Tupelo stood for the Old South, Memphis—situated on the Western border of Tennessee along the Mississippi river, with a population of around 400,000 citizens—in many ways signified the New South, a place where rural institutions and archaic social hierarchies clashed with rapid urbanization and industrialization.[15] As the only major city within a 200-mile radius, Memphis was regarded as the unofficial capital of the Mid-South, and the bustling economic hub of the Mississippi Delta. Yet it had retained many of its old-fashioned, almost feudal, structures, and Southern elites still dominated the city's political and social life almost completely. Still a highly segregated city, Memphis was also a major hub of postwar black culture, partly as a result of the massive migration of African Americans from rural areas to cities during and after the Second World War.[16] The

---

[11]Dundy, *Elvis and Gladys*, 47–8.
[12]Guralnick, *Last Train*, 18–19.
[13]Ibid., 27–8.
[14]Lee County Library (Tupelo, MS), Elaine Dundy collection, Turner to Dundy, April 19, 1981.
[15]For an intriguing study of Memphis during the second half of the twentieth century, see Wanda Rushing, *Memphis and the Paradox of Place: Globalization in the American South* (Chapel Hill, NC: University of North Carolina Press, 2009).
[16]Between 1940 and 1960, the percentage of African Americans living in cities grew from 49 to 73 percent. See Glenn C. Altschuler, *All Shook Up: How Rock 'n' Roll Changed America* (Oxford: Oxford University Press, 2003), 11.

black community's social life centered on Beale Street, an area of roughly four blocks with shops, nightclubs, and barbeque stands.[17] It also featured a vibrant musical community, attracting rural performers from around the Mississippi Delta as well as established stars like Duke Ellington or Count Basie. A particularly popular new trend at the time was rhythm 'n' blues, an upbeat fusion of urban blues and jump band jazz. In 1949, the term gained nationwide prominence when the music industry's major trade journal *Billboard* used it to replace its previous category of "race music" in their charts.[18]

*Billboard*'s adaptation of the term may also have had to do with the fact that the popularity of rhythm 'n' blues was no longer confined solely to African American communities; by the early 1950s, the music was also starting to become popular among some younger white audiences. It was a trend that was facilitated by wider changes in the media landscape: with the rapid rise of television as a mass medium, radio stations sought to find new audiences by aiming at previously underrepresented market segments.[19] In Memphis, the city's rapidly expanding African American population was an obvious target. In 1949, WDIA became the first radio station in the entire United States with an all-black cast of disc jockeys, and its broadcasts occasionally featured rhythm 'n' blues music. Surprisingly, WDIA proved popular not only with black audiences, but also among white youngsters, who tuned in with their transistor radios while their parents focused on their television sets. The trend was quickly noticed by WDIA's main "white" competitor WHBQ, which rose to the challenge by introducing its own rhythm 'n' blues program after WDIA had gone off-air in the evenings: a show called *Red, Hot and Blue*. It was hosted by Dewey Phillips, an eccentric disc jockey with a loose mouth and indiscriminate musical taste who soon acquired a substantial fan base among the Memphian youth.[20] By the mid-1950s, the enthusiasm for rhythm 'n' blues music by white teenagers had come to attract national attention. "Teen-Agers Demand Music with a Beat, Spur Rhythm-Blues," *Billboard* claimed on April 24, 1954, going on to describe how rhythm 'n' blues had developed "into one of the fastest growing areas of the entire record business" because a "teenage tide" had "swept down the old barriers which kept this music restricted to a segment of the population."[21]

[17]Rushing, *Memphis*, 125–6.

[18]Paul Friedlander, *Rock and Roll: A Social History* (Boulder, CO: Westview Press, 1996), 16; Weinstein, *Rock'n America*, 29.

[19]Weinstein, *Rock'n America*, 24; Richard Aquila, *Let's Rock! How 1950s America Created Elvis and the Rock & Roll Craze* (Lanham, MD: Rowan & Littlefield, 2017), 125.

[20]Robert Gordon, *It Came From Memphis* (Boston/London: Faber and Faber, 1995), 17; Louis Cantor, *Dewey and Elvis: The Life and Times of a Rock 'n' Deejay* (Urbana and Chicago, IL: University of Illinois Press, 2005).

[21]*Billboard*, April 24, 1954.

One slightly older Memphis resident who not only noticed the growing popularity of rhythm 'n' blues, but who was also himself fascinated by it, was Sam Phillips, founder and owner of the small independent record label Sun Studios. Phillips, who had developed a fascination with rural blues music during his childhood on the cotton fields of Alabama, made it his mission to indiscriminately record any artist, black or white, at Sun Studios, and in so doing hoped to give a platform to the many rhythm 'n' blues artists who were still ignored by the big music businesses. "I knew the physical separation of the races," he later reflected somewhat hyperbolically, "but I knew the integration of their souls."[22] Yet, although some of Sun Studio's black artists like Howlin' Wolf or Rufus Thomas had enjoyed notable successes, commercial opportunities remained restricted by the still largely segregated record market—teenagers might have listened to rhythm 'n' blues on the radio, but they would not actually buy the records in stores.[23] "If I could find a white man who had the Negro sound and the Negro feel," Phillips famously sighed around the time, "I could make a billion dollars!"[24]

Early 1950s Memphis, then, was a city that reflected tensions between old and new; a city where urbanization and postwar modernity clashed with deeply ingrained social hierarchies and class segregation. The young Elvis felt such tensions perhaps more acutely than many others at the time. Living with his family in a public housing project near downtown Memphis rather than in some segregated suburb, Elvis soon started to explore the opportunities that this urban environment offered to him. Apart from listening to rhythm 'n' blues music on WDIA and WHBQ radio, he spent a lot of time browsing record stores like Poplar Tunes or Charlie's Records, a small shop with a soda fountain whose owner allowed teenagers to use listening booths even if they could not afford to actually buy the records. Elvis also continued to attend the Assembly of God church on McLemore Avenue, and regularly participated in monthly all-night gospel singings at the Ellis Auditorium. Occasionally, he also sneaked off to a nearby "colored" church to witness the singing of the famous Reverend W. Herbert Brewster. Indeed, Elvis displayed absolutely no hesitation to get in touch with black culture more generally. He often hung around the Lansky Brothers clothing shop on Beale Street, for example, glazing at the flashy, colorful clothes on display and promising its owner that he would buy him out if he ever

---

[22]Quoted in Peter Guralnick, *Sam Phillips: The Man Who Invented Rock 'n' Roll* (London: Weidenfeld & Nicolson, 2015), xiv.

[23]Guralnick, *Sam Phillips*, 199.

[24]A quote that has since been often misunderstood as a statement for cultural appropriation and exploitation, whereas Phillips was actually voicing his frustration with the still segregated record market that compromised the commercial opportunities for many of his black artists. For a discussion, see again Guralnick, *Sam Phillips*, 207.

became rich.[25] In due course, Elvis started to wear dress pants, black bolero jackets, or pink h-boy collar shirts himself, and he also grew sideburns and groomed his hair obsessively with Rose Oil hair tonic and Vaseline.[26] It was a most peculiar look, and one that drew heavily on black styles. As his cousin Billy Smith recalled, "My family thought, 'Why doesn't he just go down on Beale Street and live with em?'"[27]

If Elvis was a product of the urban environment that surrounded him, he was also distinctive in several respects. Apart from his eccentric looks, Elvis stood out for his eclectic taste in a great variety of music.[28] He had a particular liking for rhythm 'n' blues, admiring groups like The Clovers as well as individual performers like LaVern Baker or Fats Domino. Indeed, when the songwriters Jerry Leiber and Mike Stoller first met the by-then-already-famous Elvis a few years later, they were struck by his encyclopedic knowledge. "Jerry and I shared the uppity view that he and I were among the few white guys who knew about the blues," Stoller later recalled. "In the first five minutes of our conversation with Elvis, we learned we were dead wrong. Elvis knew the blues ... There wasn't any R&B he didn't know. He could quote from Arthur 'Big Boy' Crudup, B.B. King, and Bib Bill Broonzy."[29] Elvis had also retained his childhood love for gospel quartets like The Blackwood Brothers or The New Statesmen, and he absolutely loved ballads by Dean Martin or Roy Hamilton. Above all, however, Elvis admired Mario Lanza, a semi-operatic crooner known for his dramatic interpretations of songs like "Come Back to Sorrento" or "O Sole Mio."[30] It was a truly eclectic range of musical tastes that would later feature heavily in his own repertoire. As he put it in an interview in March 1956, he was a fan of "anybody that's good regardless of what kind of singer they are. Whether they're religious rhythm and blues, hillbilly or anything else. If they're great, I mean I like 'em. From Roy Acuff on up to Mario Lanza. I just admire 'em if they're really great."[31]

Elvis distinguished himself not only by his eccentric looks and musical talent, but also by his relentless personal ambition. From an early age on, he had become consumed by popular images about the so-called American Way of Life; the idea of individual advancement, and capitalist success in a land of allegedly unlimited opportunities. While American self-understandings

---

[25]Guralnick, *Last Train*, 45–7; Simpson, *Rough Guide to Elvis*, 419. Whether Elvis actually frequented Beale Street regularly before he became famous is discussed in Guralnick's footnotes, 510–11.

[26]Guralnick and Jorgensen, *Day by Day*, 9.

[27]Quoted in Simpson, *Rough Guide to Elvis*, 382–3.

[28]Ibid., 191.

[29]Jerry Leiber and Mike Stoller, *Hound Dog: The Leiber and Stoller Autobiography* (New York, NY: Simon&Schuster, 2009), 112.

[30]A lot of information in this section is drawn from Paul Simpson's excellent overview of Elvis's music taste in Simpson, *Rough Guide to Elvis*, 167–226.

[31]Jerry Osborne, *Elvis: Word for Word* (New York, NY: Harmony Books, 2000), 13.

based on mass consumption and consumerism had been central since at least the turn of the century, such popular constructions of US identities now gained additional political currency amid the ideological confrontation of the Cold War. By the mid-1950s, the obtainment and display of consumerist items not only signified individual success; they also served as a bigger statement of an American identity.[32] Cars, of course, were particularly powerful symbols of capitalist success, and Elvis became attached to them from an early age.[33] Already in Tupelo, he had promised his mother Gladys that she should "worry none … When I grow up, I'm going to buy you a fine house and pay everything you owe at the grocery store and get two Cadillacs – one for you and Daddy, and one for me";[34] a few years later, he similarly predicted to a local Memphis musician at Charlie's Records that "someday I'm going to be driving Cadillacs."[35]

By the early 1950s, Elvis started to sense that his musical talent might offer him an opportunity to actually achieve such dreams at some point in the future. In April 1953, he performed at his high school's annual Minstrel show, and provoked enthusiastic reactions from the audience. From that point onward, the dream of becoming a successful musician seems to have manifested itself in Elvis's mind. Yet he also experienced several setbacks, such as his unsuccessful auditions at the local Hi-Hat Club and the Blackwood Brothers' junior group.[36] And when he finally mustered the courage to enter Sun Studios to make a private recording for his own use, he failed to impress Sam Phillips, who was in any case distracted by a protracted business feud with a partner. Only the studio's secretary Marion Keisker seemed to have seen something in him, putting Elvis's name on a list of potential future artists and noting next to it: "Good ballad singer. Hold."[37]

# The Making of a Local Phenomenon: Class, Race, and Gender

The story of Elvis's first professional recording has been told often, and does not need to be repeated at length here.[38] Nonetheless, its key elements

---

[32]Regina Lee Blaszczyk, *American Consumer Society, 1865–2005: From Hearth to HDTV* (Hoboken, NJ: John Wiley & Sons, 2008), 265; Charles F. McGovern, *Sold American: Consumption and Citizenship, 1890–1945* (Chapel Hill, NC: University of North Carolina Press, 2006), 1–9; Cohen, *Consumers' Republic,* 10–12.

[33]Gary S. Cross, *Machines of Youth: America's Car Obsession* (Chicago, IL: University of Chicago Press, 2018).

[34]As quoted in Guralnick, *Last Train,* 16.

[35]Ibid., 45.

[36]Guralnick and Jorgensen, *Day by Day,* 12, 15.

[37]Guralnick, *Last Train,* 62–5.

[38]For the best description, Guralnick, *Last Train,* 89–97.

are pivotal to understand many of the most central myths surrounding Elvis's legacy, so it is worth recounting the story briefly. Again, it starts with Elvis's personal determination and persistency. Although disappointed that nothing had happened in the weeks and months after his first recording at Sun Studios, he decided to stick around. Now working as a truck driver for Crown Electrics, he frequently drove past the studio during his lunch breaks, occasionally dropping in and making some awkward small talk with Marion Keisker. He also enquired regularly whether there was not any band around that might need a singer.[39] In January 1954, he then made another private recording at his own cost, but yet again provoked little reaction by Sam Phillips. On June 26, 1954, however, things changed when Marion Keisker finally called Elvis to ask whether he could come over and try his luck with a demo tape. Although it soon became evident that the song did not work for Elvis, Phillips now started to see something in Elvis's way of singing, and asked him to go through a number of songs he knew.[40] Philips then teamed Elvis up with two experienced country musicians, guitarist Scotty Moore and bass player Bill Black, in the hope that the mix might lead to some sort of creative fusion.

On July 5, 1954, Elvis Presley, Scotty Moore, and Bill Black all showed up at Sun Studios, recording Bing Crosby's "Harbor Lights" and Leon Payne's country ballad "I Love You Because." Again, however, things did not really work out. During an exhausted break, the discouraged Elvis picked up his guitar and started to fool around with "That's All Right Mama," a rhythm 'n' blues standard by Arthur "Big Boy" Crudup. Phillips was stunned. Not only was he surprised that Elvis, who had previously restricted himself to ballads and gospel, knew the song in the first place, but he was even more taken by the way in which he sang: Elvis's voice was dark and raw, and he displayed an acute sense of timing and enunciation, much of it clearly taken from rhythm 'n' blues singers. Moore and Black eventually joined in, adding some lighthearted country-style beats that make the record sound faster than the original version. Struck by what he just heard, Phillips recorded the song straight away. The final product was something truly new and original; a unique fusion of rhythm 'n' blues with traditional country and some pop elements. The band was shocked by what it had created. "[G]ood God," Scotty Moore exclaimed; "they'll run us out of town!"[41]

As Moore's statement already suggests, "That's All Right Mama"'s racial ambiguity stood at the heart of its appeal. Sam Phillips, for one, instinctively knew that he had created something remarkable, but he was not at all sure what to do with it. He thus invited his partner-in-crime Dewey Phillips over to the studio, and played him the acetate several times. "What I was

---

[39]Guralnick, *Last Train*, 64–5, 84.
[40]Ibid., 84–6.
[41]Quoted in ibid., 96.

thinking was," Sam Phillips later recalled, "where you going to go with this, it's not black, it's not white, it's not pop, it's not country, and I think Dewey was the same way. He was fascinated by it – there was no question about that – I mean he loved the damn record, but it was a question of where do we go from there?"[42] In an attempt to find out, Dewey played the acetate on his radio show the next evening, where it received an enormous response: he allegedly received forty-seven phone calls asking for the record to be played again, and ended up playing it fourteen times.[43] Struck by such an enormous response, Sam Phillips hastily got the band back together to record a B-side. They opted for "Blue Moon of Kentucky," a country standard by Bill Monroe. This time, they turned things upside down: rather than fusing a rhythm 'n' blues standard with country elements, they took a country ballad and interpreted it in a rhythm 'n' blues style. Taken together, "That's All Right, Mama/Blue Moon of Kentucky" constituted the very definition of a stylistic crossover; an original and creative fusion of two popular, yet distinct, styles. It was released on July 19, 1954, and sold 20,000 copies by the end of the year.[44]

Early reactions to the record reveal how complex issues of race were tied to Elvis's reception from the very beginning. Many listeners of Dewey's radio show, for example, simply could not make out whether Elvis was a white or black singer. When Dewey spontaneously invited Elvis to the studio for a quick interview, he therefore asked Elvis innocently which school he had just graduated from, given that the educational system was still almost completely segregated in the immediate aftermath of *Brown v. Board of Education*. "I wanted to get that out," Dewey later recalled, "because a lot of people listening thought he was colored."[45] The B-side "Blue Moon of Kentucky" only added to the record's ambiguity, although it proved highly popular among almost all listeners' segments. Less than two weeks after the initial release, the local evening newspaper *Memphis Press-Scimitar* ran its first short feature on Elvis, which quoted Marion Keisker who claimed that "That's All Right, Mama" was "equally popular on popular, folk and race record programs." It seemed, she went on, like Elvis offered "something that seems to appeal to everybody."[46] On August 7, the national trade journal *Billboard* published a short review of the record, describing Elvis as "a potent new chanter who can sock over a tune for either the country or the r.&b. markets. On this new disk he comes thru with a solid performance on an r.&b.-type tune and then on the flip side does another fine job with a country ditty."[47]

---

[42]Ibid., 99.
[43]Cantor, *Dewey and Elvis*, 150–1.
[44]Duffett, *Elvis*, 26.
[45]Quoted in Guralnick, *Phillips*, 214.
[46]*Memphis Press Scimitar,* July 30, 1954.
[47]*Billboard,* August 7, 1954.

The record clearly hit a nerve, but it also profited from a marketing hype that was consciously built up around it from the very beginning. Sam Phillips immediately handed out copies to all other Memphian disc jockeys like Dick Stuart, Bob Neal, or Sleepy Eyed John, and started advertising it to his forty-two distributors and numerous jukebox operators all across the South.[48] In this quest, Phillips was aided by a powerful network of like-minded people who too believed in the new type of music. At the *Memphis Press-Scimitar*, for example, local reporter Robert "Bob" Johnson was instrumental in cementing Elvis's local fame, regularly and positively reporting on the new star from the earliest days. Perhaps even more important to Phillips was the support he received from *Billboard* editor Paul Ackerman, who had been behind the review of "That's All Right Mama" and continued to encourage Phillips in countless phone calls and letters.[49]

At the same time, however, Phillips also encountered strong resistance because of the record's crossover character. Many Southern disc jockeys or music stores refused to play or sell it because of its evident closeness to rhythm 'n' blues: a local distributor from Miami, for example, wrote to Phillips that jukebox operators in northern Florida "wouldn't touch the record" because they deemed it "too racy."[50] When Phillips tried to enthuse the Shreveport disc jockey T. Tommy Cutrer about it, he received the reply that they would "run me out of town."[51] Partly in response to such resistances, Elvis and his band were initially promoted as "country," "hillbilly," or "bop" performers, a strategy that consciously emphasized their country roots while downplaying the rhythm 'n' blues elements.[52] Such framing was given additional credibility by joint tours with country singers like Slim Whitman or Hank Snow, as well as by his appearances on country shows like the *Grand Old Opry* and the *Louisiana Hayride Show*. The latter in particular was pivotal in promoting Elvis beyond Memphis, since the weekly country show was broadcast live by radio with over 50,000 watt all across the South and thus helped build up a significantly larger fan base than personal appearances would have achieved alone.[53]

What caused even more furor than the music, however, were Elvis's performances on stage. Almost immediately after the recording of "That's All Right, Mama," Elvis and his band started performing in local Memphis clubs and other small venues. On July 30, 1954, they got enlisted for their first major commercial gig at Overton Park Shell, already as part of a country package show. Clearly nervous about the appearance, Elvis—perhaps

[48]Guralnick, *Last Train*, 111–14.
[49]Guralnick, *Phillips*, 232, 278.
[50]Ibid., 221.
[51]Quoted in ibid., 112.
[52]Doll, *Understanding Elvis*, 54–8.
[53]Guralnick, *Phillips*, 221.

Figure 1.1 *A young Elvis during one of his first appearances on the Louisiana Hayride show in October 1954.*

involuntarily—started shaking his legs in time with the music, in movements that might have been accidental but bore some resemblance to his favorite gospel singer "Big Chief" Wetherington from the Statesmen Quartet. The crowd's response was strong and immediate. In August 1956, Elvis recalled the experience in an interview:

> The very first appearance after I started recording, I was on a show in Memphis where I started doin' that. I was on a show as an extra added single, a big jamboree at an outdoor theater ... outdoor auditorium. And, uh, and I came out on stage and I was ... I was scared stiff. And it was my first big appearance in front of an audience ... And I came out and I was doin' a fast-type tune, one of my first records, and everybody was

hollerin' and I didn't know what they were hollerin' at. Everybody was screamin' and everything. And then I came offstage and my manager told me they was hollerin' because I was wigglin' my legs ... And so I went back out for an encore and I did a little more. And the more I did, the wilder they went.[54]

Even if Elvis had really stumbled on the leg-shaking by accident, he clearly noticed the audience's strong reactions, and soon turned it into an integral part of his performance. It caused sensation wherever he appeared. As the band started touring Tennessee, Louisiana, and Texas, even some local newspapers occasionally reported on the phenomenon, with reactions ranging from mild amusement to bewilderment. The *Biloxi Daily Herald*, for example, described Elvis's performance as "bounding on the microphone, imitating the action of broken springs of an old sofa, and singing at the same time."[55]

Yet, it would be misleading to belittle Elvis's earliest performances as the goofy gimmicks of a teenager. Behind all the fun stood a strong synergy between Elvis and his audiences; perhaps a rare opportunity to let out some excess energy in the highly conscripted social environment at the age of Fordism and widespread nuclear anxiety.[56] The enthusiasm of Elvis's audiences soon became notorious wherever he appeared, with female fans trying to get autographs and kisses, ripping off his clothes, and at one point even chasing him across an entire football field. On May 13, 1955, for example, Elvis caused a full-scale riot in Jacksonville, Florida, when he announced, "Girls, I'll see you backstage" to the 14,000-strong audience; they took him by his word and chased him into the dressing room.[57] During the same tour, the *Orlando Sentinel*'s Jean Yothers, one of Elvis's earliest supporters in Florida, graphically described her experience of an Elvis concert in her regular column. "What Hillbilly music does to the hillbilly music fan is absolutely phenomenal," she wrote,

It transports him into a wild, emotional and audible state of ecstasy. He never sits back sedately patting his palms politely and uttering bravos of music appreciation as his long-hair counterpart. He thunders his appreciation for the country-style music and nasal-twanged singing he loves by whistling shrilly through teeth, pounding the palms together with the whirling momentum of a souped-up paddle wheel, stomping the floor and ejecting yip-yip noises like the barks of a hound dog when

---

[54]Quoted from the full transcript published in Osborne, *Word for Word*, 53–4. Elvis's manager at the time was actually his guitarist Scotty Moore, but it seems more likely that Elvis referred to Bob Neal here, a local country music promoter who became Elvis's manager in January 1955.

[55]*Biloxi Daily Herald*, 21 June 1955.

[56]Medevoi, *Rebels*, 91–134.

[57]Guralnick and Jorgensen, *Day by Day*, 37–8.

it finally runs down a particularly elusive coon ... [W]hat really stole the show was this 20-year-old sensation, Elvis Presley, a real sex-box as far as the teenage girls are concerned. They squealed themselves silly over this fellow in orange coat and sideburns who "sent" them with his unique arrangement of Shake, Rattle and Roll.[58]

Yothers's column offers an early indication of how sexuality became a major part of Elvis's popularity during the 1950s. The uninhibited reactions by female fans to Elvis's on-stage gyrations constituted new and unprecedentedly open expressions of sexual desire; often turning Elvis's concerts into unrestrained displays of teenage sexuality.[59] It also pushed social conventions about appropriate female behavior in public. Local journalists often denounced Elvis's concerts as immoral displays of seductive mass hysteria, reports that were often accompanied by images of screaming or crying teenage girls. In August 1955, for example, the *Florence Times* claimed that "pandemonium broke loose" when Elvis had entered the stage; the *Breckenridge American* reported in similar vein how Elvis's audience of "mostly teenage girls" had "near swooned with his every appearance on stage."[60] It also claimed to have noted that some male attendees had apparently "viewed the singer's stage antic differently," unintentionally highlighting the singer's evident sexual appeal: "Various statements marked their distaste and one was heard to remark, 'I'd like to meet him out behind the barn,' while another added, 'I'd better not see any girlfriend of mine going up after autographs from that singer'."[61]

If Elvis's concerts shook the conventions of female public behavior in 1950s America, then his eccentric personal looks seemed even more dubious. Elvis was not simply a one-dimensional masculine teenage rebel; he was an altogether more fluid figure with an androgynous look that challenged established norms of masculinity: he often included pink colors in his outfits, for example, and occasionally wore mascara and eye shadow for his performances.[62] The fact that Elvis's flamboyant looks borrowed heavily from black culture also suggested a certain racial mixing that many Southern elites continued to viciously oppose.[63] Many local newspapers therefore reported extensively on Elvis's eccentric style. In November 1955, the *Biloxi*

---

[58] *Orlando Sentinel*, May 16, 1955.
[59] For an intriguing and much more detailed study of rock 'n' roll's impact on female sexuality that also focuses on the South, see Susan K. Cahn, *Sexual Reckonings: Southern Girls in a Troubling Age* (Cambridge, MA: Harvard University Press, 2012), 241–68.
[60] *The Florence Times*, August 3, 1955; *Breckenridge American*, June 11, 1955.
[61] *Breckenridge American*, June 11, 1955.
[62] Simpson, *Rough Guide to Elvis*, 382; Medovoi, *Rebels*, 193–4; more generally in a European context, Uta G. Poiger, "Rock 'n' Roll, Female Sexuality, and the Cold War Battle over German Identities," *The Journal of Modern History* 68/3 (September 1996), 577–616.
[63] Cahn, *Sexual Reckonings*, 249–50.

*Daily Herald* claimed that Elvis had "acquired one of the biggest collections of unusual and flashy clothes any artist owns, preferring the 'cool cat' type of dress rather than Western apparel"; and the *Breckenridge American* too described at length his attire of "apricot or orange slacks and sport shirt ... A black sports jacket further added a 'cat-look' to his appearance by having inserts of orange in the back of the jacket ... P.S. – Girls, Presley left Thursday morning via his pink Cadillac wearing pink slacks and an orchid sport shirt!"[64]

Such gender-bender looks might have been Elvis's way to articulate some sort of nonverbal rebellion against established racial norms, but he was also media-savvy enough to use it for self-promotion. Asked in an interview whether he had recently bought a pink suit just to match his pink Cadillac, for example, he answered affirmatively: "I kinda thought that would be a gimmick and really, it drew a lot of attention in the trade papers, about the pink suit and the pink car."[65] At the *Memphis Press-Scimitar*, reporter Bob Johnson was among the first to realize the potential market power of Elvis's personal branding. "While he appears with so-called hillbilly shows," Johnson wrote in February 1955, his clothes were "strictly sharp. His eyes are darkly slumberous, his hair sleekly long, his sideburns low, and there is a lazy, sexy, tough, good-looking manner which bobby soxers like. Not all record stars go over as well on stage as they do on records. *Elvis sells.*"[66]

Throughout 1955, the hype only accelerated. By the end of the year, Elvis had played in hundreds of cities ranging from Mississippi and Arkansas to Ohio, Florida, and Texas. His records continued to sell well, and they occasionally even tapped into the national market: "Baby Let's Play House" became his first single to appear on the national Country & Western *Billboard* charts, and it continued to get airplay throughout the country.[67] The Elvis phenomenon also came to attract the attention of many agents, promoters, and record companies. One of them was Colonel Tom Parker, an illegal Dutch immigrant who had made his name as a carny man and manager of country singers like Eddy Arnold.[68] In early 1955, he started attending some of Elvis's shows, and was amazed by the strong reaction the singer seemed to trigger among his audiences. After a brief period of courting Elvis and his parents, Parker eventually became his lifelong personal manager, and made it his mission to expose the local phenomenon to a national audience.[69] On November 21, 1955, Parker

---

[64]*Biloxy Daily Herald*, November 1, 1955; *Breckenridge American*, June 11, 1955.
[65]Osborne, *Word for Word*, 8.
[66]*Memphis Press Scimitar*, February 5, 1955.
[67]Guralnick, *Phillips*, 255, 260.
[68]For a generally well-researched, if sensationalist, biography of Parker, see Nash, *The Colonel*.
[69]Officially, Parker did not become Elvis's exclusive manager until March 26, 1956, because Elvis was still under contract with the local country music promoter Bob Neal, but Parker had effectively taken over operations by late 1955.

completed a deal that signed Elvis to the major RCA Victor label for the unprecedented sum of $35,000 (plus $5,000 as sign-up bonus), coupled with a publishing deal with Hill and Range. He also used his long-standing relationship with Abe Lastfogel, head of the William Morris talent agency, to book Elvis for national television appearances.[70] These decisions were pivotal for Elvis's meteoric rise the following year.

# The National Controversies Surrounding Elvis's Rise

In 1956, the United States was caught in a big national debate over the vices and virtues of a seemingly new phenomenon: the rise of the so-called teenager, a term that had first emerged in 1944 to describe young people between the ages of 14 and 18 as a distinct and socially relevant group.[71] While many features of teenager culture can actually be traced back as far as the nineteenth century, the major socioeconomic transformations following the end of the Second World War led to an unprecedented number of young and increasingly affluent adolescents between childhood and full adulthood responsibility.[72] By the early 1950s, the so-called teenagers were starting to use mass media and leisurely consumption as ways to create distinct youth cultures that differentiated them from their parents. The influence of traditional civic institutions like churches or schools seemed to fade, as advertisers and the media suddenly seemed to hold a lot of power over the American youth. While the emerging youth culture generally centered around cars, fast food, clothing, and dating, it occasionally took more threatening forms, including a general rise in juvenile delinquency in the postwar years. Hollywood stars like James Dean and Marlon Brando too projected powerful images of youthful alienation and teenage rebellion in movies like *The Wild One* (1953) or *Rebel without a Cause* (1955). As parents felt their control over their children slipping away, a big national debate emerged over youthful misbehavior, social order, and the role of advertising and the media. In 1953, the Democratic senator Estes Kefauver even set up a Senate Subcommittee on Juvenile Delinquency, which identified new mass media like comic books, radio, movies, and television as the main source behind teenage unrest.[73]

---

[70]Guralnick and Jorgensen, *Day by Day*, 54.
[71]Jon Savage, *Teenage: The Creation of Youth 1875–1945* (London: Pimlico, 2008), xiii.
[72]For more general accounts, see Gilbert, *Cycle of Outrage*, 3. Linda Martin and Kerry Segrave, *Anti-Rock: The Opposition to Rock 'n' Roll* (Hamden, CT: Archon Books, 1988); Medovoi, *Rebels*, 24–30.
[73]Gilbert, *Cycle of Outrage*, 3.

The rise of rock 'n' roll became inextricably intertwined with bigger debates over parental control and the burgeoning youth culture.[74] Already prior to Elvis's arrival, rock 'n' roll had become highly popular in the United States, due not least to the disc jockey Alan Freed's pioneering championship of the new music. To many teenagers, rock 'n' roll's energetic, pulsating rhythms seemed like an ideal outlet for youthful freedom and adolescent pleasure, and in so doing utilized it to construct new social and cultural identities amid the conformity and sterility of mid-1950s America.[75] Perhaps the major catalyst of the new music was the movie *Blackboard Jungle*. Released in 1955, it told a socially critical story of teenage alienation and anti-social behavior at an inner-city school, and featured Bill Haley & His Comets' "Rock Around the Clock" over its opening and closing credits. Teenagers enthusiastically embraced the movie, which led to packed theaters and triggered occasional vandalism. These events not only turned Haley's tune into a major youth anthem, but it also cemented the connection between rock 'n' roll and juvenile delinquency in public minds.[76] One parent, for example, wrote to the Kefauver Committee that rock 'n' roll had thrown "the juvenile world into open revolt against society," and that "the gangster of tomorrow" was "the Elvis Presley type of today."[77]

Although Elvis was by no means the first rock 'n' roll star to emerge on the US national stage, he became the new generation's major figurehead and prime pop-cultural icon within a matter of weeks. Elvis's unique combination of rock 'n' roll with the rebellious styles of Hollywood stars like Marlon Brando or James Dean made him the ideal figure around which the new trend could crystallize. Above all, however, Elvis's rise was due to the rapidly rising importance of television, which exposed Elvis to millions of American households almost in an instant. While previous stars like Frank Sinatra or Rudolf Valentino had already achieved mass adoration by youngsters, it was television that took the personality hype surrounding Elvis to new and unprecedented levels. It would have been impossible only a few years earlier: whereas only 9 percent of American households owned

---

[74]For general histories of rock 'n' roll in the 1950s United States, see Altschuler, *All Shook Up* and Aquila, *Let's Rock*. They differ in their assessments: whereas Altschuler stresses the music's rebellious nature and transformative power, Aquila suggests that rock 'n' roll was more conservative and conformist than previously depicted, reinforcing, rather than challenging, traditional values and mainstream attitudes.

[75]Altschuler, *All Shook Up*, 8.

[76]For an excellent history of the song's national and international career, see Jim Dawson, *Rock Around the Clock: The Record That Started The Rock Revolution!* (San Francisco, CA: Backbeat Books, 2005).

[77]Quoted in Brian Ward, *Just My Soul Responding: Rhythm and Blues, Black Consciousness, and Race Relations* (Berkeley, CA: University of California Press, 1998), 110.

television sets in 1950, that number had risen to 64.5 percent by 1956.[78] For Elvis, such mass exposure was crucial in two respects: not only did it enable his teenage fans to observe their idol's look and movements at first hand, but it also exposed him to hordes of unsuspecting adult viewers who might otherwise have remained oblivious to the new singer.[79]

Elvis's fairly regular appearances on Saturday night shows throughout 1956 became the center of his rise to fame, as well as the main source of the controversies surrounding him. From January to March 1956, Elvis's six appearances on *The Dorsey Brothers Stage Show* (CBS) already revealed the new singer's suitability for television, as ratings increased week by week. They were followed by two appearances on *The Milton Berle Show* (NBC) in April and June, the second of which became particularly notorious for Elvis's sexually charged performance of "Hound Dog." On July 1, Elvis then did a one-off performance on *The Steve Allen Show*, where he was put in a tuxedo and forced to perform the song to a real basset dog. The television run culminated in three appearances on *The Ed Sullivan Show* (CBS) from September 1956 to January 1957, for which Elvis received the unprecedented fee of $50,000 (for comparison, The Beatles would receive only $10,000 for their three appearances eight years later).[80] The first show was watched by 82.6 percent of the US television audience, thereby setting a new record, and Sullivan's announcement that he would film the singer only from the waist up during his final appearance became an integral part of Elvis's legacy.[81]

Initial reactions to Elvis's television appearances were strong, and almost uniformly negative. In many cases, the establishment's flat-out rejection of Elvis reflected a cultural snobbism that had been inherent in the misleading but popular dichotomy between "highbrow" and "lowbrow" culture since the nineteenth century, and which was strengthened by Elvis's class background and association with rural white Southern culture.[82] Major national newspapers as well as influential magazines like *Time, Life,* or *Cosmopolitan* all derided and ridiculed Elvis, seemingly competing over the most insulting descriptions. *Life,* for example, described him as a "21-year-old hillbilly who howls, mumbles, coos and cries his way through," wondering why the "$35-a-week Memphis truck driver" was now "the biggest singing attraction for teen-agers in the U.S.A."[83] The *Washington Post* followed suit. "Elvis Presley is not, as his name might lead you to believe, a Shakespearean actor, a Blue Book registerite or a college dean," it claimed in May 1956;

[78]Aquila, *Let's Rock!*, 125.
[79]For the paramount importance of television in facilitating Elvis's rise, see above all Wiener, *Channeling Elvis.*
[80]Wiener, *Channeling Elvis*, 75.
[81]Ibid., 88, 81.
[82]Levine, *Highbrow/Lowbrow*, 1–10; Doll, *Understanding Elvis*, 73–5.
[83]*Life Magazine*, April 30, 1956.

rather, he was "a tall, shyly earnest, shambling, 21-year-old native of Tupelo, Mississippi" who "cain't hol'" still' on stage and whose rise to fame had been "so fast even he 'cain't understand it'."[84] Writing in *Cosmopolitan* magazine, the jazz musician Eddie Condron simply asked, "What Is An Elvis Presley?" before declaring him to be final proof that one did not "have to have an enormous talent to get to the top."[85] Perhaps most indignant was the *New York Times* television critic Jack Gould, who denounced Elvis as a "virtuoso of the hootchy-kootchy" with "no discerning singing ability. His specialty is rhythm songs which he renders in an undistinguished whine; his phrasing, if it can be called that, consists of the stereotyped variations that go with a beginner's aria in a bathtub."[86]

Although cultural snobbism and class contempt often lay behind such coverage, journalistic outrage centered primarily on Elvis's on-stage movements. Mirroring some of the debates that had already taken place on a local level, the national media almost uniformly denounced Elvis's gyrations as inappropriate, vulgar, or immoral, depicting him as a threat to the prevailing moral and social norms of the day. The *New York Times*, for example, claimed that Elvis's movements had previously been "identified with the repertoire of the blonde bombshells of the burlesque runway,"[87] and *Life* magazine similarly talked about "a bump and grind routine usually seen only in burlesque."[88] Some regional newspapers spelled out their contempt rather more explicitly. *The Charlotte Observer*, for example, described Elvis's performances as "unbelievable burlesque, combining the elements of a strip teaser's bumps with the slapstick gawkiness of a Harpo Marx," whereas a writer at *The Sioux City Journal* declared it to have been "the most disgusting exhibition this reporter has ever seen."[89] Such rejections of open displays of sexuality occasionally combined with deeper underlying fears about racial mixing.[90] The *Dallas Morning Star* characterized Elvis's performance as a "really classical Indian war dance" with "sheer voodoo acrobatics," whereas the *Oakland Tribune* depicted Elvis and his band as "three young men blaring a jungle rhythm," with teenage girls howling "like banshees" in response.[91]

Such denouncements of Elvis's performances suggest underlying fears about the loosening of sexual and racial boundaries, which parts of the establishment perceived as a challenge to existing political and social orders.[92]

---

[84] *Washington Post*, May 27, 1956.
[85] *Cosmopolitan*, December 1956.
[86] *New York Times*, June 6, 1956.
[87] Ibid.
[88] *Life Magazine*, August 27, 1956.
[89] *The Charlotte Observer*, June 27, 1956; *The Sioux City Journal*, May 24, 1956.
[90] Cahn, *Sexual Reckonings*, 249.
[91] *Dallas Morning Star*, October 12, 1956; *Oakland Tribune*, June 5, 1956.
[92] Cahn, *Sexual Reckonings*, 267–8.

The loose and uninhibited reactions Elvis provoked among his female fans were thus perceived as a threat to the sexual conservatism and conformist ideals of the nuclear family.[93] "Each twitch of Presley's hip, each alternate pounding of the heels drove the young ladies present into a pandemonium of screams, shouts and shrieks," the *Oakland Tribune* reported; and the *Minnesota Star Tribune* similarly declared that Elvis had "turned a rainy Sunday afternoon into an orgy of squealing in St Paul auditorium."[94] On May 25, 1956, the *Kansas City Times* offered a particularly graphic description of the uninhibitedness of Elvis's concerts at the time:

> A girl got past the police, bounced up on the stage, and hugged and kissed her panting crocodile ... A policeman got her off again, but the signal for the avalanche was on. As the cool cats would say, they were determined to get really with him. They poured over the front and over the sides of the stage. They surrounded their almost prostrated hero, reaching for buttons, a piece of his shirt, a lock of his ducktail or anything they could grab. The Presley gyrations stopped suddenly. He was immobilized.[95]

As the public outcry over Elvis intensified, major national publications picked up and sensationalized such local reports. *Life Magazine*, for example, reported in April 1956 how "shortly girls" had "kicked through a plate-glass door in Amarillo" to get Elvis "to autograph their arms and underclothes"; a few months later, it described how Elvis's "easily aroused fans" had "ripped nearly all his clothes off" during a performance in Florida.[96] It also reported extensively on the civic resistance Elvis had encountered; according to *Life*, a local judge had observed Elvis's performance with pre-prepared warrants for "impairing the morals of minors," and a Baptist preacher had denounced Elvis in sermon for having "achieved a new low in spiritual degeneracy."[97] Many other publications featured similar stories of public outrage. In several cities, rock 'n' roll concerts were banned on the grounds of being vulgar and contributing to juvenile delinquency, and a number of high schools prohibited Elvis-style haircuts and expelled students if they did not obey by such rules.[98] The crassest denouncements of Elvis, however, came from Asa Carter, the segregationist leader of the White Citizens' Council of Alabama, who claimed that rock 'n' roll was "the basic, heavy-beat music of Negroes" designed to bring out "animalism and vulgarity," as well as an

---

[93]May, *Homeward Bound*, xiv.
[94]*Oakland Tribune*, June 5, 1956; *Minnesota Star Tribune*, May 14, 1956.
[95]*Kansas City Times*, May 25, 1956.
[96]*Life Magazine*, April 30 and August 27, 1956.
[97]*Life Magazine*, August 27, 1956.
[98]For some reports, see *Corpus Christi Caller Times*, April 16, 1956; *New York Times*, February 25, 1957; *Washington Post*, November 17, 1956.

attempt by the National Association for the Advancement of Colored People (NAACP) to pull "the white man down to the level of the Negro."[99]

Such heated reactions against Elvis already show how his music and performances revealed some of the major social tensions in mid-1950s United States. In the most general sense, many teenagers endorsed Elvis as a sign of nonverbal rebellion against the sterility and conformity of their social lives.[100] Many fans also seem to have used Elvis's concerts as outlets for feelings and emotions they felt otherwise suppressed at the age of anxiety. "[I]t is simply impossible to sit still while Elvis is on stage," one fan wrote to *Life Magazine*. "His belting style drives us wild. We have to do something. Kick the seat in

Figure 1.2 *Elvis performs to an ecstatic crowd in Florida, August 1956.*

---

[99]As quoted in both Altschuler, *All Shook Up*, 38, and Martin and Segrave, *Anti-Rock*, 41.
[100]This is the main thrust of Altschuler, *All Shook Up*, who suggests that rock 'n' roll played a key part in reconstructing 1950s youth identities.

front or let out a 'rebel yell' or something."[101] It is interesting that Elvis's own perceptions seemed to mirror such views. In an interview recorded on August 29, 1956, for example, he claimed that "rhythm and blues really knocks it out. I watch my audience and listen to 'em and I know that we're all getting something out of our system. None of us knows what it is. The important thing is that we're getting rid of it and nobody's getting hurt."[102]

Indeed, Elvis's personal background seems to have been a major point of identification to many fans, as the singer's image also came to serve as a negotiating platform for bigger issues of class. "I didn't like Sinatra in his day but I like Elvis," one slightly older supporter told *The Charlotte Observer* in June 1956. "He's country and I am too."[103] Rather than linking Elvis's rural Southern background to stereotypes of backwardness and primitivism, then, his fans instead regarded it as a sign of the singer's authenticity, and therefore utilized it to differentiate their tastes against the dominant mainstream culture of the time.[104] "Man, he looks and acts just like one of us crazy mixed-up kids," a teenager told the *Lubbock Evening Avalanche Journal* in April 1956, "Only when he gets up steam, he blows it off."[105]

The Elvis phenomenon also unleashed torrents of sexual energy, and it enabled girls in particular to freely express desire in an otherwise highly conservative social environment. Such rebellion against the era's rigid moral codes manifested itself in largely nonverbal ways, such as in uninhibited screams, ecstatic dancing, and general ecstasy during Elvis's concerts.[106] Some fans also called out the hypocrisy behind critics' moral codes rather more explicitly. "No one complains about the female strip-teasers but when it comes to Elvis, it's a different story," a reader from Rochester, NY, wrote to *Life Magazine*; "When he was on the Milton Berle show the criticisms started flying. But when a girl danced the way an uncivilized native would, no one said a thing. That really scorched me."[107] A self-proclaimed "U.S. Citizen" even suspected a certain male insecurity behind the critics' sharp opposition to Elvis in the *Washington Post*: "I think you, like all other men, are just jealous of Elvis because he has a large female following ... Get off of Elvis' neck."[108] At the same time, there remained limits to rock 'n' roll's emancipatory impact. The overwhelming majority of press reports, for example, depicted the open expressions of female sexuality at Elvis's concerts as unconscious and passive reactions to the singer's seductive powers, rather than acknowledging girls' own agency, and only rarely did such teenage

---

[101]*Life Magazine*, May 21, 1956.
[102]Osborne, *Word for Word*, 78–9.
[103]*The Charlotte Observer*, June 27, 1956.
[104]Duffett, *Elvis*, 7.
[105]*Lubbock Evening Avalanche Journal*, April 11, 1956.
[106]Cahn, *Sexual Reckonings*, 251.
[107]*Life Magazine*, September 17, 1956.
[108]*Washington Post*, July 1, 1956.

rebellion extend into established political or social environments like churches or the family.[109]

A similarly ambivalent picture emerges as regards questions of race. To some extent, of course, Elvis personified a new generation whose unprejudiced embrace of rhythm 'n' blues music signaled an open and sincere endorsement of African American culture.[110] By extension, youths' embrace of Elvis might similarly be seen as evidence of greater racial tolerance: if the establishment rejected Elvis's music because of its racial connotations, then its endorsement by white teenagers can be read as the stark rejection of such views. Indeed, it is significant that many black rhythm 'n' blues artists at the time did not see Elvis as a cultural appropriator, but rather as a crossover artist who enabled rhythm 'n' blues to break into the mainstream of US popular music. "Let me tell you this," Little Richard asserted once, "when I came out they wasn't playing no black artists on no top 40 stations ... [I]t took people like Elvis and Pat Boone and Gene Vincent to open the door. And I thank God for Elvis Presley, I thank the Lord for sending Elvis to open the door so I could walk down the road, you understand?"[111]

Not only did the popularity of rock 'n' roll facilitate opportunities for black performers to break into the mass market, but Elvis himself was also initially popular among black audiences.[112] During the 1950s, Elvis's records were frequently played on black radio stations, and he was the fourth most programmed artist on *Billboard*'s rhythm 'n' blues airplay charts in 1956—after Little Richard, Fats Domino, and the Platters.[113] In his hometown Memphis, local African American newspapers praised Elvis as a "race man," and reported that he had recently broken segregation laws by visiting a local amusement park on a designated "colored night."[114] On December 7, 1956, Elvis made headlines by attending a segregated fund-raiser show organized by WDIA, after all the radio station that called itself the "Mother Station of the Negroes." Although Elvis's contract prohibited him from actually performing on stage, his short appearance from behind the curtain caused furor among the all-black audience, and he spent several hours backstage with other performers like Rufus Thomas and B.B. King afterward.[115] "Remember, this was the fifties, so for a young white boy

[109]Cahn, *Sexual Reckonings*, 260–1, 265.

[110]This, of course, is the main argument of the most authoritative study on the subject, Bertrand, *Race, Rock, and Elvis*, 231–2. More generally, see also Ward, *Just My Soul Responding*; Altschuler, *All Shook Up*, 35–66.

[111]As quoted in Simpson, *Rough Guide to Elvis*, 188.

[112]Ward, *Just My Soul Responding*, 44.

[113]Although the charts did not distinguish between black and white disc jockeys at the time. See Ward, *Just My Soul Responding*, 139; 134–42.

[114]Guralnick, *Last Train*, 369–70.

[115]Ibid., 368–70; Bertrand, *Race, Rock, and Elvis*, 203–4.

to show up at an all-black function took guts," King later reflected in his
memoirs; "I believe he was showing his roots. And he seemed proud of
those roots ... Elvis didn't steal any music from anyone. He just had his own
interpretation of the music he'd grown up with. Same was true for me; the
same's true for everyone. I think Elvis had integrity."[116]

Figure 1.3 *King Creole (1958) is one of Elvis's few movies that allude to the
African-American roots of his music*

---

[116]B.B. King, *Blues All Around Me: The Autobiography of B.B. King* (New York, NY: Avon
Books, 1996), 186.

Elvis's initial acceptance among the black community was helped by the fact that he continued to exhibit absolutely no racial prejudice, and that he publicly acknowledged his debt to black rhythm 'n' blues artists on several occasions. In an interview in Los Angeles in June 1956, for example, he defended rhythm 'n' blues as being simply "a music … it's a craze, but it's a very good craze in that there is some very beautiful songs recorded in rhythm and blues, if the people will just take time … some of the people that don't like it … would just take time to listen to it."[117] He also admired Jackie Wilson, whom he had seen perform in Las Vegas several times, and later confessed to Carl Perkins and Jerry Lee Lewis at the famous *Million Dollar Quartet* jam session at Sun Studios that Wilson's version of "Don't Be Cruel" was "much better" than his own. He also imitated some of Wilson's movements and pronunciations during his final Ed Sullivan appearance.[118] Elvis's most explicit statement of his debt to African American culture came on June 1, 1956, when he told the *Charlotte Observer*:

The colored folks have been singing it and playing it just like I'm doin' now, man, for more years than I know. They played it like that in the shanties and in their juke joints, and nobody paid it no mind 'til I goosed it up. Down in Tupelo, Mississippi, I used to hear old Arthur Crudup bang his box the way I do now, and I said if I ever got to the place where I could feel all old Arthur felt, I'd be a music man like nobody ever saw.[119]

Yet Elvis's popularity with black audiences took a sharp nosedive in April 1957, when the (white-owned) *Sepia* magazine published a highly negative article with the headline "How Negroes Feel About Elvis," in which it claimed that Elvis had allegedly slurred that "the only thing Negroes can do for me is shine my shoes and buy my records" during a visit to Boston. Although both *Jet* and *Tan* magazine subsequently went out of their ways to conclusively prove the rumor wrong—they interviewed several black performers who testified to the singer's lack of racial prejudice, had Elvis himself deny it ("I never said anything like that, and people who know me know I wouldn't have said it"), and even conducted research that Elvis had never been to Boston his entire life—it was a rumor that stuck in public memory, and one that still resurfaces occasionally to this day.[120] There are other limitations to the view of Elvis as a forerunner of cultural integration. Even though many white teenagers enjoyed black rhythm 'n' blues music, for example, their embrace rarely constituted an explicit challenge to the racial order at the time. As the historian Brian Ward

---

[117]Osborne, *Word for Word*, 33.

[118]Wiener, *Channeling Elvis*, 78; Simpson, *Elvis Films FAQ*, 375. Elvis's remarks can be heard on several recent releases of the Million Dollar Quartet sessions.

[119]Quoted in Guralnick, *Last Train*, 289.

[120]Bertrand, *Race, Rock, and Elvis*, 219–22; Guralnick, *Last Train*, 426.

points out, it was completely normal to enjoy rhythm 'n' blues music from a jukebox at a diner and still conform to the racial orthodoxies of 1950s US society.[121] Neither did the endorsement of rock 'n' roll automatically or necessarily translate into greater racial tolerance.[122] Many fans simply remained ignorant of rock 'n' roll racial connotations, and one teenager apparently saw no contradiction in describing herself as an Elvis Presley fan while posing with a Confederate flag in *Look* magazine.[123]

Most importantly, there remained the highly contentious issue of commercial exploitation. Although accusations of cultural appropriation did not really emerge until the late 1960s,[124] the issue of economic exploitation was already hotly debated in the 1950s. Black artists were routinely denied access to mainstream airwaves of television or radio, and they also suffered heavily from discriminatory pay scales or a lack of royalties. The African American songwriter Otis Blackwell, for example, was forced by Colonel Parker to share his songwriting credits for "All Shook Up" and "Don't Be Cruel" with Elvis, which left him with rather mixed feelings.[125] Elvis's management eventually ended these practices in 1957, fearing public criticism.[126] Arthur Crudup too professed to like Elvis's version of his song "That's All Right Mama," but was upset by the lack of public recognition for himself. "I was hearing my songs on the jukeboxes and places," he recalled; "but I wasn't getting enough money to make a living."[127] Ultimately, Elvis's commercial success was still partly rooted in the prevailing power relations of the day, regardless of what he may have personally thought of racial divides.

## The Politics of the Marketplace

The intense public controversies surrounding Elvis's rise served to negotiate highly complex questions of class, race, and gender, but they also reflected debates over the roles and responsibilities of civic authorities and the media in a rapidly changing cultural landscape. As the new phenomenon of mass media, above all television, enabled teenagers to pursue their own distinct tastes and interests, previous societal stakeholders felt their control over youths' tastes, as well as perhaps their wider cultural hegemony, slipping away. Yet, although many perceived the influence of mass media as a threat, others saw it as a transformative tool toward a greater cultural egalitarianism.[128]

---

121 Ward, *Just My Soul Responding*, 38.
122 Bertrand, *Race, Rock, and Elvis*, 232.
123 Altschuler, *All Shook Up*, 49.
124 Ward, *Just My Soul Responding*, 141–2.
125 Ibid., 45.
126 Duffett, *Elvis*, 43.
127 Quoted in Bertrand, *Race, Rock, and Elvis*, 202.
128 Gilbert, *Cycle of Outrage*, 4, 212.

In the case of Elvis, such debates crystallized yet again around the singer's controversial television performances. Elvis's raunchy rendition of "Hound Dog" during his second Milton Berle appearance caused particular outrage, and ensured that all his future television appearances would be closely scrutinized by the public. They also brought issues of censorship to the forefront of the debate. The *New York Times* columnist Jack Gould, for example, attacked the mass media for having facilitated Elvis's rise in the first place. "When Presley executes his bumps and grinds," he wrote after Elvis's first Sullivan appearance in September 1956, "it must be remembered by the Columbia Broadcasting System that even the 12-year-old's curiosity may be overstimulated ... [S]elfish exploitation and commercialized overstimulation of youth's physical impulses is certainly a gross national disservice." For Gould, the Elvis hype seemed final proof of the entertainment industries' obsession with commercial profit at the expense of wider societal considerations. "If the profiteering hypocrite is above reproach and Presley isn't," he concluded, "today's youngsters might well ask what God do adults worship."[129] The Archbishop of New York Francis Spellman agreed, declaring that the root cause of society's malaise lay not with teenagers but "with us – their priests, parents and teachers who do not constantly and actively work and pray to arrest the avalanche of lewd comic books, equally lewd films and television features, indecent magazine picture stories, obscene, suggestive dancing to which they are daily subjected."[130] Many parents expressed feelings of powerlessness against the mass media in readers' letters to newspapers and magazines. "When television entrepreneurs present such performers to millions of viewers and pronounce them great, when such deplorable taste is displayed in the presentation of primitive, shoddy and offensive material, one begins to understand the present day attitude of our youth," a high school teacher wrote to the *Washington Post*. "We in the classroom can do very little to offset the force and impact of these displays in our efforts to stem the tide toward a cultural debacle."[131]

The irony of such debates was that they only served to increase Elvis's popularity even further. When Milton Berle received scores of angry protest letters about Elvis's recent appearance, for example, he simply told Colonel Parker that he now had a star on his hands.[132] The thoughts of television veteran Ed Sullivan followed similar patterns. Although he had initially pledged to never have Elvis appear on his show, he changed his mind once his direct rival Steve Allen had beaten his ratings for the first time by inviting Elvis.[133] Less than two weeks later, Sullivan announced that he had

---

[129]*New York Times*, September 16, 1956.
[130]*New York Times*, October 1, 1956.
[131]*Washington Post*, June 18, 1956.
[132]Quoted in Wiener, *Channeling Elvis*, 42.
[133]Ibid., 57.

signed Elvis for three appearances, apparently because of the "thousands of letters from teen-agers asking him to have the singer on his show."[134] Such hypocrisy did not escape the attention of attuned observers. The *Washington Post*, for example, pointed out that Elvis's managers only profited from the singer's "public indignation. They convert outrage into cash when the freak followers line up at the box office." The reason that "no steps have been taken to ban Presley" was due to the fact that "rock 'n' roll is the hottest fad to strike the musical frenzy since the Charleston. It is big business. The kids love it."[135]

Another reason why rock 'n' roll was not banned lay in the fact that public perceptions of Elvis and his fans also changed over time. Commentators and journalists came to perceive the new musical trend no longer as an all-out assault on American life, but instead depicted it as a much smaller-scale teenage rebellion that could fairly easily be contained by US society. From their perspective, Elvis seemed less like a fundamental threat to the American youth than as a harmless teenage fad.[136] When the *New York Times* hosted a panel to discuss the new teenage phenomenon, for example, an invited psychiatrist proclaimed that rock 'n' roll was merely the expression of teenagers' "rebellious attitudes" that were "more or less a phase."[137] The *Washington Post* too quoted a Columbia Records representative who described rock 'n' roll as merely "a safe form of rebellion against mother, father and teacher. It's a way they can take out their feelings of independence without hurting those they love."[138] Interestingly, a lot of parents seemed to agree with such views. "The actions of those teen-age girls made me realize how silly and simple I was when I almost went haywire over Johnny Ray," one of them wrote to *Life Magazine*; "I guess it is just a phase we all go through."[139] Some parents even joined their children in battle. When a student in Macomb County, MI, unsuccessfully appealed against his high school's decision to expel him for an Elvis haircut, his mother defended him defiantly. "We're going to try to get Robert into another school," she told the *Washington Post*. "We don't want to live under a dictatorship."[140]

It helped, of course, that Elvis's off-stage personality did not at all match the prevalent stereotype of the juvenile delinquent. As journalists rarely failed to point out, Elvis always appeared well behaved and polite in interviews, at times appearing almost deferential in public. "Offstage Presley" was a "shy young

---

[134] *New York Times*, July 14, 1956; Bernie Ilson, *Sundays with Sullivan: How the Ed Sullivan Show Brought Elvis, The Beatles, and Culture to America* (Lanham, MD: Taylor Trade Publishing, 2009), 53.

[135] *Washington Post*, June 23, 1956.

[136] Aquila, *Let's Rock!*, xiv, 146–8; Gilbert, *Cycle of Outrage*, 196–211.

[137] *New York Times*, November 26, 1956.

[138] *Washington Post*, June 25, 1956.

[139] *Life Magazine*, September 17, 1956.

[140] *Washington Post*, November 17, 1956.

man" who did not smoke and drink, the *Daily Oklahoman* reported on April 20, 1956, and he unfailingly addressed his opposites as sir or madam.[141] When Elvis received a polio shot in New York as part of a vaccination campaign, the *New York Times* similarly described him as "a polite, personable, quick-witted and charming young man."[142] After Elvis's final Ed Sullivan appearance, the host famously declared to the nation that Elvis was "a real decent, fine boy ... we want to say that we've never had a pleasanter experience on our show with a big name than we've had with you."[143]

The ambiguity between Elvis's personality and the sound and fury surrounding his performances was striking. In a rare television interview with Hy Gardner, the singer took care to stress that he "was raised in a pretty decent home and everything. My folks always made me behave whether I wanted to or not."[144] Yet he also defended his fans strongly against derogatory accusations by the media. "Sir, those kids that come here and pay their money to see this show, come to have a good time," he angrily exclaimed to an interviewer a few months later;

> If they wanna pay their money to come out and jump around, and scream and yell, it's their business. They'll grow up someday and grow out of that. But while they're young let 'em have their fun. Don't let some old man that's so old he can't get around, sit around and call 'em a bunch o' idiots, because they're just human beings like he is ... I'm not tryin' to be vulgar, I'm not tryin to sell any sex, I'm not tryin' to look vulgar and nasty. I just enjoy what I'm doin' and tryin' to make the best of it.[145]

# The Power of the Marketplace

Whether in spite or because of the public controversies surrounding Elvis, 1956 was a year of unprecedented commercial triumph and personal success. Elvis appeared on all major television shows in the country, scored five number-one singles ("Heartbreak Hotel," "I Want You, I Need You, I Love You," "Don't Be Cruel," "Hound Dog," and "Love Me Tender"), and broke all previous records with the sales figures of his singles, EPs, and albums. On April 25, 1956, Elvis even signed a Hollywood contract with Paramount's producers Hal Wallis, the ultimate sign of 1950s superstardom.

But not everything was well. Colonel Parker in particular was concerned that the scandals surrounding Elvis's television appearances might ultimately

---

[141]*Daily Oklahoman*, April 20, 1956.
[142]*New York Times*, October 29, 1956.
[143]Wiener, *Channeling Elvis*, 96.
[144]Osborne, *Word for Word*, 43.
[145]Ibid., 51.

limit his wider appeal, not least among the teenage fans' parents on whose revenue the singer ultimately depended.[146] Parker's fears were shared by Chick Crumpacker, a representative of Elvis's record company RCA, as well as by Hal Wallis.[147] After Elvis's second Milton Berle appearance, Wallis's partner Joseph Hazen claimed that there was "no doubt that Presley went completely overboard," and that even RCA were "having their heads beaten in by the public protest."[148] Parker clearly saw the signs, and repeatedly urged his client to tame down his performances. Indeed, Elvis's television appearances became significantly more choreographed and somewhat more restrained over time. At his final Sullivan appearance, he performed ballads like "Love Me Tender" or "When My Blue Moon Turns to Gold Again" as well as his rock 'n' roll standards, and finished the show with the gospel "Peace in the Valley" that Sullivan declared it to be a tribute to the Hungarian Uprising.[149] Elvis also released a gospel EP and a Christmas album in 1957.

There remained controversies over Elvis's live performances, which frequently seemed to escalate. In August 1956, a local judge in Jacksonville, FL, threatened Elvis with arrest if he did not tone down his act; Elvis responded by moving only his little finger throughout the performance and the crowd went wild nonetheless.[150] At his Los Angeles debut in October 1957, he faced an unprecedented press onslaught for having rolled around on stage with a life-size stuffed animal version of RCA's mascot Nipper. Elvis's "disgraceful exhibition ... was absolutely frightful in its cynical pandering to the most violent sexuality, not too far short of Sodom and Gomorrah," Jack O'Brian wrote in the *New York Journal* afterward, proclaiming that the details of "Presley's contortions and violent exhibition rolling on the stage floor with a stuffed dog" were "far too indecent to mention."[151] The *Los Angeles Mirror-News* even echoed historical fears about the alleged seductiveness of mass culture by musing that Elvis's "Frantic Sex Show" had "looked like one of those screeching, uninhibited party rallies which the Nazis used to hold for Hitler."[152] In response to the outrage, the LA Police Department decided to film Elvis's second appearance the following night, which toned down the act considerably. In April and August 1957, Elvis's five appearances in Canada caused additional scandal, as newspaper

[146] *Wiener, Channeling Elvis*, 62.
[147] Ibid., 4.
[148] Hazen to Wallis, June 11, 1956. [M]argaret [H]errick [L]ibrary, Los Angeles, CA (United States), Hal Wallis Papers, Presley, Elvis, contract correspondence, f.2112.
[149] Wiener, *Channeling Elvis*, 93–4, 96.
[150] For a great recollection with lots of pictures (*Life* magazine was present at the gig as well), see "Elvis Presley | Jacksonville, FL," https://www.elvispresleymusic.com.au/pictures/1956-florida-state-theater-august-10-11.html [last accessed December 12, 2019].
[151] *New York Journal*, November 8, 1957.
[152] *Los Angeles Mirror-News*, October 29, 1957.

columnists almost universally denounced Elvis as the prime example of the negative effects of US cultural dominance. Eight students at the Notre Dame Convent in Ottawa were expelled for having attended Elvis's performance.[153] The conservative newspaper *Vancouver Sun,* however, suggested a simpler solution. "[I]f any daughter of mine broke out of the woodshed tonight to see Elvis Presley in the Empire Stadium," its columnist Mac Reynolds declared, "I'd kick her in the teeth."[154]

Partly as a result of such scandals, the marketing of Elvis shifted increasingly toward an all-round marketing of his public persona as a charming but harmless teenage celebrity. Indeed, Parker wasted no time in building up a colossal marketing machine for Elvis, enlisting the services of Hollywood merchandising expert Henry Saperstein. The results were phenomenal: by the end of the year, Elvis fans could buy over eighty items of merchandise, ranging from charm bracelets and Elvis-themed lipsticks to dolls and glow-in-the-dark posters.[155] "Elvis Presley today is a business," Saperstein told the *Wall Street Journal* in December 1956, bragging how orders of around $22 million had been placed in the last quarter of the year alone.[156] Parker also professionalized the emerging fan scene by setting up an official "Elvis Presley Fan Club," where subscribers had to pay in order to receive newsletters and photographs of their idol. The consumption of Elvis products thus became an integral part of fans' identification with the singer.[157]

The personal marketing surely played some part in the shift in adult perceptions of rock 'n' roll music from a societal danger to a commercial product.[158] The market researcher Eugene Gilbert, for example, claimed at the time that Elvis distinguished himself from other stars first and foremost by the way in which he was sold. Presley, Gilbert argued, was getting "a colossal build up by some of the top brains in every aspect of merchandising to the teen level. They are attempting to make the Presley name the watchword to look for on every sort of product catering to the teen and pre-teen taste."[159] Indeed, Gilbert was the avant-garde of an increasing number of entrepreneurs who came to see the enormous commercial potential of the emerging youth market, and who deliberately set out to tackle it.[160] As the

---

[153]Guralnick and Jorgensen, *Day by Day,* 102.

[154]*Vancouver Sun,* August 31, 1957.

[155]For further background on Parker's and Saperstein's marketing activities, see Nash, *The Colonel,* 119, 127. For a fan book that investigates EPE's early marketing and includes a fascinating A–Z catalogue of all available items, see Bob Pakes, *The EPE Catalog: A Comprehensive A to Z Guide of Vintage Elvis Presley Enterprises Memorabilia* (Oslo: KJ Consulting, 2017).

[156]*Wall Street Journal,* December 31, 1956.

[157]Aquila, *Let's Rock!,* 135.

[158]Gilbert, *Cycle of Outrage,* 205–10.

[159]Quoted in an extensive profile on Eugene Gilbert in the *New Yorker,* November 29, 1958.

[160]Gilbert, *Cycle of Outrage,* 215.

journalist Eric Sevareid reflected only half-ironically in the *Washington Post*, "Teen-agers used to be told what to think. Now swarms of motivational researchers are going around asking them what they think."[161]

Elvis's superstardom and unprecedented commercial success eventually came to dominate his public image. Even the most critical reports on Elvis invariably stressed his fame and income, occasionally listing the precise amount of money he had earned thus far. *Life* magazine, for example, told its readers in August 1956 that Elvis had "fallen just short of grossing half a million dollars" to date: "$100,000 for over 125 public appearances, $350,000 in record loyalties, $20,000 from TV, and $50,000 more due in the fall for three Ed Sullivan appearances."[162] Local newspapers too rarely failed to mention the particular salary Elvis had received for his appearances. At times, such references to Elvis's commercial success were also used as the justification of Elvis's presence in American public life. As the *Tampa Daily Times* put it in August 1956, "The 21-year-old former Tupelo, Miss., truck driver answers critics who say he 'can't carry a tune in a bucket' with his $1,000,000 bankroll, his fleet of flashy automobiles and his great following, The Teenager."[163] Some of Elvis's fans put such market logic in somewhat blunter terms. "Maybe he isn't the best educated person in the world," a teenager told the *San Antonio Express and News* in October 1956, "but he makes a lot of money."[164]

Such statements not only reflected underlying debates about the value of labor in Fordist society, but they also tied into bigger narratives of upward mobility and capitalist success in the United States. Mass consumerism had of course played a powerful part in popular constructions of US identities since at least the turn of the century; at the height of the Cold War, however, the act of consumption acquired even more political symbolism.[165] It is thus no surprise that Elvis, whose imagination had been captured by the pop-cultural images of capitalist success from an earliest age, celebrated his newly acquired wealth with the purchase of flashy clothes, eccentric jewelry, and expensive cars. "Wearing a lavender checked sport coat, ruffled ivory shirt open at the neck and charcoal slacks that draped over his heels," the *Long Beach Independent* told its readers in June 1956, "Presley arrived in a new black Cadillac convertible, one of three he owns";[166] the *St Petersburg Times* reported in similar vein that the "ex-truck driver" now owned "four new Cadillacs in a rainbow assortment of colors, a fancy Harley-Davidson motorcycle and a three-wheeled Messerschmidt. Other holdings include

---

[161]*Washington Post*, December 16, 1956.
[162]*Life Magazine*, August 27, 1956.
[163]*Tampa Daily Times*, August 6, 1956.
[164]*San Antonio Express and News*, October 14, 1956.
[165]Cohen, *Consumers' Republic*, 10–12; McGovern, *Sold American*; Roland Marchand, *Advertising the American Dream: Making Way for Modernity, 1920–1940* (Berkeley, CA: University of California Press, 1985).
[166]*Long Beach Independent*, June 8, 1956.

a ranch home in Memphis, complete with swimming pool, and a tidy wardrobe that includes 30 sports coats and 40 sport jackets, the Presley trademarks."[167] When Elvis purchased Graceland, the *Memphis Press-Scimitar* ran the headline "Mansion Fit for a (Rock 'n' Roll) King."[168]

Elvis's unabashed display of his newly found wealth soon became an integral part of his public image. It framed him into more mainstream narratives of postwar American society, which increasingly tended to sideline or altogether ignore Elvis's rural Southern background.[169] Symbols of Elvis's wealth and fame also found their way into his performances. On March 28, 1957, Elvis performed in Chicago in a $2,500 gold-leaf suit, combined with gold slippers and bow tie. Although the suit had been designed on the instructions of Parker and Elvis himself did not really like it, he wore it several more times, and it became a key part of his iconography.[170] It achieved additional fame through the album cover of *Elvis' Gold Records, Vol. 2* (1959), which featured several pictures of Elvis in the golden lamé suit and the slogan "50,000,000 Elvis fans can't be wrong." In public statements and rare interviews, Elvis tended to embrace the American Dream narratives that were constructed around him, even if he occasionally added a self-ironic twist. In August 1956, for example, he told an interviewer about the fate of his famous pink Cadillac:

Well when I was drivin' a truck, every time a big shiny car drove by it started me sort of daydreaming. I always felt that someday, somehow, something would happen to change everything for me, and I'd daydream about how it would be. The first car I ever bought was the most beautiful car I've ever seen. It was a second hand but I parked it outside of my hotel the day I got it, and sat up all night just lookin' at it. And the next day, the thing caught fire and burned up on the road.[171]

What did more than anything to re-shape Elvis's public image, however, was the singer's move to Hollywood. From a management perspective, it seemed like the logical move to take: Hollywood was not only the place where Elvis could be marketed most lucratively, but it was also where his image could be most tightly controlled.[172] After 1956, Parker drastically limited Elvis's live performances, refused all offers for future television

---

[167]*St Petersburg Times*, July 24, 1956.
[168]*Memphis Press Scimitar*, March 24, 1957.
[169]Doll, *Understanding Elvis*, 119.
[170]Guralnick, *Last Train*, 399–400.
[171]Osborne, *Word for Word*, 79.
[172]Elvis's Hollywood career will be discussed a lot more extensively in Chapter 4. For the relationship between Elvis's 1950s movies and more general rock 'n' roll movies at the time, see David E. James, *Rock "N" Film: Cinema's Dance with Popular Music* (Oxford: Oxford University Press, 2016), 73–91.

**Figure 1.4** *Elvis performs in his $2,500 gold-leaf suit in March 1957.*

appearances, and concentrated firmly on Elvis's movie career.[173] It helped that Elvis, who had harbored acting ambitions ever since his childhood, was eager to prove himself in Hollywood, and that the movie industry could not wait for the new singer either: when the famous Paramount producer Hal Wallis saw Elvis's appearance on the *Dorsey Brothers* show, he was so taken by the singer's charisma that he immediately decided to invite him for a screen-test.[174] Yet, Elvis's movie debut actually took place with 20th Century Fox, to

[173]Wiener, *Channeling Elvis*, 97.
[174]Hal Wallis and Charles Higham, *Starmaker: The Autobiography of Hal Wallis* (New York: Macmillan Publishing, 1980), 147–8.

which he was loaned out for a Civil War western originally titled *The Reno Brothers* but later renamed *Love Me Tender* (1956). It was enthusiastically received by fans and virulently denounced by newspaper critics.[175]

By contrast, Elvis's subsequent three 1950s movies all constituted conscious efforts to reshape Elvis's star image in the public imagination.[176] Perhaps the most interesting one in that regard is Elvis's first Paramount production *Loving You* (1957), a semi-biographical but heavily sanitized analogy to Elvis's career. Elvis plays a naïve but good-natured delivery man called Deke, whose miraculous singing talents are discovered by an aging country band leader and his manager. The two scrupulous music business professionals then take Deke under their wings and engineer his breakthrough, but Deke arouses controversy with his music and eccentric on-stage movements. In a highly poignant scene toward the end, the manager defends Deke in front of a city council. "You cannot blame the behavior of young people or old people on music," she proclaims; "thirty years ago people were alarmed by what they thought jazz was doing to the country ... Now you're adopting the same attitude toward rock 'n' roll, because you can't use it to blow off steam." She even concludes her speech with a passionate plea for American values: "The name of your city is Freegate ... How about living up to its name?" It is a particularly blatant example of how Elvis's image was reconstructed into a good-natured country boy pursuing an exciting but essentially apolitical musical trend; an image that became central to many later depictions of Elvis's life and career.

Before entering the army in March 1958, Elvis starred in another two movies—*Jailhouse Rock* (1957) and *King Creole* (1958). While *Jailhouse Rock* might be considered another loosely biographical take that depicted Elvis as a juvenile delinquent rising to singing fame, *King Creole* in many ways constituted Elvis's most ambitious movie.[177] Set in the French quarter of New Orleans, it featured Elvis as the school dropout Danny Fisher who sings in a local nightclub but gets drawn into various brawls and family feuds. Directed by Casablanca director Michael Curtiz, it showcased Elvis as a serious dramatic actor, and it has since often been praised as one of his best acting efforts.[178] Throughout 1957 and 1958, Elvis also achieved several more number-one hits ("Too Much," "All Shook Up," "(Let Me Be Your) Teddy Bear," "Jailhouse Rock," "Don't"), and celebrated commercial successes with soundtrack albums as well as the *Elvis' Golden Records* (1958) compilation. But there were no further television appearances after January 1957, and his three performances in Honolulu in November 1957 were the last time he appeared in front of a live audience during the 1950s. It set the tone for the things that were to follow.

---

[175]Simpson, *Elvis Films FAQ*, 1–18; Neibaur, *Elvis Movies*, 9–15.
[176]Doll, *Understanding Elvis*, 105.
[177]James, *Rock "N" Film*, 73–91; Neibaur, *Elvis Movies*, 27–37.
[178]Neibaur, *Elvis Movies*, 38–48.

# Conclusion

Elvis Presley's emergence in the mid-1950s United States was intrinsically connected to some of the country's major societal tensions. With his class background and unique music and performance style, Elvis came to embody as well as to challenge the prevalent, yet fragile, Cold War consensus at the time, particularly along the lines of class, race, and gender. While Elvis's background as a poor Southern white triggered harsh rejections and class contempt, for example, it also endowed him with seeming authenticity among thousands of teenagers with similar backgrounds. As regards race too, Elvis's creative fusion of African American rhythm 'n' blues music and hillbilly country was simultaneously derided by large parts of the American establishment and embraced by countless teenagers who, like Elvis, showed few hesitations to get in touch with black culture. And while Elvis's provocative stage shows triggered some virile denouncements by those who saw their cultural hegemony under threat, they also provided teenagers with new opportunities to freely express their sexuality, as well as to rebel against the conscripted nature and sterility of daily life in the mid-1950s United States.

Rather than being a symbol of one-sided rebellion or conformity, then, Elvis rather seems to reflect the contradictions and duplicity of American society in the mid-1950s. Elvis himself clearly did not have any particular political or social agenda; the rebel image was usually endowed onto him by others. And while he always defended the African American origins of his music as well as the behavior of his fans in public, he also displayed traditional conservative values, such as his clean lifestyle, religiosity, and strong allegiance to his family. Ultimately, these bigger ambiguities of Elvis's public image became contained in the bigger American Dream narrative that was constructed around him; a narrative that located Elvis within the wider civic ideology of consumerism while sidelining the more controversial issues of class, race, and gender that were initially associated with him.

It is also questionable whether Elvis's teenage fans really embraced Elvis as an all-out challenge to the prevailing social and racial norms of the day, or whether he ultimately constituted a relatively harmless outlet for teenage rebellion and nuclear anxiety that was still safely contained within the larger political and social framework of US society.[179] Indeed, as Susan Cahn and Brian Ward have suggested, it was fairly common for 1950s teenagers to embrace African American rhythm 'n' blues music, and to uninhibitedly express their sexuality in sound and dance, while still being safely contained within traditional societal structures that reinforced, rather than challenged, racial and patriarchal inequalities.[180] Paradoxically, then, Elvis Presley ultimately ended up both challenging and reinforcing American Cold War identities in the mid-1950s.

---

[179]Medovoi, *Rebels*, 34–5, 38; Aquila, *Let's Rock!*, xiv.
[180]Cahn, *Sexual Reckonings*, 265; Ward, *Just My Soul Responding*, 38.

# 2

# Cold War Elvis: The 1950s Abroad

In 1956, Elvis Presley came to be known around the world almost as quickly as within in the United States. Although Elvis never performed abroad during his entire lifetime,[1] he turned into an international phenomenon within months, as his record company RCA aggressively pushed his records into emerging new markets, journalists everywhere reported on the new American singer, and some radio stations transmitted his songs even behind the Iron Curtain. At a time of profound economic and social transitions, youths around the world adopted Elvis to escape from the conscripted nature of their postwar lives, and, just like in the United States, thereby encountered the frequent resistance of parents and other traditional stakeholders. The singer's international popularity during the 1950s was thus part of a much wider generational—and highly transnational—struggle at an important juncture in postwar history, which played out not only in the United States but in many other corners of the world as well. Elvis became a symbol of the almost global spread of American influences after 1945, seemingly signifying both the vices and virtues of US popular culture.

Elvis's rise to international fame was not caused by the Cold War, but the burgeoning East–West conflict nonetheless conditioned the singer's reception abroad.[2] In Western Europe in particular, Elvis benefited heavily from the US' unprecedented political and economic expansion after 1945, and quickly became a symbol in much wider confrontations over mass

---

[1]The exceptions are five shows in Canada and three shows in Hawaii in 1957, which did not become part of the United States until 1959.
[2]For a stimulating take on the relationship between the Cold War and the wider international history of the second half of the twentieth century, see Odd A. Westad, "The Cold War and the International History of the Twentieth Century," in Melvyn P. Leffler and Odd A. Westad (eds.), *The Cambridge History of the Cold War, Vol. I: Origins* (Cambridge: Cambridge University Press, 2010), 1–19.

consumerism and postwar modernity that were often waged in a language of "Americanization." In other parts of the world too, Cold War mindsets shaped the singer's reception. While his records and movies were highly popular in Western-oriented countries like Japan, for example, Communist states like China or the Soviet Union rigorously banned them as unwanted American imports, even if rock 'n' roll occasionally found its way across the Iron Curtain in spite of such governmental censorship. A particularly interesting case study is Eastern Europe, where initial dynamics closely mirrored West European patterns but some governments' crackdown on rock 'n' roll turned Elvis into a symbol of political resistance and subversion.

# The Cold War, Youth, and the rock 'n' roll Wave Abroad

After 1945, the rapidly growing antagonism between the United States and the Soviet Union shaped the postwar world in myriad ways. As both superpowers sought to impress their respective ideologies all around the globe, the Cold War turned into a conflict between two radically different ways of seeing the world, and dealing with the massive changes brought by modernity and the age of industrialization. From the late 1940s onward, both superpowers therefore invested heavily to project their ideological visions to countless nations all around the world.[3] The Soviet Union clamped down heavily on unwanted non-socialist influences at home while putting unprecedented resources into its propaganda apparatus, and the United States too professionalized its long-standing attempts at cultural diplomacy, not least by the establishment of the United States Information Agency (USIA) in 1953.[4] Since neither side seemed able to penetrate the other hemisphere directly, however, the superpowers' propaganda efforts soon came to center on other regions, particularly Eastern and Western Europe.[5]

Trying to win over hearts and minds on the war-torn and politically divided European continent, the United States focused its message first and foremost on economic growth and the benefits of capitalism. Its

---

[3]David Caute, *Dancer Defects*, 1–16; Jessica Gienow-Hecht, "Culture and the Cold War in Europe," in Leffler and Westad (eds.), *Cambridge History of the Cold War, Vol.* 1, 398–419.

[4]Krenn, *United States Cultural Diplomacy*, 4–5; Belmonte, *Selling the American Way*; Kenneth Osgood, *Total Cold War: Eisenhower's Secret Propaganda Battle at Home and Abroad* (Lawrence, KS: University Press of Kansas, 2006); Scott Lucas, *Freedom's War: The U.S. Crusade against the Soviet Union, 1945–1956* (New York: New York University Press, 1999); Frances S. Saunders, *Who Paid the Piper? The CIA and the Cultural Cold War* (London: Granta Books, 1999).

[5]For the centrality of Europe in the early Cold War, see Federico Romero, "Cold War Historiography at the Crossroads," *Cold War History* 14/4 (2014), 685–703.

propaganda messages styled the United States into the very embodiment of capitalist progress and social mobility, celebrating the so-called American Way of Life and proclaiming that capitalism and democracy provided the best possible life.[6] The images it projected thus reflected above all the US' postwar affluence, particularly the alleged virtues of everyday consumerism and modern goods like cars, television sets, and household appliances. Such achievements of capitalism were usually connected to the country's political values of opportunity, freedom, and democracy, while they side-lined or completely ignored the country's profound inequalities and racism.[7] In spite of such major omissions, the United States largely seems to have succeeded in projecting its messages favorably, particularly in Western Europe: one USIA survey in August 1956 found that the United States enjoyed "a crushing superiority over Russia in comparative general esteem" there.[8]

Such propagandistic emphasis on mass consumerism was aided immeasurably by the US' unprecedented economic expansion after 1945. Although American businesses and entrepreneurs had been heavily invested in foreign markets since the turn of the century, the political imperatives of the Cold War now led to further spike in US engagement during the 1950s. In so doing, American companies not only exported industrial or consumption goods, but they also injected more concrete meanings into previously fairly abstract concepts like modernization, mass culture, or indeed the so-called American Way of Life.[9] The lure of postwar America manifested itself not only in household items like refrigerators or dishwashers, but it also popularized leisurely goods like chewing gums, Coca-Cola, or blue jeans, which fascinated the younger generation in particular.[10]

Yet the US' strong propagandistic focus on everyday affluence and capitalism also reinforced some deeply ingrained historic European stereotypes about American materialism, and the alleged decadence of its mass culture. Such debates often played out in the cultural realm, where longer-term European self-understandings as highly sophisticated and deeply cultured nations were pitched against American civilization and its

---

[6]Walter L. Hixson, *Parting the Curtain: Propaganda, Culture, and the Cold War, 1945-1961* (Basingstoke: Macmillan, 1998), xi; Osgood, *Total Cold War*, 255-6.
[7]Belmonte, *Selling the American Way*, 179.
[8]"S-4-56: Opinion Trends among America's European Allies," August 1956; [R]oosevelt [I]nstitute for [A]merican [S]tudies, Middelburg (Netherlands), Records of the U.S. Information Agency (USIA), Part 1: Cold War Era Special Reports, Series A: 1953–1964, Reel 8. See also "The Degree of Interest in Features of American Life Expressed by Possible Target Groups," September 11, 1957; [N]ational [A]rchives and [R]ecords [A]dministration, College Park, MD (United States), [R]ecord [G]roup 306, Program and Media Studies 1956–62, Series A1/1011, Box 10, File C-9.
[9]Nolan, *Transatlantic Century*, 5; De Grazia, *Irresistible Empire*.
[10]For general studies on popular culture in postwar Europe, see Wagnleitner and May, *Foreign Politics of American Popular Culture*; Ramet and Crnković, *American Impact on European Popular Culture*. Country-specific works are listed in the relevant sections below.

alleged lack of tradition.[11] After 1945, such stereotypes became a crucial ingredient in the propaganda war, not least because the Soviet Union played on such European notions by projecting itself as the true bearer of Europe's cultural heritage and placed heavy emphasis on its classical traditions like literature, the performing arts, or ballet.[12] Indeed, in the cultural realm, the United States remained on the defensive throughout the Cold War, almost desperately trying to convince the Europeans of its cultural achievements through efforts like the Congress for Cultural Freedom (CCF). "Not only does the weight of opinion rate American contemporary culture below that of Europe," one USIA survey sighed in 1956, "but a majority believes that the general level of culture in America is low in itself."[13]

These bigger patterns of the cultural confrontation between East and West shaped the role of music in the early Cold War. In their attempts to counter the Soviet Union's emphasis on its so-called "high arts," the United States tried to respond in kind, utilizing its own soloists or orchestras like the New York Philharmonic in their cultural diplomacy.[14] The strategy had only limited success, however, not least because there was nothing distinctively "American" about a traditional symphony orchestra playing mostly European classical music.[15] More authentic jazz music, however, was utilized only very reluctantly, not least because of its association with African American culture.[16] Although jazz had proven very popular in Europe during the interwar years, and prominent musicians like Louis Armstrong or Miles Davis toured the continent extensively in the late 1940s, it was not until the mid-1950s that Dizzy Gillespie became the first jazz musician to embark upon a tour that was officially sponsored by the State Department.[17]

Rock 'n' roll was yet another different matter. Like many parts of the American establishment at the time, US officials considered rock 'n' roll to be a morally wrong or even dangerous trend, and feared that its widespread association with juvenile delinquency might reinforce already negative impressions of the American youth abroad.[18] Some USIA studies suggested that these fears were not without foundation: in September 1957, a major

---

[11]Gienow-Hecht, "Culture and the Cold War," 400–1; Gienow-Hecht, *Transmission Impossible,* 10–11; Lüdtke, Marßolek, and von Saldern, "Amerikanisierung," 13–14.
[12]Gienow-Hecht, "Culture and the Cold War," 399–404.
[13]"Culture and Politics Studies: Exposure to American Media of Culture, and Ratings of America's Cultural Level," November 20, 1956. NARA, RG306, International Survey Research Reports, 1954–1964, HMS: P 78, IRI FR 43, Box 3.
[14]Fosler-Lussier, *Music in America's Cold War Diplomacy,* 17.
[15]Osgood, *Total Cold War,* 225–6.
[16]Penny M. von Eschen, *Satchmo Blows Up the World: Jazz Ambassadors Play the Cold War* (Cambridge, MA: Harvard University Press, 2006); Lisa E. Davenport, *Jazz Diplomacy: Promoting America in the Cold War Era* (Jackson, MI: University Press of Mississippi, 2009).
[17]Caute, *Dancer Defects,* 457.
[18]"The Image of American Youth and American Women in Western Europe," September 1960. NARA, RG306, Program and Media Studies, 1956–62, Series A1/1011, PMS-41.

survey of the influence of US popular music on the country's image abroad found a "predominant dislike" in all surveyed West European countries. One British respondent, for example, complained that "Rock and roll drives kids crazy and has a poor influence on home life"; another thought that British youths "don't seem like Englishmen [any more] as they hang around juke boxes." Findings from West Germany revealed similar patterns. "You just have to look at the young hooligans," one respondent told the USIA; "they prefer American music and thus hang out at places of entertainment where it is played ... [W]e aren't Negroes or primitives from the backwoods, that's a throwback to barbarism."[19]

State Department officials therefore stayed well clear of utilizing rock 'n' roll music throughout the 1950s; if anything, it was seen as a liability rather than as an asset in shaping perceptions of the United States abroad. But Elvis Presley and rock 'n' roll found their way outside the United States nonetheless—and came to shape perceptions of American culture as much, or perhaps even more, than official cultural diplomacy.

## The Dissemination of Elvis in 1950s Western Europe

Elvis Presley arrived in Western Europe almost the minute he had found fame in the United States. This was due to the dense web of transatlantic networks and companies that was expanding ever more rapidly as a result of the US' unprecedented engagement in the immediate postwar years.[20] By the mid-1950s, a highly interconnected cultural and media landscape had emerged: many American publications were freely available in Western Europe, and several European newspapers had full-time correspondents in the United States.[21] As a result, Elvis became known in Western Europe within weeks of his domestic breakthrough. On December 25, 1955, the UK's music magazine *Melody Maker* published the first known European report on Elvis, only days after the singer had signed for RCA. It was written by an American disc jockey, who described Elvis as follows:

[T]he new rage – sings hillbilly in R-and-B time. Can you figure that out? He wears pink pants and a black coat and owns a Cadillac painted

---

[19]"West European Reactions to American Jazz, 11 September 1957," NARA, RG306, Program and Media Studies, 1956–62, Series A1/1011, PMS-18. At the time, "jazz" was often (misguidedly) used as a description of "rock 'n' roll" in the public discourse.
[20]Geir Lundestad, "Empire by Invitation? The United States and Western Europe, 1945–1952," *Journal of Peace Research* 23/3 (1986), 263–77; Nolan, *Transatlantic Century*, 230.
[21]Peter Hoeres, *Außenpolitik und Öffentlichkeit: Massenmedien, Meinungsforschung und Arkanpolitik in den deutsch-amerikanischen Beziehungen von Erhard bis Brandt* (München: Oldenbourg, 2013), 527–30.

pink with a black top. He's a big curly-headed, fine-looking chap – very popular with the girls. He's going terrific, and if he doesn't suffer too much popularity he'll be all right. He's been making records, and now one of the big companies has got him.[22]

It was no surprise that Elvis's name would first be mentioned in a British publication. The country had long been one of the most important European entry points of American influences, and its close links to the United States had only recently been reinforced by the two countries' unprecedentedly close wartime cooperation.[23] The bonds of a common language and centuries-long transatlantic networks made Britain a particularly fruitful ground for American commercial and cultural influences, a process intensified by the presence of almost three million G.I. soldiers on British soil during the Second World War.[24] Indeed, Elvis was initially only one in a long line of American singers who were also popular in Western Europe: in Britain, reports over the hysteria surrounding Elvis's concerts evoked comparisons to the frenzy that had surrounded Frank Sinatra or Johnnie Ray a few years earlier.[25]

In spite of his early arrival, Elvis remained a distant and fairly abstract medial construction in Western Europe at first.[26] Apart from the fact that it was impossible to see Elvis in concert, the dissemination of his music and performances was also much more uneven. Television, for example, had not yet reached the status of a mass medium in Western Europe, and the singer's television appearances were not broadcasted at all outside the United States during the 1950s.[27] It was also significantly more difficult to buy Elvis's records. Although Elvis's rise coincided with his label's attempt to build up a global network of distributors, availability varied hugely between West European countries.[28] For example, whereas Elvis records could be bought as

---

[22]*Melody Maker*, December 25, 1955.

[23]For a classic and nuanced overview, see David Reynolds, "A 'Special Relationship'? America, Britain, and the International Order since the Second World War,", *International Affairs* 62/1 (1985), 1–20.

[24]David Reynolds, *Rich Relations: The American Occupation of Britain, 1942–1945* (New York: Random House, 1995), 437–9.

[25]Almost every edition of the British *New Musical Express* (NME) between April and June 1956 featured passionate debates over the respective merits of Elvis and/or Johnnie Ray. See, for example, NME April 27, May 4, May 11, May 18, and June 1, 1956. More generally, Gillian A.M.Mitchell, "Reassessing 'the Generation Gap': Bill Haley's 1957 Tour of Britain, Inter-Generational Relations and Attitudes to Rock 'n' Roll in the Late 1950s," *Twentieth Century British History* 24/4 (2013), 594.

[26]See also Nygaard, "High Priest of Rock and Roll," 333.

[27]Frank Bösch, *Mediengeschichte: Vom asiatischen Buchdruck zum Computer* (Frankfurt and New York: Campus, 2019), 208.

[28]RCA's previous worldwide licensing agreement with the British EMI had run out at the end of 1955. For more detail, see Sigbjorn Stabursvik and Hans Otto Engvold, *How RCA Brought Elvis to Europe: The Nordic Elvis Presley Discography 1956–1977* (Oslo: KJ Consulting, 2016), 61–2.

early as March 1956 in the UK and had started to appear in France, Belgium, and Italy by May, the first record was not released in West Germany until October 12, 1956—although RCA's local licensee then dropped eight records at the same time. In Northern Europe, Sweden was the earliest and biggest hub of Elvis records, whereas they were largely unavailable in Denmark until mid-1958 due to copyright and distribution disputes. The President of the Copenhagen Elvis Presley Fan Club later recalled how he usually had to travel to Sweden to buy Elvis records at the time, "or one could be lucky and get some which were smuggled in from Germany."[29] In Southern Europe, availability was often determined by political circumstances: whereas RCA's branch in Spain released them immediately and often with unique Spanish cover designs, Portugal censored US products well into the 1960s, which meant that almost no Elvis record could be found there until 1965. In Greece, the first known Elvis record dates from 1959; in Turkey, they were released from 1961, although it is possible that some imports had been circulating a bit earlier in the Istanbul area.[30]

Even in places where Elvis records were available, they did not always enjoy widespread popularity. In 1950s Western Europe, rock 'n' roll constituted by and large a minority phenomenon, as record markets continued to reflect national styles and tastes. In France, the *chanson* still dominated the national music scene almost completely, while traditional folk music and *Schlager* retained their popularity in West Germany well into the 1960s.[31] Although American pop songs occasionally occupied prominent places in West European charts, they usually took the form of instrumental versions by national orchestras, or covers by domestic stars singing in their own language: the German singer Freddy Quinn's "Heimat," for example, was a cover version of Dean Martin's "Memories Are Made of This."[32] Most public broadcasters ignored, and occasionally banned, rock 'n' roll altogether. The British Broadcasting Corporation (BBC), for example, refused to play rock music until the late 1960s; in West Germany, most broadcasters similarly snubbed the trend, although there were a few

---

[29]*Elvis Monthly*, 2/1, January 1961.

[30]All facts and dates from Stabursvik and Engvold, *How RCA Brought Elvis to Europe*, 16–29.

[31]Dietmar Hüser, "'Rock Around the Clock'. Überlegungen zu amerikanischer Populärkultur in der französischen und westdeutschen Gesellschaft der 1950er und 1960er Jahre," in Chantal Metzger and Hartmut Kaelble (eds.), *Deutschland—Frankreich—Nordamerika: Transfers, Imaginationen, Beziehungen* (München: Franz Steiner Verlag, 2006), 199–200; Klaus Nathaus, "Nationale Produktionssysteme im transatlantischen Kulturtransfer. Zur „Amerikanisierung" populärer Musik in Westdeutschland und Großbritannien im Vergleich, 1950–1980," in Werner Abelshauser, David A. Gilgen and Andreas Leutzsch (eds.), *Kulturen der Weltwirtschaft* (Göttingen: Vandenhoeck & Ruprecht, 2012), 210.

[32]Nathaus, "Nationale Produktionssysteme," 206–7; Monika Burzik, "Von singenden Seemännern und Musikern vom Sirius. Die Musik der fünfziger Jahre," in Werner Faulstich (ed.), *Die Kultur der Fünfziger Jahre* (München: Wilhelm Fink Verlag, 2007), 258.

notable exceptions.[33] In Scandinavia too, Elvis's records received almost
no airplay in public radio, although the radio disc jockey Bent Henius did
present a half-hour special on Elvis in December 1956.[34] All of these trends
severely limited Elvis's exposure in Western Europe: his first number one hit
came as late as July 1957 when "All Shook Up" topped the charts in Britain;
in most other West European countries, he would not reach the top spot
until his move toward lighter pop music in the early 1960s.[35]

At the same time, it would be misleading to reduce Elvis's cultural impact
in 1950s Western Europe merely to sales figures or his absence from public
radio. Rather than buying expensive records, for example, many younger
fans swapped records with their friends and hosted private rock 'n' roll
parties, or they utilized the exploding number of juke boxes in milk bars
or cafés.[36] They also used portable transistor radios to listen to foreign
commercial radio stations like Radio Luxembourg or Europe No. 1, which
deliberately broadcasted English language programs with rock 'n' roll music
to break state monopolies and target the growing market of teenagers.[37]
Others tuned into the broadcasts of the American Forces Network (AFN)
or the British Forces Broadcasting Service (BFBS), which catered primarily
to their own soldiers but also played rock 'n' roll occasionally.[38] Even if
both Elvis and rock 'n' roll remained a minority taste in the 1950s, the new
trend nonetheless served an important social function, enabling teenagers
to ignore established entertainment preferences and carve themselves a
distinct cultural niche. The result was that Elvis became part of the much
bigger generational conflict in postwar Europe, and one in which issues of
generational control and postwar modernity were frequently negotiated in
the language of "Americanization."

---

[33]The Westdeutscher Rundfunk (NWDR) briefly experimented with music shows hosted by
the American disk jockey Mal Sondock and the British singer Chris Howland in the early
1960s. Christoph Hilgert, *Die unerhörte Generation: Jugend im westdeutschen und britischen
Hörfunk 1945–1963* (Göttingen: Wallstein, 2015), 146–50; Konrad Dussel, "The Triumph of
English-Language Pop Music: West German Radio Programming," in Axel Schildt and Detlef
Siegfried (eds.), *Between Marx and Coca-Cola: Youth Cultures in Changing European Societies,
1960–1980* (New York and Oxford: Berghahn Book, 2006), 127–48. For the BBC, see Dick
Bradley, *Understanding Rock 'n' Roll: Popular Music in Britain, 1955–1964* (Buckingham:
Open University Press, 1992), 13.
[34]Nygaard, "High Priest of Rock 'n' Roll," 333.
[35]Bradley, *Understanding Rock 'n' Roll*, 64.
[36]Adrian Horn, *Juke Box Britain: Americanisation and Youth Culture, 1945–60* (Manchester:
Manchester University Press, 2009).
[37]Anna Jehle, *Welle der Konsumgesellschaft: Radio Luxembourg in Frankreich 1945–1975*
(Göttingen: Wallstein, 2018), 235–43.
[38]Anja Schäfers, *Mehr als Rock'n'Roll: der Radiosender AFN bis Mitte der sechziger Jahre*
(Stuttgart: Steiner, 2014), 303; Christoph Hilgert, "Der junge Hörer, das unbekannte
Wesen: Programmangebote für Jugendliche im westdeutschen Hörfunk in der Mitte des
20. Jahrhunderts," in Aline Maldener and Clemens Zimmermann (eds.), *Let's Historize It!
Jugendmedien im 20. Jahrhundert* (Köln: Böhlau, 2018), 137.

Figure 2.1 *Teenagers listening to the latest records at Imhof's Melody Bar in London, November 1955.*

# Rejecting Elvis: Western Europe I

Elvis Presley emerged in Western Europe at a time of profound political, economic, and cultural transition. After the devastation of the Second World War, many West European countries had come to experience a slow but sustained economic recovery by the mid-1950s, with levels of production and consumption now frequently exceeding prewar figures.[39] The emergence of a US-style mass consumerist society, however, was not embraced unconditionally in Western Europe; indeed, it was received in highly ambivalent ways.[40] This applies in particular to the realm of popular entertainment, where erstwhile cultural guardians reactivated longer-term

---

[39]Tony Judt, *Postwar: A History of Europe since 1945* (London: Vintage, 2005 [2010]), 324–69; Axel Schildt, *Moderne Zeiten: Freizeit, Massenmedien und "Zeitgeist" in der Bundesrepublik der 50er Jahre* (Hamburg: Christians Verlag, 1995).

[40]Rob Kroes, *If You've Seen One, You've Seen the Mall: Europeans and American Mass Culture* (Urbana and Chicago, IL: University of Illinois Press, 1996).

anti-American stereotypes to protest against the alleged erosion of national heritage and traditions, as well as against the primitivity and tastelessness supposedly inherent in mass culture.[41]

What distinguished the reception of Elvis from previous transatlantic celebrities was his widespread association with rock 'n' roll and juvenile delinquency. Just like in the United States, Europe's postwar economic recovery and its associated socioeconomic changes had triggered the emergence of a new type of youth culture that utilized consumerism and popular culture to differentiate itself from previous generations.[42] In the early 1950s, juvenile street gangs and rowdy teenagers who consciously appropriated symbols of American popular culture in order to challenge authorities and conventions were popping up in several West European countries. In the working-class areas of East and South London, for example, these gangs were termed *Teddy Boys* because of their creative mix of older Edwardian and newer American influences.[43] In West Germany too, the so-called *Halbstarke* (half-strong) often wore leather jackets and styled their hair like James Dean or Marlon Brando, and some of them listened to rock 'n' roll on their transistor radios or met up at fun fairs where the music was played.[44] The close association of such juvenile gangs with American popular culture can even be traced in the way in which they were referred to in the public discourse: in France, for example, the "blousons noirs" (black jackets) triggered a medial craze about the threat of American influences to the "civilisation francaise."[45]

Cinema cemented the link between youthful unrest and rock 'n' roll in the minds of the West European public, since American rock 'n' roll movies

---

[41]Ibid., 43–68; Nolan, *Transatlantic Century*, 230–48.

[42]For the interrelations between the rise of consumerism and the emergence of youth cultures in late 1950s Europe, see Axel Schildt and Detlef Siegfried, "Youth, Consumption, and Politics in the Age of Radical Change," in Axel Schildt and Detlef Siegfried (eds.), *Between Marx and Coca-Cola Youth Cultures in Changing European Societies, 1960–1980* (New York, NY and Oxford: Berghahn Books, 2006), 2–3, 12–16; Arthur Marwick, "Youth Culture and the Cultural Revolution of the Long Sixties," in Schildt and Siegfried (eds.), *Marx and Coca-Cola*, 39–40.

[43]Bill Osgerby, *Youth in Britain since 1945* (Oxford: Blackwell, 1998), 13; Bradley, *Understanding Rock 'n' Roll*, 12, 86.

[44]Thomas Grotum, *Die Halbstarken: Zur Geschichte einer Jugendkultur der 50er Jahre* (Frankfurt am Main: Campus, 1994); Hans-Jürgen von Wensierski,'„Die anderen nannten uns Halbstarke"—Jugendsubkultur in den 50er Jahren', in: Heinz-Hermann Krüger (ed.), „Die Elvis-Tolle, die hatte ich mir unauffällig wachsen lassen": Lebensgeschichte und Jugendliche Alltagskultur in den fünfziger Jahren* (Opladen: Leske und Budrich, 1985), 103–28.

[45]Hüser, "Rock Around the Clock," 193, 198; Florence Tamagne, "La Nuit de la Nation. Jugendkultur, Rock 'n' Roll und *moral panics* im Frankreich der sechziger Jahre," in Bodo Mrozek, Alexa Geisthövel and Jürgen Danyel (eds.), *Popgeschichte, Band 2 Historische Fallstudien 1958–1988* (Bielefeld: transcript Verlag, 2014), 41; William J. Risch, "Introduction," in William J. Risch (ed.), *Youth Cultures, Music, and the State in Russia and Eastern Europe* (Lanham, MA: Lexington Books, 2015), 3.

quickly became the focal point of teenage rebellion. Already in 1955, *Blackboard Jungle* had caused some furor among some audiences; yet it was Bill Haley's *Rock Around the Clock* that acquired notoriety in Western Europe. In September 1956, showings of the film triggered several riots in UK cinemas, with overenthusiastic audiences dancing, screaming, and even tearing out seat rows.[46] A few months later, West German youths mimicked the behavior of their British counterparts, as movie screenings triggered outrage in the German cities of Mannheim and Bielefeld.[47] Although these events constituted relatively harmless expressions of youthful rebellion rather than full-scale riots, they triggered Europe-wide press debates over the allegedly malign influence of rock 'n' roll on the European youth. Ironically, West European newspapers often drew closely on American newspapers in their denouncements of rock 'n' roll, and in so doing replicated the chauvinism, class contempt, and racism inherent in much of the early US coverage. The British *Daily Mail*, for example, labelled it as "cannibalistic" and claimed that it had "surely originated in the jungle," whereas *The Times* described rock 'n' roll concerts "[o]utbursts of violence spurred by the heavy, pulsing beat of this latest derivative of Negro blues."[48]

Elvis Presley was initially perceived as only one part of the larger rock 'n' roll phenomenon. Following Elvis's controversial second appearance on the Milton Berle show, West European newspapers again took their cues more or less directly from US publications like *Time* or *Life* magazine to profess their outrage over the new singer.[49] Their coverage was almost uniformly negative and frequently derogatory. In the UK, for example, *Aberdeen Evening Express* denounced Elvis as the "high priest of rock 'n' roll" who sang "semi-inarticulate commercialized blending of negro rhythm-and-blues and cacophonous cornbelt hillbillyism"; Danish journalists described him in similar vein as "the 'high priest' of rock-madness" with "legs shaking like jelly below him in obscene movements."[50] In September 1956, the West German magazine *Der Spiegel* offered a particularly graphic account of an Elvis concert:

His forelock hangs in his face, his eyes are closed, his arms bent like a spasm. His body – in a trendy gabardine suit, black shirt with white

---

[46]Bradley, *Understanding Rock 'n' Roll*, 32–4.
[47]Mrozek, *Jugend—Pop—Kultur*, 252–65.
[48]*Daily Mail*, September 4 and 5, 1956; as quoted in Gillian A. M. Mitchell, *The British National Daily Press and Popular Music, c. 1956–1975* (London and New York: Anthem Press, 2019), 2; *The Times*, September 15, 1956. For more detail, also Mitchell, *British National Daily Press*, 13–30.
[49]Wolfgang Rumpf, *Pop & Kritik: Medien und Popkultur* (Münster: Lit Verlag, 2004), 48–9, 52.
[50]*Aberdeen Evening Express*, June 23 and October 11, 1956; the Danish quotations are from Nygaard, "High Priest," 336.

tie – swings rhythmically with the motions of a striptease dancer. With a powerful baritone, he stereotypically bellows the staccato syllables of poor-in-words lyrics into the microphone, accompanied by the inflaming rhythms of the band ... The rhythm gets ever more compelling, the movements in the hall become ever more hectic. Here and there, some fellows get up and tear their shirts off their bodies; their blunt eyes do not reveal whether they still notice their environment, only the uber-rhythm seems to push them forward ... [They are] staggering around as if in a trance ... dancing just for themselves like possessed medicine men of a jungle tribe.[51]

Although the initial press coverage of Elvis in Western Europe closely followed US patterns, there was an important difference: both Elvis and rock 'n' roll were frequently denounced as dangerous American influences completely alien to European cultural heritage. The resentments against the emerging youth culture among European elites were thus articulated in the language of Americanization, labeling Elvis as an unwanted cultural infiltration and threat to the European youth.[52] Even in Britain, anti-American sentiments dominated the early coverage of Elvis. "This man is dangerous," the UK *Picturegoer* magazine warned its readers on July 21, 1956, exclaiming that it did not "want to see British youngsters hacking out his name on their arms with clasp-knives, or see sex treated as an appallingly commercial freakshow. This is what is happening in America."[53] The music magazine *Melody Maker* also saw a commercial threat in Elvis.[54] "If our publishers and record men ... are in favour of the BBC studying the American market in order to anticipate the next teen-age craze over here, then I am against them," one of its columnists proclaimed. "That would be to abdicate our musical independence, the last crap of it – and it would completely turn Britain into a 49th State in the world of entertainment."[55] At the UK release date of "Hound Dog" in October 1956, columnist Steven Race even deemed the end of civilization to be nigh. "I fear for this country," he wrote, "which ought to have had the good taste and the good sense to reject music so decadent."[56]

In West Germany, comparable debates over Elvis and rock 'n' roll tied into even longer-term patterns of German receptions of American popular

---

[51]*Der Spiegel* 39/1956.

[52]For the way in which emerging European youth cultures were frequently denounced in a language of Americanization, see Rob Kroes, "American Mass Culture and European Youth Culture," in Schildt and Siegfried (eds.), *Marx and Coca-Cola*, 82, 93.

[53]*Picturegoer*, July 21, 1956. Emphases in original.

[54]Nick Johnstone, *Melody Maker History of 20th Century Popular Music* (London: Bloomsbury, 1999), 90–117.

[55]*Melody Maker*, June 23, 1956.

[56]*Melody Maker*, October 20, 1956.

culture.[57] During the Weimar Republic, for example, many Germans had become attracted to jazz music and Hollywood films as vibrant signs of modernity, whereas others had dismissed them as an infiltration of traditional bourgeois German "high culture."[58] In the 1930s, the National Socialist regime had then built on such anti-American sentiments in its all-out propagandistic attack on US mass culture, and jazz in particular was denounced in highly racist and anti-Semitic terms.[59] These historical legacies gave West German debates over Elvis additional potency, since many such longer-term anti-American stereotypes had survived the caesura of 1945 and were now projected onto US popular culture.[60] The *Frankfurter Allgemeine Zeitung*, for example, dismissed Elvis's performances as "ridiculous by European standards," whereas *Der Spiegel* claimed that he signified nothing more than "a cleverly-marketed commodity of the U.S. entertainment industry" who in any case was "by his own admission half-illiterate."[61] Indeed, *Der Spiegel*'s major cover story on Elvis featured even crasser nationalistic sentiment: it professed its hopes that German reactions to the singer would reveal the differences between the "youth of the old world and the youth of the young world," and even quoted a spokesman of his German label who proclaimed that the "German youth" simply had "a different blood type" than its American counterparts.[62]

# Embracing Elvis: Western Europe II

Such resistance against American cultural influences, however, was only part of the story, for many others in Western Europe eagerly embraced them as signs of postwar affluence, a new type of leisurely lifestyle, and modernity in general. Young adolescents in particular endorsed consumer goods and pop-cultural influences from the United States, as items like Coca-Cola, blue jeans, and chewing gum all became symbols of the so-called American Way of Life, as well as bigger symbols of individual freedom and youthful

---

[57]Kaspar Maase, "Establishing Cultural Democracy: Youth, 'Americanization', and the Irresistible Rise of Popular Culture," in Hanna Schissler (ed.), *The Miracle Years: A Cultural History of West Germany, 1949–1968* (Princeton, NJ: Princeton University Press, 2001), 430.
[58]For differences between American and German conceptions of "culture," see Gienow-Hecht, *Transmission Impossible*, 10–11; 180. For jazz, see Jonathan O. Wipplinger, *The Jazz Republic: Music, Race, and American Culture in Weimar Germany* (Ann Arbor, MI: University of Michigan Press, 2017); for Hollywood, Thomas J. Saunders, *Hollywood in Berlin: American Cinema and Weimar Germany* (Berkeley, CA: University of California Press, 1994).
[59]Maase, "Establishing Cultural Democracy," 432.
[60]Poiger, *Jazz, Rock and Rebels*, 170–85; Maria Höhn, *GIs and Fräuleins: The German-American Encounter in 1950s West Germany* (Chapel Hill, NC: The University of North Carolina Pres, 2002), 9–10.
[61]*Frankfurter Allgemeine Zeitung*, December 31, 1956; *Der Spiegel*, 50/1956.
[62]*Der Spiegel*, 50/1956.

hedonism.[63] In the eyes of many teenagers, Elvis Presley thus became the very embodiment of how they imagined the postwar United States: a country full of excitement, colorfulness, and vibrancy.

It was not only the novelty of Elvis's music that excited teenagers; it was also his unique looks and styles that were projected through countless newspapers and magazines, and which seemed to be completely different to the perceived greyness and boredom of life in postwar Europe. In Britain, the release of "Heartbreak Hotel" in March 1956 seems to have had a particularly strong impact. One fan from Sunbury-on-Thames, for example, later recalled how she "literally jumped up and down" the first time she heard the song: "I couldn't believe anything could sound so great. It had been out a week and I bought it the next day. I also bought the 'Picturegoer' and it contained the first photo of Elvis seen over here."[64] Indeed, the combination of Elvis's visual attraction and musical novelty stood at the very heart of his early reception in Britain. When the mother of the nine-year-old Reginald Kenneth Dwight, who later changed his name to Elton Hercules John, bought the record one Friday afternoon, the young boy recognized the name on the cover straight away. "The previous weekend I'd been looking through the magazines in the local barber shop … when I came across a photo of the most bizarre-looking man I'd ever seen," he recently reflected in his autobiography; "Everything about him looked extraordinary: his clothes, his hair, even the way he was standing. Compared to the people you could see outside the barber shop window … he might as well have been bright green with antennae sticking out of his forehead."[65] As David Bowie, who also grew up in 1950s London, later put it, "Elvis had it all. It wasn't just the music that was interesting, it was everything else. And he had a lot of everything else."[66] Interestingly, neither David Bowie nor Elton John could even understand Elvis's lyrics. Elton John recalls about listening to "Heartbreak Hotel" that he managed to get "that his baby had left him" but "completely lost the thread" afterward; Bowie liked about "Hound Dog" that he "couldn't understand the lyrics and that really made an impression on me – there was some secret information there that I didn't have. I think that's been something that's been important to me ever since."[67]

In West Germany, Elvis's association with a new type of American lifestyle gained additional political connotations in light of the country's more general transition into a Western liberal democracy after 1945. Many young Germans embraced American popular culture not just for fun, but also as a bigger symbolic statement of their embrace of US-style consumerism and

[63]Maase, BRAVO Amerika, 10; Höhn, GIs and Fräuleins, 226.
[64]Elvis Monthly 79, August 1966.
[65]Elton John, Me (London: Macmillan, 2019), 9.
[66]Quoted in Dylan Jones, David Bowie: A Life (New York, NY: Crown Archetype, 2017), 10–11.
[67]John, Me, 9; ibid., 10.

the bigger notions of individual liberty and freedom of expression that were associated with it.[68] Just like in Britain, many German youngsters were as attracted by Elvis's looks and lifestyle as they were by his music. They often went at great lengths to imitate Elvis's quaff and ducktail, for example, and in so doing also articulated nonverbal opposition against established tastes and authorities.[69] Elvis's luxurious lifestyle too fascinated many West German teenagers. "It was in the fall of 1956 that I first heard of, or rather read about, a certain Elvis Presley," a fan from Saarbrücken recalled a few years later; "I was almost seventeen years old then and didn't care about pop music and singers. But I remember quite well the report and the photos that were shown in that particular magazine. One of them showed his home at Audubon Drive, another himself with his fleet in the yard of the house." He even appropriated the hostile coverage of Elvis in parts of the West German press to his own ends. "I read a big article in our leading news mag *Der Spiegel* which told me all about Elvis including the titles and numbers of all his records," he recalled. "It even had Elvis on the front cover. Up to this day I still treasure this story which actually made me an Elvis fan."[70]

The behavior of most Elvis fans in Western Europe did not at all fit the stereotype of the dangerous juvenile delinquent so prevalent in the press at the time.[71] They often tended to pursue their musical interests individually or in small groups, listening to Elvis records in private and collecting all sorts of materials about the singer. In so doing, they created a teenage culture that centered not on street gangs, but rather on the consumption of pop-cultural products like records, youth magazines, and other items commonly associated with US teenage lifestyles. Fan clubs became particularly important arenas for exchanges between fans, and also offered opportunities for identification and the creation of emotional bonds.[72] Already in the 1950s, numerous Elvis fan clubs emerged in Western Europe, ranging from Sweden and Germany to Malta, France and the Netherlands.[73] They often gathered in private or semi-private settings to share records, and to listen to their newest Elvis records together. In a reader's letter to the *New Musical Express* (*NME*) from July 1956, a teenager from Birmingham offered a fascinating glimpse into such rituals:

---

[68]Maase, *BRAVO Amerika*, 10–14.
[69]Ibid., 100–1.
[70]*Elvis Monthly* 112, May 1969.
[71]Gillian A. M. Mitchell, *Adult Responses to Popular Music and Intergenerational Relations in Britain, c. 1955–1975* (London and New York: Anthem Pres, 2019), 4.
[72]Mrozek, *Jugend—Pop—Kultur*, 330–5.
[73]For a list of some of these fan clubs at the dawn of the 1960s, see, for example, *Elvis Monthly* 4, May 1960; *Elvis Monthly* 11, December 1960; *Elvis Monthly* 14, February 1961; *Elvis Monthly* 17, May 1961.

Every Saturday night, a whole crowd of us teenagers gather in sweaters and jeans at my home, where Mum has turned over to me the front room, which she aptly calls the "Rock-and-Roll Room." From 7 p.m. until midnight, the room simply rocks to Bill Haley, Rusty Draper, Fats Domino, Elvis Presley, the Teenagers [...]. Hot and loud and vulgar music, non-stop for five hours. Luckily, my home is detached, so there is no fear of complaining neighbours. The room, contemporary in style, hasn't much furniture. Just a gram, record cabinet, studio couch, an assortment of chairs and a soft drinks bar. So we push everything to the sides and just rock-and-roll, and suddenly the whole crazy, mixed-up world seems to be put right, alive and new. It gives me a feeling that's hard to express in writing. But on these Saturday nights, when everything is so gay and young, it really feels good to be alive.[74]

In the absence of live performances or television appearances, Elvis's movies became a major focal point for West European teenagers, and often constituted their first exposure to Elvis. "The first time I heard and saw Elvis was when I went to see 'Loving You' in my home town Glasgow," one fan recalled in the *Elvis Monthly* magazine; "I was twelve years old at the time, but I remember everyone raving about this American singer ... I thought this would be another flash in the pan but I went along with my friends and that was it, I was converted."[75] A teenager from the London borough of Hampstead had a similar experience. "I couldn't believe my eyes or ears," he wrote afterward; "I was spellbound; that cheeky grin and merry twinkle in his eyes plus that voice was all that was needed to convert me then and there."[76] In December 1956, the *Daily Mirror* reported on the scenes at the opening of Elvis's first movie *Love Me Tender* in Britain:

Hundreds of teenage girls shrieked and sighed over their idol – Elvis (the Pelvis) Presley in a London cinema last night ... When Presley began to sing many girls, dressed in jeans and tight sweaters, threw themselves on to the floor in ecstasy. Others kicked off their shoes and waved their legs to the music. Some rocked 'n' rolled in their seats. Less energetic fans just sighed blissfully. One Elvis fan, fourteen-year-old Heather Meeson, of South Berry Road, Enfield, said as she wriggled on the cinema floor: "I JUST WANT TO DIE. HE IS THE MOSTEST." Heather, wearing a black skirt with 'Elvis Presley' stitched in pink across it, added: "I've got all his records. He just sends me."[77]

---

[74]*NME*, July 27, 1956.
[75]*Elvis Monthly* 109, January 1969.
[76]*Elvis Monthly* 156, January 1973.
[77]*Daily Mirror*, December 14, 1956.

Figure 2.2 *An 18 year old Elvis fan of Tolworth in Surrey stares at a life-sized cardboard cut-out of Elvis Presley, a prize in a raffle to be drawn at the rock 'n' roll contest at Wimbledon Palais in London*

Such adaptation processes by fans helped transform perceptions of Elvis from a juvenile rebel figure into a symbol of US-inspired teenage culture, which became an integral part of Western Europe's more general embrace of postwar consumerism and leisurely entertainment.[78] It also reveals the delicate relationship between the intimate association of rock 'n' roll with the United States on the one hand, and the broader structural developments underlying the emergence of a highly transnational youth culture on the other. Bigger societal transformations and generational conflicts, as well as attitudes toward postwar consumerism and modernity, thus became negotiated through the public image of Elvis Presley.

[78]Mitchell, *Adult Responses*, 2–4; Maase, *BRAVO Amerika*, 95–103; Axel Schildt, *Moderne Zeiten: Freizeit, Massenmedien und "Zeitgeist" in der Bundesrepublik der 50er Jahre* (Hamburg: Christians Verlag, 1995).

# Mediating Elvis: Western Europe III

The emergence of a teenage culture that centered primarily on the consumption of pop-cultural products did not escape the attention of savvy entrepreneurs, who clearly saw the commercial opportunities behind the new trend.[79] In West Germany, for example, youths' ownership of record players and radios increased significantly, and the number of jukeboxes quadrupled between 1957 and 1960.[80] Numerous marketing items for Elvis and other stars also emerged in due course, including posters, fan books, clothes, puppets, and even an Elvis-themed soap.[81] Most important, however, was the emergence of music and youth magazines in numerous countries, which deliberately targeted the growing readership of affluent teenagers. They not only reshaped Elvis's public image in Western Europe, but in so doing they also transported much bigger images of American culture and society.[82]

In Britain, the *NME* was the first major publication that tried to carve itself a niche as the key provider of information and entertainment for a new teenage audience. Starting with its first major article on Elvis on May 4, 1956, it aggressively promoted the new singer as "America's Newest and Greatest Disc Sensation" and "rock age idol."[83] Rather than depicting Elvis as a threat to the British youth, it focused its coverage overwhelmingly on the singer's commercial success and popularity among teenagers, embedding his rise in the rags-to-riches narrative so familiar from US publications at the time. The young Elvis had "never had any professional instruction" and "no money to buy a guitar," it wrote on May 11, 1956, but he had worked hard "in the firm belief that one day he might reach the top." It then went on to describe Elvis's wealth and luxurious lifestyle:

> Standing 6ft. 2ins. in his stockinged feet, and weighing 160 pounds, he has dark, wavy hair, blue eyes – and is unmarried. He has a huge appetite and is reputed to eat a dozen eggs and either two steaks or a pound of bacon – for breakfast! Outside of music, Elvis's main interest lies in his two Cadillacs – one in pink and black that carries him all around the country on his personal appearances, the other in canary yellow that he drives in his leisure hours. In addition, he also owns a station wagon and a motorcycle. He spends a good deal of time buying clothes, and has recently persuaded his 39-year-old father to retire.[84]

---

[79]More generally Arthur Marwick, *The Sixties: Cultural Revolution in Britain, France, Italy, and the United States, c. 1958–c.1974* (Oxford: Oxford University Press, 1998), 45–54.
[80]Maase, *BRAVO Amerika*, 78.
[81]Mrozek, *Jugend—Pop—Kultur*, 345.
[82]Bill Osgerby, *Youth Media* (London: Routledge, 2004); Maldener and Zimmermann, *Jugendmedien*.
[83]*NME*, May 4, 1956.
[84]*NME*, May 11, 1956.

Such extensive descriptions of Elvis's wealth highlight the role of Elvis as a role-model for many teenagers, who were as interested in his lifestyle and looks as in his music. The strategy worked. One of Elvis's earliest British fans, for example, later recalled how she "eagerly" anticipated the *NME*'s new edition every Friday, "exclaiming at Elvis' chart positions and at the photos of him."[85] In due course, it also came to feature advertisements for Elvis records, fan clubs, and all other sorts of "Presley-endorsed merchandise."[86] It also never got tired of promoting its closeness to Elvis, advertising "exclusive pictures" or "intimate details of his fabulous career."[87] At one point, it even printed an article that had allegedly been written by Elvis himself.[88] Other publications eventually followed suit. In October 1956, the *Daily Sketch* tried to replicate the *NME*'s strategy by publishing a four-part special on Elvis's life that, as the editorial made clear, was deliberately targeted at teenagers. The special again conveyed many positive images of teenage life in the postwar United States. "Exactly what does the hero of the world's most astonishing rags-to-riches fable think of it all?" it asked at one point. "After kissing 20 of the thousands of girls who met him recently at Los Angeles airport he grinned, wiped his mouth, carefully unwrapped fresh chewing-gum and said: 'This sure beats truck driving for livin'."[89]

In West Germany, the recently founded entertainment magazine *BRAVO* styled itself into Elvis's biggest champion.[90] Just like the above-mentioned British publications, it sought to transform Elvis from a juvenile rebel figure into a prime figurehead of a new teenage culture based largely on consumption, and in so doing conveyed numerous images of capitalist life in the United States. In its first major special on Elvis, for example, it depicted Elvis's life story as the quintessential rags-to-riches story of upward mobility and capitalist advancement, focusing on his miraculous career rather than on his music. "Whether you love him or him," it declared, "his life story is unique." It then went on to describe Elvis's looks and possessions extensively, not least his "six Cadillacs in all colors, a Mercedes 300, a jaguar ... and a ranch worth $40.000."[91]

---

[85]*Elvis Monthly* 211, August 1977.
[86]*NME*, August 31, 1956. See also June 15 or August 31, 1956.
[87]*NME*, June 8, 1956.
[88]*NME*, September 7, 1956. In the article, "Elvis" told readers that he was still "afraid to wake up each morning" because he could not "believe all this has happened to me," and that everything was "going so fine for me that I can't believe it's not a dream." He also thanked his fans for "the way they respond to my style. I get around 10,000 fan letters a week. So many people all over the country are starting fan clubs for me."
[89]*Daily Sketch*, October 19, 1956.
[90]Maase, *BRAVO Amerika*, 104–12.
[91]*BRAVO*, 8/1957.

In compiling its extensive features on Elvis, *BRAVO* benefited from its Hollywood correspondent Thomas Beyl's surprisingly close relationship with Elvis. At one point, it even printed a handwritten letter by Elvis, in which he proclaimed somewhat hyperbolically that "teen-agers the world over like pretty much the same thing, though they may be separated by wide oceans of water."[92]

Music and youth magazines like *BRAVO* or the *NME* thus played an important part in instigating the more general shift in perceptions of rock 'n' roll from a societal threat into a rather harmless teenage phenomenon. Such interpretations were undoubtedly helped by a growing political consensus that popular music essentially constituted a private, rather than public, matter.[93] In January 1957, the *Daily Mirror* reported that many parents had apparently "come to terms with this wildest of Tin Pan Alley crazes," and that some even allowed their children to host rock 'n' roll parties. "The music is shocking," one mother told the *Mirror*, "but they'll grow out of it."[94] Like the *NME*, the *Mirror* had by now come to realize the commercial opportunities behind the trend, and in so doing embraced Elvis in its attempt to tap into the growing market of a young affluent working-class readership.[95] While parents and clergymen might denounce Elvis as obscene, it declared in December 1956, Elvis signified "sex, love, hate, sorrow, joy ... for countless teenagers the world over."[96]

Yet Elvis was not embraced unconditionally in Western Europe. Like all other American cultural influences, Elvis was perceived and understood only selectively through numerous lenses, and his music and image were often adapted and modified to particular national tastes and traditions.[97] Perhaps the most telling example was the emergence of the British singer Tommy Steele, who was hailed by the *NME* as Britain's "answer to Elvis Presley" and acted as an important cultural mediator.[98] Discovered by a savvy manager while performing a cover version of "Heartbreak Hotel" at a Soho coffee shop, Steele—or Thomas Hinks, as he was actually called—was marketed as a South London working-class boy who remained deeply anchored in his community and thus embodied

---

[92]*BRAVO*, 10/1957.
[93]Mitchell, *Adult Responses*, 2–4; Poiger, *Jazz Rock and Rebels*, 187.
[94]*Daily Mirror*, January 21, 1957.
[95]Mitchell, *British National Daily Press*, 47–63; Mitchell, "Reassessing 'the Generation Gap'," 573–605.
[96]*Daily Mirror*, December 28, 1956.
[97]Horn, *Juke Box Britain*; more generally Kroes, "American Mass Culture," 86.
[98]*NME*, November 2, 1956.

core British values of locality and class.[99] "Tommy' Steele's greatest talent is that he is an ordinary, likeable British kid," the *Picture Post* proclaimed in 1957, which made him seem "infinitely nearer to the boy next door than any of the top American stars, like Presley, who come from places and home conditions that the ordinary English working girl can never understand."[100] In spite of such patronizing marketing, many British fans still preferred the American original. "How dare you describe Tommy Steele as Britain's answer to Elvis Presley!" one of them complained in a reader's letter to the *NME*; "Just because Steele is Britain's first rock 'n' roller doesn't give you cause to compare him with one of the greatest artists in the pop field today."[101]

While Steele was highly successful not only in Britain but also in many other parts of Western Europe, where he was often regarded as a somewhat "Europeanized" version of rock 'n' roll, he was only one of countless European *Ersatz-Elvises* who modified the new musical trend to fit traditional national tastes.[102] In Italy, for example, a young Adriano Celentano found initial fame with his Italian-style rock 'n' roll, while in Scandinavia, the Swedish singer Little Gerhard and the Dane Otto Brandenburg stormed the charts.[103] There were also several German *Ersatz-Elvises*, such as Peter Kraus or the somewhat more macho Ted Herold. Kraus in particular found a surprisingly large market with his German-style rock 'n' roll, which featured more traditional instrumentalizations and "clean" German lyrics pinned with occasional Americanisms, like "Sugar Baby" or "Teenager-Melodie."[104] A particular interesting case is

---

[99]Gillian A. M. Mitchell, "A Very 'British' Introduction to Rock 'n' Roll: Tommy Steele and the Advent of Rock 'n' Roll Music in Britain, 1956–1960," *Contemporary British History* 25/2 (2011), 213–17.

[100]*Picture Post*, February 25, 1957; as quoted in Charlotte Rørdam Larsen, "'Above all, it's because he's English … ' Tommy Steele and the Notion of 'Englishness' as Mediator of Wild Rock 'n' Roll," in Jørgen Sevaldsen, Bo Bjørke and Claus Bjørn (eds.), *Britain and Denmark: Political, Economic and Cultural Relations in the 19th and 20th Centuries* (Copenhagen: Museum Tusculanum Press, 2003), 503.

[101]*NME*, November 9, 1956.

[102]I am grateful to Bertel Nygaard for coining the brilliant term "Ersatz-Elvis" during a lovely conference dinner in Aarhus in December 2017.

[103]Mrozek, *Jugend—Pop—Kultur*, 207; Nygaard, "High Priest," 342–3.

[104]Michael Fischer, "'Musik, Stars, Medien: Peter Kraus als Beispiel einer domestizierten Amerikanisierung der deutschen Musikkultur," in Michael Fischer und Christofer Jost (eds.), *Amerika-Euphorie—Amerika-Hysterie: Populäre Musik made in USA in der Wahrnehmung der Deutschen 1914–2014* (Münster and New York: Waxmann, 2017), 211–26; Rüdiger Bloemeke, *Roll over Beethoven: Wie der Rock 'n' Roll nach Deutschland kam* (Andrä-Wördern: Hannibal Verlag, 1996), 127–8.

France, where rock 'n' roll emerged only with a significant time lag in the early 1960s.[105] Here, singers even adapted English-sounding stage names like Richard Anthony, Dick Rivers or Eddy Mitchell; the most prominent example is of course Johnny Hallyday, whose actual name was Jean-Philippe Smets. Interestingly, the cover of his first single featured a sticker with the slogan "chanteur américain de culture française."[106] Rather than illustrating an all-out endorsement or rejection of US popular culture, then, the *Ersatz-Elvis* phenomenon illustrates the complex ways in which American cultural influences were adapted, modified, recontextualized, and appropriated by European audiences.[107] Similar processes took place in many other parts of the world, albeit in rather different political environments.

**Figure 2.3** *The German* Ersatz-Elvis *Peter Kraus performs in the movie* Wenn die Conny mit dem Peter, *1958*.

---

[105]Jonathyne Briggs, *Sounds French: Globalization, Cultural Communities, and Pop Music in France, 1958–1980* (Oxford: Oxford University Press, 2015), 14–43.
[106]Quoted in Hüser, "Rock Around the Clock," 202.
[107]Kroes, "American Mass Culture," 82–108; Pells, *Not Like Us*; Wagnleitner and May, *Foreign Politics of American Popular Culture*.

# Fighting Elvis: Behind the Iron Curtain

Although Elvis became known almost globally within months of his national arrival, his impact was often debated controversially. Just like in Western Europe, the overarching Cold War mindset conditioned the reception of Elvis in other parts of the world as well. Predictably most hostile was the Soviet Union, where both Elvis and rock 'n' roll were seen as unwanted and dangerous capitalist American influences.[108] In the 1950s, the Soviet regime exercised tight control over its youth through the mass organization Komsomol, trying to protect it from hostile Western influences by offering supposedly superior socialist alternatives like state-sponsored clubs and cafés.[109] If US cultural products were imported at all, they appeared only in very limited numbers as the result of official exchanges or agreements.[110] It is thus of little surprise that there were no Elvis records or films released in the Soviet Union throughout Elvis's lifetime, and that rock 'n' roll was heavily denounced by Soviet propaganda from the very beginning.[111] In March 1957, for example, the Secretary of the Central Committee Dmitri Shepilov proclaimed that American popular music was similar to "the wild orgies of cavemen"; rock 'n' roll in particular was "devoid of any elements of beauty and melody" and represented "an uncontrolled release of base passions, a burst of the lowest feeling and sexual urges."[112]

In spite of such state interference, however, parts of the Soviet public appeared enthusiastic about rock 'n' roll. In February 1957, the *New York Times* reported boastfully how Elvis was "the latest craze of the Soviet zoot-suiters, or stilyagi, as they are called," claiming that Soviet teenagers liked Elvis because their own lives under communism were "so boring [and] so dull."[113] Many Soviet youths gathered in private places, listening to foreign broadcasts, underground copies of rock 'n' roll records, or to an increasing number of pirate radio stations.[114] As the Anglo-American writer Sally

---

[108]Risch, "Introduction," 6–7. For Soviet perceptions of the United States during the 1950s more generally, see Rosa Magnúsdóttir, *Enemy Number One: The United States of America in Soviet Ideology and Propaganda, 1945–1959* (Oxford: Oxford University Press, 2019).

[109]Gleb Tsipursky, *Socialist Fun: Youth, Consumption, and State-Sponsored Popular Culture in the Soviet Union* (Pittsburgh, PA: University of Pittsburgh Press, 2016).

[110]Marsha Siefert, "From Cold War to Wary Peace: American Culture in the USSR and Russia," in Alexander Stephan (ed.), *The Americanization of Europe: Culture, Diplomacy, and Anti-Americanism after 1945* (New York: Berghahn, 2006), 187–8.

[111]Although a few Elvis tunes bizarrely found their way onto some Melodiya compilation albums during the 1960s, see Staburvik and Engvold, *How RCA Brought Elvis to Europe*, 40–1.

[112]*New York Times*, April 4, 1957.

[113]*New York Times*, February 3, 1957.

[114]Juliane Fürst, *Stalin's Last Generation: Soviet Post-war Youth and the Emergence of Mature Socialism* (Oxford: Oxford University Press, 2010), 348–9; Magnúsdóttir, *Enemy Number One*, 108.

Belfrage, who was living in Moscow at the time, later recalled, rock 'n' roll seemed to be everywhere in the city's university quarter, and one could "hardly go to any young person's house without finding everyone doing it, or playing it, or at least discussing it."[115] There also existed a vibrant underground rock 'n' roll scene, where copies of Elvis records made on discarded medical X-ray plates could be bought for 50 rubles a copy, at the time around $12.50.[116] In 1959, Soviet authorities clamped down on such underground trade, imprisoning two of the dealers for two years.[117] Like in other parts of the world, Soviet teenagers not only liked Elvis's music, but they also replicated his style and looks. "Some of the Moscow and Leningrad youth ... sport long, combed-back, Presley-like pompadours," the *New York Times* reported, although sideburns apparently constituted "a custom that antedate[d] Presley."[118] Interest in rock 'n' roll occasionally extended beyond the big metropolis of Moscow. In the Soviet city of Dnipropetrovsk, some comparatively wealthy university students sought to imitate the *stilyagi* style from Moscow, asking local tailors to narrow their trousers and shirts to make them look like the dresses of Elvis or other Western stars.[119]

There were some limited opportunities for the Soviet youth to explore Western influences in more direct ways. In 1957, the Moscow World Youth Festival led to an influx of thousands of Western visitors, many of whom offered first-hand examples of what was seen as the looser, more relaxed public behavior of young people in the West.[120] The few Soviet citizens who were themselves able to travel the United States or Western Europe during the 1950s often used these trips to explore American popular culture. In October 1957, for example, the CDSA Moscow football team, which had traveled to Britain for three friendly matches, went to a local cinema to see Elvis's latest film *Loving You*, even though Soviet officials had apparently wanted them to visit Shakespeare's hometown Stratford-upon-Avon instead.[121] The Soviet author and later dissident Viktor Nekrasov also made sure to watch an Elvis movie during his New York visit in 1960. "We were attracted by advertisements for the famous Elvis Presley, the idol of American teenagers," he recalled a few years later;

[115]As quoted in Caute, *Dancer Defects*, 457.
[116]Stabursvik and Engvold, *How RCA Brought Elvis to Europe*, 36.
[117]*New York Times*, January 13, 1960; Timothy W. Ryback, *Rock Around the Bloc: A History of Rock Music in Eastern Europe and the Soviet Union* (New York, NY and Oxford: Oxford University Press, 1990), 33.
[118]*New York Times*, February 3, 1957.
[119]Sergei I. Zhuk, *Rock and Roll in the Rocket City: The West, Identity, and Ideology in Soviet Dniepropetrovsk, 1960–1985* (Baltimore, MY: Johns Hopkins University Press, 2010), 72–3.
[120]Fürst, *Stalin's Last Generation*, 348; Magnúsdóttir, *Enemy Number One*, 110–19.
[121]Reported in *Daily Mirror*, October 28, 1957.

It was a trivial comedy, amusing at times ... He spent most of the time sighing over a girl and she did the same over him, and they kissed a few times, and that was it. This entertainment cost us a dollar each, and I can tell you confidentially, it was also partly responsible for that lecture we had to endure in the first briefing session in front of the U.N., especially three of us, the movie-goers.[122]

In Eastern Europe, access to rock 'n' roll music varied according to each state's degree of relative political autonomy from the Soviet Union, although censorship in general was somewhat laxer.[123] The still communist but non-aligned Yugoslavia, for example, displayed a fairly liberal attitude toward Western cultural imports, trying to position itself somewhere between East and West in the cultural realm.[124] In 1957, roughly half of the music played by Yugoslavian radio stations was popular music from both East and West, and over half of the films shown in Yugoslavian cinemas came from the United States.[125] In the early 1960s, RCA's local licensee Jugoton even started producing its own Elvis records: for many teenagers throughout Eastern Europe, their import constituted the only possibility to get hold of Elvis's music well into the 1970s.[126] At the same time, however, Yugoslavian authorities remained concerned about the degree of popularity of Western products, fearing that it might compromise the attractiveness of its own cultural products or weaken the youths' support for its communist agenda.[127]

The regimes of the East European countries that were formally integrated in the Soviet bloc officially displayed an almost uniform dislike of both Elvis and rock 'n' roll. As the result of the centralization and nationalization of East European music industries during the late 1940s, there were thus almost no opportunities to legally purchase Elvis records until at least the 1970s. Yet, the sharpness of East European regimes' reactions varied significantly according to wider political considerations. In Hungary, for example, the early Kádár regime displayed a surprisingly liberal attitude toward US popular culture, perhaps in an attempt to calm tensions in the aftermath of the Hungarian revolution. It even installed jukeboxes equipped with Western records in some youth clubs, and the Eastern Railroad Station in Budapest featured a record shop where people could borrow (although not buy) recordings by Elvis or Tommy Steele on an hourly basis.[128]

---

[122]The movie was G.I. Blues. Viktor Nekrasov, *Both Sides of the Ocean: A Russian Writer's Travels in Italy and the United States* (New York: Holt, Rinehart and Winston, 1964), 112.

[123]Siefert, "Cold War to Wary Peace," 188.

[125]Ibid., 25.

[124]Dean Vuletic, "Swinging between East and West: Yugoslav Communism and the Dilemmas of Popular Music," in William Jay Risch (ed.), *Youth and Rock in the Soviet Bloc: Youth Culture, Music, and the State in Russia and Eastern Europe* (Lanham: Lexington Books, 2015), 25–42.

[126]Stabursvik and Engvold, *How RCA Brought Elvis to Europe*, 42–3.

[127]Vuletic, "Swinging between East and West," 26–7.

[128]Ryback, *Rock Around the Bloc*, 21–2.

In Poland and Czechoslovakia, authorities generally exercised restraint in their response to rock 'n' roll, and Western popular music occasionally even featured on public radio during the 1950s.[129] At the time of de-Stalinization, the Gomulka regime in Poland appeared fairly liberal about Western cultural products in general, which manifested itself not least in the success of local bands like Drazek I pieciu that occasionally played rock 'n' roll and even covered some Elvis hits.[130] The first major Polish rock band was called Rhythm and Blues and was formed in 1959, although it soon morphed into Czerwono-Czarni: among many other rock 'n' roll tunes, it covered Elvis's "Love Me" and "Jailhouse Rock." From 1963 onward, Poland allowed the limited import of Elvis records from Yugoslavia, and even produced its own playable Elvis postcard records in the late 1960s.[131] In Czechoslovakia too, emerging rock 'n' roll bands were a plenty, including the young singer Jiri Suchý who was dubbed the "Czech Elvis" by Western journalists; the Reduta Club in Prague became a particular hot spot for rock 'n' roll enthusiasts.[132]

Other East European regimes, by contrast, clamped down more heavily on 1950s rock 'n' roll. In Bulgaria, for example, an initially vibrant rock 'n' roll scene was crushed violently by the government;[133] and in some more remote areas, Elvis merely triggered curiosity because most people had never heard of the singer. In September 1957, the American journalist Harrison E. Salisbury, who would publish a book about the US' own "shook-up" generation a few months later, reported in the *New York Times* about a recent trip to Romania:[134]

At any time of day or night you are likely to hear a youngster improvising on a piano in the best Western style. Even so, in a random group of nineteen youngsters, only one had heard of Elvis Presley. "He has something to do with rock 'n' roll," a knowledgeable youngster said. This immediately produced a storm of questions: What is rock 'n' roll? Is it true that all American youngsters are crazy over rock 'n' roll? Why are such bad things said about it in the newspapers?[135]

---

[129]Ibid., 22–3.

[130]Alex Kan and Nick Hayes, "Big Beat in Poland," in Sabrina P. Ramet (ed.), *Rocking the State: Rock Music and Politics in Eastern Europe and Russia* (Boulder, CO: Westview Press, 1994), 41–2.

[131]Stabursvik and Engvold, *How RCA Brought Elvis to Europe*, 39.

[132]Ryback, *Rock Around the Bloc*, 24–5; Sabrina P. Ramet, "Rock Music in Czechoslovakia," in Sabrina P. Ramet (ed.), *Rocking the State: Rock Music and Politics in Eastern Europe and Russia* (Boulder, CO: Westview Press, 1994), 56.

[133]Ryback, *Rock Around the Bloc*, 25, 27.

[134]Harrison E. Salisbury, *The Shook-Up Generation* (New York, NY: Harper, 1958).

[135]*New York Times*, September 8, 1957.

The East European state where rock 'n' roll had the by far most controversial impact, however, was the German Democratic Republic (GDR).[136] After 1949, the GDR had evolved into one of the Soviet Union's most rigid satellite states, as the leadership dogmatically implemented its own brand of Marxism-Leninism and exercised far-reaching controls into their citizens' lives.[137] Since the GDR regime regarded the East German youth as pivotal in the creation of its envisioned socialist society, rock 'n' roll acquired an immediate political resonance: it feared that the generational conflict over rock 'n' roll might also stretch into the realm of politics.[138] The East German government therefore did not simply regard rock 'n' roll as an unwanted teenage trend; it considered it a dangerous US political weapon apparently designed to infiltrate and benumb the European youth.[139] "Nobody can say that this rock 'n' roll noise has anything to do with art," GDR leader Walter Ulbricht proclaimed in 1958; in his eyes, it reflected "the anarchical conditions of capitalist society." He therefore saw it as the GDR's task to "defend German culture against this 'American way of life'."[140]

As Ulbricht's statement already suggests, the East German debate over Elvis reveals some remarkable similarities with simultaneous debates in the West, where historical German anti-American stereotypes similarly dominated the discourse. Yet, the GDR's self-stylization into the true upholder of Germany's cultural heritage vi-á-vis the capitalist West led to even more graphic denunciations at times. In many cases, East German newspapers simply replicated West German reports on Elvis, with some even mentioning explicitly that they had acquired their information from West German publications, but then added their own ideological spin. On December 13, 1956, for example, the *Berliner Zeitung*'s major article on Elvis built almost exclusively on *Der Spiegel*'s cover story that had appeared a few days earlier.[141] Accompanied by the headline "Appealing to the sapient," it proclaimed that there was "nothing special" about Elvis: "[H]e looks rather stupid, other people do that too; his face is always a bit blurred, like the faces of some other people too; he cannot play the guitar, that

---

[136]For several more detailed studies, see Mark Fenemore, *Sex, Thugs, and Rock 'n' Roll: Teenage Rebels in Cold-War East Germany* (New York, NY and Oxford: Berghahn Books, 2007); Wiebke Janssen, *Halbstarke in der DDR: Verfolgung und Kriminalisierung einer Jugendkultur* (Berlin: Ch. Links Verlag, 2010); Michael Rauhut, *Beat in der Grauzone: DDR-Rock 1964 bis 1972* (Berlin: BasisDruck, 1993); Thomas Fuchs, "Rock 'n' Roll in the German Democratic Republic, 1949–1961," in Wagnleitner and May (eds.), *Foreign Politics of American Popular Culture*, 192–206.

[137]Stefan Wolle, *Der große Plan. Alltag und Herrschaft in der DDR 1949–1961* (Berlin: Ch. Links, 2013).

[138]Janssen, *Halbstarke*, 52–3.

[139]Poiger, *Jazz, Rock and Rebels*, 193–4.

[140]*Berliner Zeitung*, November 13, 1958.

[141]*Berliner Zeitung*, December 13, 1956. The article mentioned explicitly that it got its information about Elvis out of *Der Spiegel*.

does not distinguish him either; neither can he sing." Such contemptuous depictions of Elvis were then followed up by exaggerated descriptions of his stage shows: "he only has to senselessly shake and vibrate with his hips" to "let hell loose amongst the audience, particularly among the underage womanhood."[142] The newspaper of the GDR's socialist youth organization followed suit, accusing Elvis of "wild hip-swinging à la Marilyn Monroe" and "jump[ing] around like a lunatic, shaking his crotch as if he had been given undiluted hydrochloric acid, and roar[ing] like some wounded deer, just not as melodious."[143]

If the GDR's political rejection of Elvis revealed some remarkable similarities to West German debates, then the East German youth too adapted Elvis in strikingly similar ways to their West German counterparts.[144] Youth groups gathered on streets and squares in industrialized cities like Leipzig or Halle in order to listen to foreign radio stations on portable transistor radios, and several East German youth clubs even featured juke boxes stocked with rock 'n' roll records. There were also signs of organized fandom in the GDR: in many cities, fan clubs with names like "Presley Disciples" or "Presley Admirers" were formed, and some of the more violent street gangs too occasionally referred to Elvis in their names.[145] Many fans met up regularly in their private homes to listen to pirate recordings of rock 'n' roll music from the West; and they often created their own fan insignia, such as Elvis buttons for their jackets, so that they could publicly display their fandom. In Halle, several students were caught swapping Elvis photographs which they had imported from the West; in Karl-Marx-Stadt, some local apprentices were found decorating the inside of their lunch boxes with Elvis pictures.[146] There were several fan clubs that established contacts with their West German counterparts: in August 1959, for example, the GDR's security service and secret police *Stasi* intercepted a letter exchange between Margaret, an Elvis fan from Rostock, and the secretary of the Elvis Presley Club in Munich.[147] As the fourth chapter shows, such transnational fan exchanges that occasionally even transcended the East–West border would become much more common in the 1960s.

The GDR regime tried to counteract rock 'n' roll in two ways. First, it stepped up its efforts to create its own brand of socialist-style popular culture. "It is not enough to condemn capitalist decadence in words," SED leader

---

[142]Ibid.

[143]*Junge Welt*, February 5, 1957. Quoted in Michael Rauhut, *Beat in der Grauzone: DDR-Rock 1964 bis 1972* (Berlin: BasisDruck, 1993), 31.

[144]Janssen, *Halbstarke*, 101–27; Poiger, *Jazz, Rock and Rebels*, 175–82.

[145]More generally Mrozek, *Jugend—Pop—Kultur*, 350–62; Fenemore, *Sex, Thugs, and Rock 'n' Roll*, 23–4.

[146]Janssen, *Halbstarke*, 102.

[147]Fenemore, *Sex, Thugs, and Rock 'n' Roll*, 80.

Walter Ulbricht famously declared in 1959, "we have to offer something better [ ... than] the 'hot music' and ecstatic 'singing' of a Presley."[148] Apart from promoting home-grown singing talents like Alo Koll and issuing a decree that restricted the amount of Western music played in public to 40 percent, it famously commissioned the creation of the so-called Lipsi dance as a socialist alternative to rock 'n' roll.[149] Yet, such efforts failed to impress the East German youth: on several occasions, young protestors interrupted parades of the GDR's youth organization FDJ with the chant "We need no Lipsi and no Alo Koll, we need Elvis Presley and his rock 'n' roll."[150] Some East German fans also utilized Elvis for more overt political purposes. At a Leipzig youth forum in November 1958, for example, Ulbricht was asked provocatively why East German youths should not have the freedom to purchase "Presley records" in West Berlin,[151] and during at least one GDR parade, protestors alternated their familiar chant "Long live Elvis Presley" with an occasional "Down with Ulbricht."[152] Confronted with popular resistance, the GDR regime eventually resorted to political persecution, leading to several lengthy prison sentences and an upsurge in violent clashes between rock 'n' roll gangs and the GDR police.[153]

Such acts of suppression and violence were, of course, transmitted to the United States, which in turn only enhanced the music's growing association with American ideals like individual liberty and freedom of expression. The *New York Times,* for example, routinely expressed its outrage over the prosecution and arrest of Elvis fans in spite of its evident dislike of the singer; in November 1959, for example, it reported with disgust about the imprisonment of "Leipzig Presley Fans."[154] The political dimension of Elvis's reception in Eastern Europe did not bypass Elvis's American fans either. "We, as free Americans are appalled at such harsh treatment," one of them declared in *Elvis Monthly.* "What courage and devotion these fans must have to brave such outrageous measures to keep them from listening to their idol's music! ... If their youth *would* model themselves after the Elvis we know, how much better off the youth of the world would be! Elvis is *not* illiterate. He is smart, bright and an ambitious and hard-working young man."[155]

---

[148]As quoted in Rauhut, *Beat in der Grauzone*, 37.

[149]Fuchs, "Rock 'n' Roll," 202; Janssen, *Halbstarke*, 107–8; Poiger, *Jazz, Rock and Rebels*, 185; Rauhut, *Beat in der Grauzone*, 44.

[150]Poiger, *Jazz, Rock and Rebels*, 196; Janssen, *Halbstarke*, 108.

[151]*Berliner Zeitung*, November 13, 1958. Ulbricht claimed in response that he was against any sort of manipulation of youth and that the GDR already offered all sorts of other opportunities for its young adolescents.

[152]Fenemore, *Sex, Thugs, and Rock 'n' Roll*, 151.

[153]Ibid., 150.

[154]*New York Times*, November 3, 1959.

[155]*Elvis Monthly 9*, October 1960.

# Global Elvis? Beyond the Iron Curtain

Although Elvis's impact was by far the biggest in the United States and Europe during the 1950s, the wider repercussions of rock 'n' roll stretched far beyond. In Asia-Pacific, Elvis's reception was again shaped largely by the ideological parameters of the Cold War. In Communist China, for example, little was known about Elvis for much of his lifetime; the first Chinese Elvis record was released in only 1991.[156] Elvis therefore seems to have been largely unknown among the Chinese public during the 1950s, even though there were rumors about illegal rock 'n' roll imports to Shanghai via Hong Kong in 1957.[157] In 1958, a visiting American journalist found the Chinese music scene dominated by the domestic hit record "Catch Up With Britain," a tune that was apparently "sung by factory workers, peasants and teenage Pioneers sporting the red neckerchief of China's Communist youth movement." Another such hit was "Socialism Is Good," and the Chinese government apparently urged its citizens to compose similar "songs of their own to symbolize the advance of Chinese communism."[158]

In Japan, by contrast, rock 'n' roll was highly popular and eagerly embraced by the Japanese youth. Following the Second World War and the Chinese revolution in 1949, the United States had gone at great lengths to draw Japan into the Western camp and prevent a potential drift toward communism. It pursued this quest not only through a significant reductions of reparation payments and the country's rapid integration into the world economy, but it also utilized popular culture like Hollywood films to enthuse Japanese audiences about US-style democracy.[159] Japanese audiences endorsed not only Hollywood movies but also rock 'n' roll. In the late 1950s, Japan was swept by the so-called "rockabirii" boom. Local artists appropriated rock 'n' roll to Japanese styles, and several Japanese *Ersatz-Elvises* like Kazuya Kosaka or Masaaki Hirao emerged in due course. "Like everything that makes money," the *New York Times* wrote somewhat condescendingly in June 1957, "Elvis Presley is skillfully imitated in Japan, the imitation being, except for eyes, authentic-appearing in every detail, including sideburns and voice."[160] The following year, its long-term correspondent Robert Trumbull reported how rock 'n' roll had

---

[156]Stabursvik and Engvold, *How RCA Brought Elvis to Europe*, 37.

[157]Ibid.

[158]*New York Times*, July 27, 1958.

[159]Aaron Forsberg, *America and the Japanese Miracle: The Cold War Context of Japan's Postwar Economic Revival, 1950–1960* (Chapel Hill: University of North Carolina Press, 2014); Hiroshi Kitamura, *Screening Enlightenment: Hollywood and the Cultural Reconstruction of Defeated Japan* (Ithaca, NY: Cornell University Press, 2010). For the political background, see most recently Jennifer M. Miller, *Cold War Democracy: The United States and Japan* (Harvard: University Press, 2019).

[160]*New York Times*, June 9, 1957.

turned "ordinarily bashful Japanese teen-agers temporarily into screeching dervishes in countless theatres and dimly lighted coffee houses throughout the land."[161] He suggested that some Japanese rockabirii stars managed surprisingly authentic imitations of Elvis:

> Masaaki Hirao, who at 19 is the darling, the Elvis Presley, of Japan's "rockabilly" set, gyrates and writhes to a bedlam of squealing, swaying teen-agers, mostly girls. Some are in skin-tight blue jeans, but many wear their demure school uniforms of blue pleated skirt and middy blouses ... The young man in the center of the stage, flailing a guitar as if he were trying to beat it to pieces, wears a scarlet cap over his poodle haircut, matching shirt with cuffs turned back over the sleeves of his pastel pink jacket, and skin-tight brown pants ending an inch or so above canary yellow suede oxfords ... [He] accompanies his angle-worm writhing with loud moaning sounds. The meaning of his lyrics is lost on everyone, because he has learned them by rote from a record in English – which he doesn't understand.[162]

If Hirao seems to have performed an almost perfect Elvis imitation, then the fans' reaction to the phenomenon was second to none. As the article went on to describe,

> Young men sail colored streamers onto the stage, enveloping Hirao, guitar and microphone in a squirming paper cocoon. In a final transport, some of the girls hurl panties, presumably extra pairs, across the footlights. Other ponytailed adolescents bound onto the stage and fight to plant kisses on the howling juvenile with the guitar. The panting object of all this attention finishes his number flopping about on his back like a freshly beheaded chicken while the audience goes wild.[163]

Japan is perhaps the most extreme example of the 1950s rock 'n' roll hype in Asia, but there were plenty of other examples as well. This applies particularly to former British colonies and other parts of Asia that were not under communist influence, and which now benefited from the wide availability of Western records and movies. In Hong Kong, for example, Elvis's rise coincided with a boom of Western-style consumerism that not only led to the establishment of arcades and shopping malls, but that also brought with it a spread of jukeboxes, cinemas, and radios.[164] The Hong Kong citizen Vivienne Wang, who became an Elvis fan in 1956, later recalled

---

[161]*New York Times*, April 20, 1958.
[162]Ibid.
[163]Ibid.
[164]David Clayton, "The Consumption of Radio Broadcast Technologies in Hong Kong, c. 1930–1960," *The Economic History Review* 57/4 (2004), 708–9.

how Elvis had been "well accepted" in Hong Kong from the very beginning, and how "all his songs topped our local charts."[165] Singapore offers a similar picture. "I remember it was about 10 years ago in 1959 when I was then a student in Primary 4 that I first became aware of this magnificent personality who goes by the name of Elvis Presley," a local fan later recalled; "I did not have much to spend but ... I saved just about all I can and spent it on Elvis magazines, pictures, films, etc." Before long, however, a "group of us ardent Elvis fans discovered one another and started to listen to Elvis songs during our leisure time, organizing Elvis get-togethers at one of our Elvis fan's house and marching to the local theatre where and when an Elvis film was shown."[166] In the case of Singapore, enthusiasm for Elvis often tied into more general enthusiasm for US-style modernity. "We baby boomers in Singapore in the 1960s also wanted what the teenagers in America and Europe wanted," one fan later recalled. "Their pop music symbolized the new life, the good life, and we all wanted a part of it."[167]

On the African continent, Elvis Presley's popularity was biggest in South Africa, where his music was distributed widely among the white population. In the absence of television, Elvis's early films like *Love Me Tender* or *Jailhouse Rock* enjoyed particular popularity, and they undoubtedly contributed to Elvis's big commercial success there: in 1959, the *Sunday Times* of Johannesburg identified Elvis as the "top male vocalist of all time" and declared "Jailhouse Rock" to be the country's most popular record of all times.[168] Such top-down promotion was often complemented by bottom-up fan activism: for many years, the fortnightly tabloid magazine *Personality* hosted an "Elvis's Corner" section that was written by the local fan club's secretary.[169] In December 1961, a South African reader proudly told *Elvis Monthly* about the country's "very flourishing fan club ... with a membership of almost 50,000."[170] At the height of Apartheid, however, Elvis's popularity remained by and large confined to the white population. In spite of several attempts to market rock 'n' roll to the black population, it was commonly regarded as an US import performed by white singers for white audiences. The import of US rock 'n' roll records was restricted to white performers, and there were no records available by Chuck Berry or Little Richard during the 1950s.[171]

In South America, in the more immediate periphery of the United States, Elvis became highly politicized too. In Mexico, for example, rock 'n' roll

---

[165]*Elvis Monthly* 100, May 1968.

[166]*Elvis Monthly* 111, April 1969.

[167]As quoted in Kai Khiun Liew, "Rock 'n' Roll and the Restringing and Resounding of the Singapore Story," in Jason Lim and Terence Lee (eds.), *Singapore. Negotiating State and Society, 1965–2015* (London and New York: Routledge, 2016), 189.

[168]Charles Hamm, *Putting Popular Music in its Place* (Cambridge: Cambridge University Press, 1995 [2006]), 188.

[169]Sewlall, "Elvis Presley in the South African Musical Imaginary," 61–4.

[170]*Elvis Monthly* 2/12, December 1961.

[171]For more detail, see again Hamm, *Putting Popular Music in its Place*, 188–90.

became intermeshed in a much wider generational struggle over the country's social fabric: whereas many adults rejected it outright as an unwarranted US-imperialist import that morally corrupted the Mexican youth, others embraced it as a symbol of Mexico's desired transition into a modern, consumerist society.[172] Elvis's personal popularity, however, suffered greatly when government officials popularized a rumor that Elvis had allegedly claimed how he would "rather kiss three black girls than a Mexican."[173] Although the rumor has since been proven conclusively wrong, the smear campaign led to a sharp decline in the singer's popularity, and triggered an upsurge in the popularity of home-grown "rocanrol" bands. The label *Orfeón* in particular invested heavily in the promotion of local artists, and groups like Los Teen Tops, Los Rebeldes del Rock, Los Loud Jets, or Los Hooligans enjoyed great popularity with their translated and often sanitized versions of American rock 'n' roll hits.[174]

The most blatant example of how Cold War politics shaped Elvis's reception, however, can be found in Cuba. Until the late 1950s, rock 'n' roll records were imported with little difficulty from the United States there, and Elvis in particular proved highly popular: the single "Don't Be Cruel," for example, sold more than 50,000 copies in 1957, whereas sales of 3,000 had previously been seen as a success in Cuba.[175] Teenagers also adapted Elvis's looks and styles: the novelist Enrique Alvarez Jané later recalled how crowds of "young people dressed and with hair styles in the American style" lined up in front of cinemas whenever a new Elvis movie appeared.[176] Such was the popularity of Elvis in Cuba that it initially even survived the revolution: in April 1959, RCA established its own Cuban affiliate *Discuba*, which manufactured its first and only Elvis record (*Elvis Regresa*, or *Elvis Is Back*) in 1960. Following the US trade embargo and the further worsening of US-Cuban relations, however, the government eventually clamped down on rock 'n' roll music. In March 1963, Fidel Castro launched an all-out attack during a speech at the University of Havana:

> Many of these people are in those places; in the poolrooms, on the corners, in the bars. All these things must be studied. The important thing is the principle that we cannot permit them to aspire to be lazy. Many of those lazy pepillos, sons of the bourgeoisie, are walking around there with trousers that are too tight. Some of them have small guitars and "ELVIS-PRESLIANAS" attitudes, and they have taken the extreme liberty of attempting to organize their effeminate shows in public places.

---

[172]Eric Zolov, *Refried Elvis: The Rise of the Mexican Counterculture* (Berkeley, LA: University of California Press, 1999), 8–10.

[173]Zolov, *Refried Elvis*, 41–4.

[174]Ibid., 62–6.

[175]Stabursvik and Engvold, *How RCA Brought Elvis to Europe*, 44.

[176]As quoted in Louis A. Pérez Jr., *On Becoming Cuban: Identity, Nationality, and Culture* (Chapel Hill, NC: The University of North Carolina Press, 1999), 393.

Let them not confuse the calmness and equanimity of the revolution with weakness, because our society cannot make room for these degenerates. The socialist society cannot permit that kind of degeneration. Youths who aspire to that sort of thing? No! For trees that grow twisted, the remedy is no longer so easy. I am not going to say that we are going to take drastic measures against these crooked trees ... But they are all linked, the little bum, the loafer, and the vagus, the ELVIS-PRESLIANO, the "pitusa".[177]

Castro's speech finished Elvis's presence in Cuba almost instantly. The public radio station immediately stopped playing Elvis music, no further Elvis records were sold, and the remaining stock of the *Elvis Regresa* LP was bought up by the Polish import firm Ars Polana, where it became the first official Elvis record on the market.[178]

# Conclusions

During the 1950s, Elvis Presley's rise to global prominence reflected a delicate mix between Cold War politics and much broader underlying transnational dynamics. While Elvis became the prime figurehead of an emerging transnational youth culture that clearly transcended national borders, his global image was also shaped by particular national characteristics and the political imperatives of the East–West confrontation. In Western Europe, for example, his status as one of the US' most visible cultural exports after 1945 meant that much bigger debates over mass consumerism and postwar modernity were waged through the singer's public image. While Elvis eventually became accepted by both the establishment and the wider public in Western Europe, he was also adapted and modified to particular national contexts, as not least the emergence of countless *Ersatz-Elvises* shows. Behind and beyond the Iron Curtain too, the Cold War heavily conditioned Elvis's reception. While his records and films were freely available and highly popular in Western-oriented countries like Japan, for example, Communist countries like China or the Soviet Union rigorously prohibited them throughout the singer's lifetime. The most drastic example of Elvis's politicization during the 1950s, however, concerns East Germany, where the regime's eventual crackdown on rock 'n' roll turned Elvis into a symbol of political resistance and subversion.

---

[177]As quoted and translated in Stabursvik and Engvold, *How RCA Brought Elvis to Europe*, 44. For the Spanish original, see "Discurso Pronunciado por El Commandante Fidel Castro Ruz, Primer Ministro del Gobierno revolucionario de Cuba, en la Clausura del acto para Commemorar el vi aniversario del as alto al Palacio Presidencial, celebrado en la escalinata de la Universidad de la Habana, el 13 de Marzo de 1963," www.cuba.cu/gobierno/discursos/1963/esp/f130363e.html [last accessed December 22, 2019].
[178]Stabursvik and Engvold, *How RCA Brought Elvis to Europe*, 45.

# 3

# American Elvis: The Army Years

John Lennon once famously remarked that Elvis died "the day he went into the army."[1] The remark suggested that Elvis's time as G.I. soldier stripped him off his authenticity and creativity, restraining and eventually commodifying the erstwhile rebel figure into a mainstream entertainer. For millions of other people, however, Elvis Presley was actually born that very day. His decision to take up the draft and serve his military duty like any other ordinary soldier endowed him with a degree of social acceptance and credibility that had been missing for much of his previous career. Not only did the effective staging of Elvis as a patriotic soldier signify a dramatic change in Elvis's public image, but it also opened up attractive new markets: the singer returned from the army as a polished mainstream entertainer at the very center of US popular culture. Just as the rock 'n' roll hype faded and most of its erstwhile heroes faded into insignificance, Elvis became elevated into a much bigger all-American icon.

The transformation of Elvis's image is in itself fascinating, but his military service also sheds light on many bigger issues in late 1950s America and its relationship to the wider world. Within the United States, the decision to draft Elvis triggered wide-ranging debates over the status of celebrities in US public life, as well as over the egalitarian principles of its army and the draft—debates that offer a fascinating glimpse into the relationship between the American people and its military force at the height of the Cold War. And in West Germany, where Elvis was stationed from October 1958 to March 1960, public attitudes toward Elvis reveal a lot about the changing images and perceptions of the United States at a crucial point in the county's transition toward a Western-style liberal democracy. Elvis's time in Germany therefore shows the extent but also some of the limits of US involvement in postwar Europe, revealing a slow but accelerating blurring between

---

[1]Quoted, for example, in Douglas Brode, *Elvis Cinema and Popular Culture* (Jefferson, NC: McFarland & Company, 2006), 58.

American and West European celebrity cultures. It also offers a fascinating case study of the many daily interactions between G.I. soldiers and local populations, which eventually turned Elvis into an informal ambassador for the so-called American way of life.

# Act I: The Draft

On January 4, 1957, a shiny, cream-colored Cadillac Eldorado pulled up in front of the Kennedy Veterans Hospital in Memphis. Journalists and cameramen watched excitedly as a 21-year-old man, wearing a bright red jacket with a black collar and black waist band and black trousers, exited the car, posed for some pictures, and then quickly disappeared behind the hospital entrance. His entourage, the Las Vegas dancer Dotty Harmony, told the assembled press that they had just witnessed a "fine physical specimen" but she would not dare predict the outcome of the examinations that were about to take place. Elvis Presley was taking his pre-army induction physical.[2]

The draft hung over Elvis almost from the day his career had begun. Conscription had been re-introduced in the United States through the Selective Training and Service Act in 1940, and it required all men between the ages of 18 and 25 to register with Selective Services within a month of their eighteenth birthday. With Elvis being in that exact age group, rumors over his potential induction had started to circulate almost as soon as the singer rose to stardom. As early as October 1956, film producer Hal Wallis inquired with Colonel Parker about Elvis's likely induction date, who was quick to reply that the Tennessee draft board had reassured him that Elvis was "not at the top of the list."[3] After Elvis's pre-army physical in January 1957, however, the fact that Elvis would be enlisted at some point felt practically certain: the Memphis draft board soon let it known to the local press that Elvis's physical constitution had been the highest possible one, while his mental score had apparently been "about average."[4] The most likely induction date was estimated at some point over the next six to eight months.

The practical certainty of Elvis's draft provoked heated debates within Elvis's management and the army over how to best handle the issue. At first glance, the obvious route would have been to enlist Elvis for Special Services, perhaps as a recruitment advertiser or troop entertainer. Indeed, it was not uncommon for celebrities at the time to be put into Special Services or to be assigned special duties, as the recent examples of the singer Tom

[2]*Memphis Press-Scimitar*, January 4, 1957; Guralnick and Jorgensen, *Day by Day*, 95.
[3]Hazen to Wallis, October 26, 1956. MHL, Hal Wallis Papers, Presley, Elvis, contract correspondence, f.2112.
[4]*Memphis Press Scimitar*, January 8, 1957.

Lehrer or baseball player Willie Mays had shown.[5] In the run-up to Elvis's induction, several army agencies proposed a wide range of rather creative schemes to recruit the singer, including the navy's idea to set up an entire "Elvis Presley company" and the air force's proposal to have Elvis tour recruitment centers around the United States for two years.[6] The public relations officer for the Memphis draft board Sergeant Walter Alden, father of Elvis's later girlfriend Ginger Alden, even tried to recruit the singer as a volunteer, only to be told that he "had decided not to enlist and would take his chances with the draft."[7]

The possibility of Elvis's draft tied into several bigger debates over military service in 1950s America. While the principle of universal service as an inherently democratic and egalitarian policy was still widely accepted, the draft's growing inequity had by the mid-1950s become a hotly debated topic. The deferment policies for college students in particular were highly contentious, and rising birth rates as well as changes in military strategy meant that comparatively few people were called up: in February 1957, a study found that only 139,000 of the 1.2 million people reaching draft age every year ended up actually serving.[8] The special treatment of celebrities also provoked occasional controversies: a few years earlier, the singer Eddie Fisher had received scorning headlines when it was revealed that he had spent much of his draft living in a luxurious apartment and working on his music; he was soon transferred to Korea.[9]

In light of these bigger debates, there was a real danger that any special treatment for Elvis would create a significant backlash among the wider public. If any further proof was needed, it came when a Memphis army spokesman carelessly assured fans that Elvis would "probably" be assigned to Special Services, and therefore be able to keep his long hair. Once the statement had found its way into the press, the Department of Defense received numerous angry letters, one of which claimed that such special treatment was evidence of the "deterioration in the discipline and morale in our Army, Navy, and Marines ... since World War II."[10] Even the Republican Senator Clifford Case wrote to Secretary of the Army Wilber Brucker asking for clarification over Elvis's exact

---

[5]Brian McAllister Linn, *Elvis's Army: Cold War GIs and the Atomic Battlefield* (Cambridge, MA: Harvard University Press, 2016), 5.
[6]Guralnick, *Last Train*, 442–3.
[7]Alden, *Elvis and Ginger*, 6.
[8]George Q. Flynn, *The Draft, 1940–1973* (Lawrence, KS: University Press of Kansas, 1993), 162, 134–65.
[9]Linn, *Elvis's Army*, 141.
[10]*Boston Herald*, January 6, 1957; Bennet to Department of Defense, January 7, 1957; NARA, RG 407, Biography File 390-E, Box 12, Elvis Presley File.

army status.[11] The Department of Defense quickly responded to such inquiries that nobody would "be given special treatment because of their prominence," and that Elvis would "go to the barber shop and then to the supply room and receive his basic training the same as any other soldier."[12]

Eventually, it was decided in cooperation between Colonel Parker and the Department of Defense that Elvis should be drafted like any other soldier, without receiving any sort of extra treatment. The arrangement benefited both sides. From the army's perspective, it avoided otherwise inevitable charges of favoritism: instead, the fact that the most prominent entertainer of his age and time would submit to all hardships of soldiering life was a perfect example of the alleged egalitarianism the army was so eager to project at the time.[13] For Elvis, in turn, the draft offered an opportunity to demonstrate to the American public that he was not a teenage delinquent but a responsible and trustworthy American who dutifully fulfilled his obligations to his country. From Parker's perspective, another consideration may have played some part too: if Elvis had been enlisted for Special Services, the army could have exploited his talent free of charge, whereas Parker was now able to set up an elaborate marketing machinery to keep Elvis's name in the public eye through several marketing stints and carefully timed releases of pre-recorded singles.[14] Indeed, Parker stubbornly refused all army attempts to have Elvis perform while on duty, and continuously urged his client to turn down any such offers as well.[15]

As always, Elvis humbly accepted Parker's judgment. Although he worried privately that the two-year hiatus from the public eye might eventually turn out to be the premature end of his career, he felt that he had little choice but to follow the reasoning of his management and the army. When he finally received his draft notice in December 1957, he asked for a two-month deferment to finish shooting for his latest movie *King Creole*, but otherwise appeared to accept the decision in good stride: "It's a duty I've got to fill and I'm going to do it," he told the Memphian *Commercial Appeal*.[16] In private, however, he appeared rather less upbeat. As his friend George Klein recalls, Elvis seemed "devastated – just down, depressed," and complained harshly that Parker had not tried harder to get him out of it.[17] Yet, Elvis kept the façade in public. "I don't know what they will want me to do," he told the *Memphis Press-Scimitar*, "I'll do what they ask." And although he admitted that his mother Gladys was anxious about the whole enterprise, he told the

[11]Alan Levy, *Operation Elvis* (London: André Deutsch Limited, 1960), 8–9.
[12]Note: Col. Franks, January 9, 1957. NARA, RG 407, Biography File 390-E, Box 12, Elvis Presley File.
[13]Linn, *Elvis's Army*, 4–5.
[14]Nash, *The Colonel*, 174.
[15]Guralnick, *Careless Love*, 11–12.
[16]*Commercial Appeal*, December 28, 1957.
[17]George Klein as quoted in Guralnick, *Last Train*, 443.

interviewer that she was "no different from millions of other mothers who hated to see their sons go."[18] A humble, responsible young American just doing his duty: this set the tone for the massive public relations campaign that was about to start.

# Act II: The Induction

The news of Elvis's induction made headlines all over the world. Within the United States, the issue quickly turned into a much wider debate over the role of military service in American society. General public acceptance of the draft was still high, and it was commonly depicted as a civic duty every American male had to fulfil. Indeed, as late as 1959, almost 80 percent of high school students professed to be in favor of universal military service, even if almost two-thirds of them also supported college deferments.[19] At the same time, however, the debates over Elvis's induction also reveal some slight cracks in the seemingly prevalent Cold War consensus at the time. To Elvis's fans in particular, the decision to enlist Elvis not only seemed to reflect the draft's inequity, but it was also seen as a blatant attempt at the domestication of their idol.

The debates surrounding Elvis's induction offer a fascinating glimpse into how bigger societal issues like the principle of military service or the status of celebrities in US public life were negotiated through Elvis's public image. Both President Eisenhower and the Department of Defense received numerous letters about Elvis from the wider public, which either supported or denounced the singer's drafting. Many agitated citizens professed their strong approval, and complained harshly whenever rumors of any special treatment surfaced. "Will the Army never learn that we are living in a democracy and that every American who is drafted deserves exactly the same treatment," one such letter read; another one even referred to "our beloved Lincol [sic]" who "once said 'All men are created equal.' ... For if you let Presley have more privilages [sic] you are breaking the constitution and are giving privilages [sic] so a rich man can get more money."[20] Ongoing debates over inequity also shone through occasionally: one man from Los Angeles even wrote to Eisenhower that any special treatment or deferment of Elvis would "break down the morale in our entire Armed Forces. I happen to have a nephew who recently graduated from collete [sic], got married and was just starting his business career when he was inducted into the Service.

---

[18]*Memphis Press Scimitar*, March 15, 1958.
[19]Flynn, *The Draft,* 148.
[20]All from "Excerpts from Letters to DA regarding Elvis Presley," undated. NARA, RG407, Biography File 390-E, Box 12, Elvis Presley File.

This, of course, has interrupted his whole life which has been the case with many other thousands of fine young Americans."[21]

Many of Elvis's fans, however, saw the draft as yet another attempt by the establishment to domesticate their idol, not least because comparatively few people of his generation actually ended up getting drafted at the time. Angry fan letters flooded both the White House and the Pentagon, as countless fans registered their strong disapproval. Many such letters referred to American values and the country's founding principles, claiming that the draft would take away Elvis's personal liberties. "It would be America without Freedom if Elvis was Drafted," one agitated fan wrote; and another warned that "if you draft Elvis all the teenagers will be mad at the Army. It would be like Russia if Elvis was in the Army." Some even evoked the American Dream narrative that had been so effectively constructed around Elvis in their attempts to bail him out. "He was poor and a truckdriver, then he won fame, please don't end it," one letter to the Department of Defense pleaded. "He hasn't done anything wrong."[22] In some of these letters, bigger issues of inequity shone through. "Elvis is not an only exception there are other boys too," one fan wrote to Eisenhower. "Take my uncle for instance he's 23 and hasn't been drafted yet, so why does the most popular guy (Elvis of course) have to be drafted. He's just 22. I am sure he can fight but so can some of the others on the opposite side."[23]

The debate over Elvis's induction also offered opportunities to renegotiate bigger questions of individualism, liberty, and freedom of expression; issues that were of course at the very heart of the youth culture that Elvis had helped shape. Elvis's hair—the question of whether or not Elvis would get a regular army cut—came to be a particular focal point; indeed, an internal count at the Department of Defense found that the greatest number of letters it had received were related to the "cutting of Mr Presley's hair."[24] This was not surprising: Elvis's long hair and sideburns had become a key symbol of nonconformity and teenage rebellion, whereas an army haircut was the very definition of the opposite. Some felt sufficiently agitated over the issue that they urged Eisenhower and the Department of Defense to enforce the haircut as a signal sign of generational control. "All over the country, educators are trying to combat his influence by getting young people to dress decently, and have neat tidy haircuts," one teacher wrote, and then "what happens – the military says this special (?) boy doesn't have to get his hair cut – this young

---

[21]Letter to Eisenhower, January 8, 1958. [E]isenhower [P]residential [L]ibrary, Dwight D. Eisenhower: Records as President, [W]hite [H]ouse [C]entral [F]iles, [A]lphabetical [F]ile, Box 2496, Presley, Elvis.

[22]All from "Excerpts from Letters to DA regarding Elvis Presley," undated. NARA, RG407, Biography File 390-E, Box 12, Elvis Presley File.

[23]Letter to Eisenhower, January 16, 1957. EPL, WHCF, AF, Box 2496, Presley, Elvis.

[24]"Fact Sheet: Letters concerning Elvis Presley," February 11, 1958. NARA, RG407, Biography File 390-E, Box 12, Elvis Presley File.

man with his disgusting gyrations that belong in burlesque atmosphere!" Another letter declared in similar vein that "[t]wenty million veterans who were given the choice of a shaved head or the guard house, sincerely regret and deeply resent the discriminatory, preferential and unfair special favor accorded a half baked hill billy."[25] Even some younger people agreed. "Dear Ike," a letter of six self-proclaimed Elvis fans to Eisenhower started, "we have read in the papers that Elvis Presley doesn't have to get his hair cut, when going in to the service. WHY? He is no better than our brothers and boyfriends that are in now."[26]

If some saw the haircut merely as demonstration of the army's egalitarianism, many fans instead regarded it as a blatant domestication attempt, as well as an attack on the styles and culture of their entire generation. "First you take Elvis away from us and put him in the Army," one fan wrote, "then you say that you are going to cut all his long hair off. And then you are going to shave his sideburns off. You just can't do it. And then I guess in a little while you will stop him from makeing [sic] records." Another letter almost pleaded to the Department of Defense: "Can't you see his hair helped him win stardom, and is his trademark? ... With other guys it doesn't matter, but with him you'll be cutting as much of his fame as you will his hair."[27] Several fans wrote desperate pleas to the President. "Please don't let the Army cut off his hair which every teen-ager in America idolizes," one hand-written letter signed by twenty-seven fans read. "You are the commander in chief of the Armed Forces, so surely you can do something about it ... If you do cut off his hair it would probably start a national war, and I am sure, you know it is bad enough having to fight other countries much less having our own in a war with each other."[28] One hand-written letter to Eisenhower even proclaimed that an army hair cut would deprive Elvis of his human dignity: "My friends and I are Elvis Presley fans, and we don't want him to go to the army because if he is in the army he will have his sideburns cut off. He looks unhuman without them."[29]

In light of such heated debates, it is of little surprise that Elvis's induction aroused much media interest. On the morning of March 24, 1958 at 6.35 am, Elvis, accompanied by his family and several friends, arrived at the Memphis Draft Board 86 in a black Cadillac, where he boarded a bus with twelve other recruits to the Kennedy Veterans Memorial Hospital to undergo several medical tests.[30] They were then transferred to Fort Chaffee in Arkansas,

---

[25]"Excerpts from Letters to DA regarding Elvis Presley," undated. NARA, RG407, Biography File 390-E, Box 12, Elvis Presley File.

[26]Letter to Eisenhower, February 8, 1957. EPL, WHCF, AF, Box 2496, Presley, Elvis.

[27]"Excerpts from Letters to DA regarding Elvis Presley," undated. NARA, RG407, Biography File 390-E, Box 12, Elvis Presley File.

[28]Letter to Eisenhower, January 16, 1957. EPL, WHCF, AF, Box 2496, Presley, Elvis.

[29]Letter to Eisenhower, February 11, 1957. EPL, WHCF, AF, Box 2496, Presley, Elvis.

[30]*Memphis Press Scimitar*, March 24, 1958.

where Elvis was welcomed by roughly one hundred screaming fans as well as Colonel Parker, who handed out balloons advertising Elvis's latest movie. Around fifty journalists had the opportunity to observe and document every little step of the singer's transition into soldiering life, taking pictures of him receiving his army equipment and making his bunk bed several times for the cameras. Interested readers around the world soon learned about Elvis's first army breakfast ("scrambled eggs, sausage, toast, cereal, jam, butter and coffee") and lunch ("half of a fried chicken, combination salad, mashed potatoes and gravy, green beans, two slices of bread, two pats of butter, olives stuffed with pimiento and a brick of chocolate ice cream"), found out his serial number (US-53310761), and were supposed to be amused by his low monthly wage ($78). Predictably, Elvis's haircut aroused the biggest interest, and was documented in film and photographs by the assembled journalists; the hair was swept up and burnt afterward to avoid having fans and journalist fight over it. "Hair today, gone tomorrow," Elvis remarked wittily if somewhat self-consciously to the assembled press corps.[31]

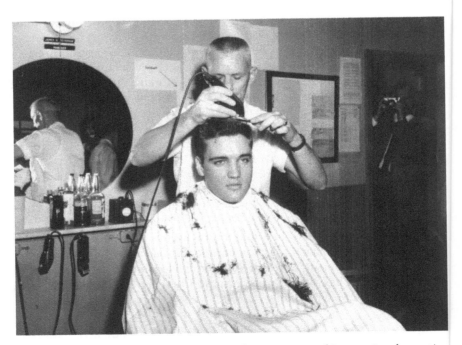

**Figure 3.1** *Elvis Presley getting his army haircut attracted international attention in March 1958.*

---

[31]For even more details, see *Commercial Appeal*, March 21, March 24, March 25 and March 27, 1958; *Memphis Press Scimitar*, March 24, March 25, and March 26, 1958; as well as Levy, *Operation Elvis*, 22–6, 46–56; Guralnick, *Last Train*, 461–5.

The narrative of Elvis as a good soldier who fulfilled his tasks humbly and dutifully dominated the press coverage from the very beginning. Still at Fort Chaffee, Elvis received a telegram from Tennessee Governor Frank Clement congratulating him for being "an American citizen first ... – a young man willing to serve his country when called upon,"[32] and his commanding officer testified that Elvis had conducted himself "in a marvelous manner" and was really "trying to be one of the boys."[33] In the *New York Herald Tribune*, columnist Hy Gardner showered praise on Elvis in what almost read like an eulogy on the ideals of the country that the singer now served:

Where else could a nobody become a somebody so quickly, and in what other nation in the world would such a rich and famous man serve ... without trying to use influence to buy his way out? In my book this is American democracy at its best – the blessed way of life for whose protection you [his fellow soldiers] and Elvis have been called upon to contribute eighteen to twenty-four months of your young lives.[34]

Once the initial furor had faded, Elvis was transferred to Fort Hood in Texas for eight weeks of basic training with the 2nd Armored Division, where he was declared off-limits to journalists.[35] During the eight weeks that followed, Elvis and his fellow recruits sweated in physical drilling exercises underneath the hot Texas sun while sharing four toilets with fifty-nine other recruits.[36] By all accounts, Elvis never asked for special favors and fitted in well with his comrades. His commanding general professed that Elvis was "treated like everyone else," working "long days and long hours" and demonstrating "that millionaires aren't given special treatment."[37] "Elvis went through it all just like the rest of us," his army buddy Rex Mansfield later recalled. "If anything it was harder on him, because he was being watched all the time by everybody."[38] Such judgments were, of course, quickly filtered through to the press, and even found their way to Western Europe, where the press reported extensively on Elvis's military achievements.[39] This was no coincidence: on May 28, 1958, the army announced that Elvis would be sent to West Germany as part of a replacement unit for the 3rd Armored Division of the Seventh US Army.[40] He spent his final weeks at Ford Hood

---

[32]Levy, *Operation Elvis*, 24.
[33]*Memphis Press Scimitar*, March 26, 1958.
[34]*New York Herald Tribune*, March 28, 1958.
[35]Guralnick, *Last Train*, 465.
[36]Linn, *Elvis's Army*, 195.
[37]Quoted in Levy, *Operation Elvis*, 72.
[38]Rex and Elisabeth Mansfield, *Elvis the Soldier* (Bamberg: Collectors Service, 1983), 14.
[39]*Der Spiegel* 23/1958; *BRAVO* 26/1958.
[40]Peter Heigl, *Sergeant Elvis Presley in Grafenwöhr* (Amberg: Buch & Kunstverlag Oberpfalz, 2007), 19; Levy, *Operation Elvis*, 67.

completing his advanced individual and unit training, qualifying as a marksman and sharpshooter, and coming out third-highest ranking in his tank gunnery unit.[41] Shortly before his departure, however, Elvis suffered a personal tragedy: his beloved mother Gladys was hospitalized for hepatitis, and died a few days later from heart failure. It was a loss that would haunt Elvis for the rest of his life.[42]

Although the narrative of Elvis as a normal G.I. soldier dominated the coverage of his military service from the very beginning, the media hype surrounding his every move was of course anything but ordinary. The singer's departure to West Germany in particular was a carefully staged event that was handled jointly by Colonel Parker and the foreign department of the Paramount film company.[43] On September 22, 1958, Elvis arrived at New York City's Brooklyn Army terminal after a lengthy train ride from Fort Hood, where he gave a forty-minute press conference for around eighty journalists in front of several recruiting posters. The assembled press corps included eleven foreign correspondents from West Germany, France, Australia, Japan, Sweden, and the UK.[44] He conducted himself well, proudly presenting his medals and professing that the first thing he wanted to do in Europe was to look up Brigitte Bardot.[45] Then, as the army band played Elvis tunes like "Don't Be Cruel" and "Tutti Frutti," he walked up and down the plankway of the USS *Randall* eight times for the assembled press corps, carrying a heavy duffel bag and waving his American fans goodbye. "Presley's personality was impressively and favorably projected," Paramount concluded in its internal evaluation of the event, immediately sending out photos and soundbites "around [the] world for local planting by Paramount people."[46] At Parker's insistence, RCA even released a recording of the press conference as the EP *Elvis Sails*, which sold an astonishing 60,000 copies.[47] The first stage of Elvis's transformation was complete.

# Act III: The Soldier in Germany

The military presence of the United States in Europe was due first and foremost to the military realities of the Cold War. Given the nuclear stalemate between

---

[41]Levy, *Operation Elvis*, 72.

[42]Guralnick, *Last Train*, 480; ibid., 73.

[43]Bernard F. Dick, *Hal Wallis: Producer to the Stars* (Lexington: University Press of Kentucky, 2004), 165.

[44]Ackerman to Nathan, September 19, 1958; "Private Presley Departs for Germany," September 22, 1958. MHL, HW, Presley, Elvis, contract correspondence, f.2112.

[45]They never met. *Memphis Press Scimitar*, September 22, 1958.

[46]"Private Presley Departs for Germany," September 22, 1958. MHL, HW, Presley, Elvis, contract correspondence, f.2112.

[47]Jorgensen, *A Life in Music*, 114. This was, however, less than the 100,000 sales that Parker had been contractually guaranteed by RCA.

the United States and the Soviet Union, as well as the Soviet superiority in conventional forces, US strategists from the late 1940s onward had deemed a strong military presence in Western Europe vital to defend itself against Soviet aggression. The Korean War had led to a further hike in American soldiers stationed abroad: in 1958, there were 220,337 military and civilian US employees stationed in West Germany alone, as well as 157,704 family dependents.[48] Such a strong and continuous US presence was not only deemed vital for the deterrence of Soviet aggression, but it also played an important part in West Germany's transition from Nazi dictatorship to a Western-style liberal democracy: G.I.s were often seen as informal ambassadors for American lifestyles, serving as living examples of a less hierarchical, affluent society with laid-back attitudes and every-day consumerism.[49] Elvis's stationing in West Germany thus served a dual purpose: not only was he an integral part of the Western alliance's military defense, but it was also hoped that he would help boost the popularity of the United States in the Federal Republic.[50]

Early signs were promising, as the hype surrounding Elvis's arrival at Bremerhaven on October 2, 1958 more than matched the frenzy that had accompanied his departure in the United States ten days earlier. Around 500 German teenagers could barely contain themselves when Elvis walked off the ship and waved to his fans, as the US Army band played, among other tunes, the German schlager "In München steht ein Hofbräuhaus."[51] In spite of tight security, one fan even managed to climb up the plankway to get an autograph from Elvis, an image that immediately found its way into the German and American presses. Although the army had declined Paramount's request for a formal press conference, Elvis's arrival was nonetheless covered prominently by all news agencies, as well as by several television and radio stations.[52] Even major West German newspapers like the *Frankfurter Allgemeine Zeitung* or the *Süddeutsche Zeitung* reported on the occasion. Elvis then quickly boarded a train to his duty station, the 3rd Armored Division in Friedberg (Hesse), where he finally gave a quick press conference and posed for journalists receiving his army equipment and shopping at an Army and Air Force Exchange Service.[53] Yet again,

---

[48]Dewey A. Browder, "Appendix: Population Statistics for U.S. Military in Germany, 1945–2000," in Thomas W. Maulucci Jr. and Detlef Junker (eds.), *GIs in Germany: The Social, Economic, Cultural, and Political History of the American Military Presence* (Cambridge: Cambridge University Press, 2013), 351.

[49]Höhn, *GI and Fräuleins*, 226.; Thomas W. Maulucci Jr. and Detlef Junker (eds.), *GIs in Germany: The Social, Economic, Cultural, and Political History of the American Military Presence* (Cambridge: Cambridge University Press, 2013).

[50]While it is tempting to conclude that the stationing of Elvis in West Germany was a deliberate political decision, no such evidence could yet be found in the archives.

[51]Peters and Reiche, *Elvis in Deutschland*, 16.

[52]Jankolovics to Ackermann, October 3, 1958, MHL, HW, Presley, Elvis, contract correspondence, f.2112.

[53]Heigl, *Sergeant Elvis Presley*, 22.

Paramount's supervisor for West Germany claimed that the media coverage had been a "complete success."[54]

Once the initial press furor had faded, however, Elvis's daily tasks closely resembled those of the other approximately 200,000 soldiers stationed with him. He was assigned to the 1st Medium Tank Battalion 32d Armor, which was composed of around 750 men and seventy-two tanks divided into five companies.[55] Its chief task was to prepare a defense against a potential Soviet invasion of West Germany through the close-by "Fulda Gap," at the time considered to be the most likely point of a Soviet invasion.[56] After an initial few days as a jeep driver for a high-ranking officer, Elvis was designated a reconnaissance scout for the battalion's headquarters, making it his main responsibility to move ahead of the tanks to explore enemy positions and set up road blocks. In case of real military conflict, he would be the first contact to the enemy.[57] On the eve of the Second Berlin Crisis, this was a tough and potentially dangerous assignment. Given that the 32d Tank Battalion was likely one of the first US units to be attacked, Elvis, as reconnaissance scout, would probably have died within the first week, if not the first day, in case of actual warfare.[58] There were real dangers involved in every-day training as well. "I simply cannot forget the fact that Elvis chose to serve in a combat unit," his commanding officer William J. Taylor Jr. recalls, "I have seen a tank loader's head smashed by a 90mm main gun recoil, hands mutilated or cut off by engine maintenance accidents, an eye put out by blank ammo fired in someone's face, a soldier's body crushed by a tank rolling over it."[59]

Perhaps the most challenging times of Elvis's military service were two extended maneuver exercises at Grafenwöhr, a US training facility close to the Czechoslovakian border and at the time often described as the "Siberia of Western Europe."[60] The first took place only a few weeks after his arrival, and required the new recruit to spend a total of seven weeks scouting in muddy fields while enduring cold winds, rain, and occasional snow. Elvis again suffered these tough conditions without complaint, and performed

---

[54]Jankolovics to Ackermann, October 3, 1958, MHL, HW, Presley, Elvis, contract correspondence, f.2112.

[55]William J. Taylor Jr., *Elvis in the Army. The King of Rock'n'Roll as Seen by an Officer Who Served with Him* (Novato, CA: Presido Press, 1995), 11.

[56]Heigl, *Sergeant Elvis Presley*, 49. The "Fulda Gap" became even more prominent during the so-called "second" Cold War in the late 1970s and early 1980s, a time when lots of West German fears about a potential Soviet invasion or nuclear warfare on the European continent resurfaced. At the time, there even existed several military board games called "Fulda Gap." See Florian Greiner and Maren Röger, "Den Kalten Krieg Spielen: Brett- und Computerspiele in der Systemkonfrontation," *Zeithistorische Forschung/Studies in Contemporary History* 16/1 (2019), 46–73.

[57]Guralnick, *Careless Love*, 10.

[58]Linn, *Elvis's Army*, 339.

[59]Taylor, *Elvis in the Army*, 165.

[60]Linn, *Elvis's Army*, 191.

well in the exercises: one time, he even managed to capture eight prisoners thanks to a clever ploy he had worked out.[61] In January 1960, the second major exercise proved even more demanding: the so-called "Operation Winter Shield" involved all divisions of the 7th Army, a total of over 60,000 men, and also included significant ground forces of the German Bundeswehr for the first time.[62] Although local spectators and the press watched out almost every day, Elvis was barely seen by the public during both exercises, although he was once discovered by some teenagers while directing traffic at an intersection.[63] He also gave some short interviews to the local Bavarian press, which afterward appeared enthusiastic about the "modest, nice young man" it had encountered.[64]

Judging by the countless recollections of those who served with him, Elvis displayed a highly professional attitude toward all the military tasks that were demanded of him throughout his time in Germany. Although Elvis,

Figure 3.2 *Elvis during a training maneuver in late 1958.*

[61]Ibid.
[62]Heigl, *Sergeant Elvis Presley*, 65.
[63]Ibid., 75.
[64]*Weidener Nachrichten*, December 15, 1958.

like many other G.I.s with family dependents, lived off-base with his father, grandmother, and some friends, the entire Presley household woke promptly every day at 5am so that Elvis could have breakfast with his family and still arrive punctually at the army base. He acquired a reputation for keeping his equipment, especially his boots, in excellent shape, and by all accounts most enjoyed working on the jeeps and tanks.[65] Lieutenant William J. Taylor Jr. professes that the entire battalion regarded Elvis as "a fine young man who did his job to the best of his ability and tried to stay out of the limelight,"[66] and General Colin Powell, the future US Secretary of State who also served with Elvis in German, similarly recalls how Elvis "looked just like another GI" and acted "as just another soldier, in the woods, kind of dirty, doing a job."[67] Toward the end of his time in Germany, Elvis was promoted sergeant in recognition of his achievements, a promotion that comparatively few recruits achieved at the time.[68] This professional attitude was crucial for the subsequent legacy-building of Elvis's army life by the media and his management.

Apart from its military function, the presence of the US Army also served as an important contact point between Americans and the West German population. Particularly in those regions where many G.I.s were stationed, they served as real-life examples of the supposedly much more liberal and laid-back lifestyles in the postwar United States. They also showcased American wealth and affluence through open displays of consumer goods like cigarettes, nylon, and cars that were seemingly easily obtainable even for low-ranking soldiers and their dependents.[69] There were also countless personal interactions in daily life and nightclubs—more than 37,000 children were born out of wedlock to G.I.s stationed in Germany and Austria in the first decade after the Second World War.[70] While direct personal interactions had become somewhat more limited by the mid-1950s, given that most US bases had morphed into fairly secluded "Little Americas" with their own shops, schools, and leisure centers, there were still frequent encounters with the local population on a daily level.[71]

Although Elvis tried to live a private life off-duty, he almost inevitably came to serve as a prominent celebrity-in-exile, and thus informal ambassador of American lifestyles. His five-bedroom house in the spa town

---

[65]Taylor, *Elvis in the Army*, 32.
[66]Ibid., xvi.
[67]BBC, "Press Releases: General Colin Powell on Elvis Presley the Soldier and Patriot," August 21, 2007, www.bbc.co.uk/pressoffice/pressreleases/stories/2007/08_august/21/elvis.shtml [last accessed September 4, 2019].
[68]Taylor, *Elvis in the Army*, xi.
[69]Höhn, *GIs and Fräuleins*; Maulucci and Junker, *GIs in Germany*.
[70]Thomas W. Maulucci, Jr., "Introduction," in Maulucci and Junker, *GIs in Germany*, 14.
[71]Thomas Leuerer, "U.S. Army Military Communities in Germany," in Maulucci and Junker, *GIs in Germany*, 121–41.

of Bad Nauheim soon became a rallying point for the local youth, not least because a sign was put up which stated that Elvis would give autographs every day between 7.30 and 8.00p.m.[72] It was a task he usually fulfilled dutifully, and when he was absent, fans inscribed the garden fence with names, messages, and even body measurements. Claus-Kurt Ilge, a sixteen-year-old local superfan, spent almost every day outside Elvis's house, trying to chat with his idol and collecting as many autographs as he could get.[73] There were also frequent visitors from other parts of Germany and far beyond: one night, a group of five Swedish teenagers broke into Elvis's garden after having tramped all the way from Sweden; a British girl from Birmingham even temporarily relocated to West Germany in order to be closer to her idol.[74] Elvis usually received around 10,000 letters of fan mail a week, roughly a third of which came from within West Germany. Elisabeth Budniak, his bilingual secretary who he also dated briefly, remembers how she opened a bag of fan mail the first night she stayed with Elvis. "I was so curious ... that I started reading the letters that night," she recalls. "Most of the mail asked for autographed pictures. Some letters had Christian Medals inside for Elvis. Many were love letters and a few hate letters from jealous boyfriends or husbands. Some letters were from people who had money problems and wanted hand-outs."[75]

The sensation caused by Elvis's presence offers a unique window into West Germany's postwar embrace of American-style modernity, as well as into the increasingly blurry lines between US and West European celebrity cultures in the late 1950s.[76] Again, Elvis's impact in West Germany could not be reduced to his music or movies alone; he also served to showcase American lifestyles and habits of consumption, as well as his astonishing affluence. Indeed, his presence in West Germany attracted many local spectators who were simply curious to gauge at the singer's openly displayed wealth. His expensive cars, for example, attracted almost as much interest as the man himself. "We come to see his cars," one German teenager told an American reporter outside Elvis's house at the time. "His cars, that is the best of him. The man is terrible."[77] When Elvis bought a white BMW 507 at a car dealer close to Frankfurt as part of a PR stunt, fans and spectators overran the store which had to be evacuated by the police.[78]

Perhaps most furor was aroused by Elvis's off-duty trips to Paris and Munich, which he each visited twice. In Paris, Elvis made headlines in all

[72]Guralnick, *Last Train*, 17; Mansfield, *Elvis The Soldier*, 51.
[73]Peters and Reiche, *Elvis in Deutschland*, 30–2.
[74]All anecdotes according to *BRAVO* 50/1959 and *BRAVO* 1/1960.
[75]Mansfield, *Elvis the Soldier*, 47.
[76]Maase, *BRAVO Amerika*, 22.
[77]Levy, *Operation Elvis*, 93.
[78]*Frankfurter Allgemeine Zeitung*, December 22, 1958.

**Figure 3.3** *Elvis is given the keys to a BMW 507 sports car as a publicity stunt for the German press, December 1958.*

major French newspapers, even giving a quick impromptu press conference in the lobby of the swanky Prince de Galles Hotel where he was staying. Such was his status in the French capital that he could not even walk the streets of Paris without causing mobs; he resigned himself to spending his days locked away in his top-floor hotel suite overlooking the Champs-Élysées—and the nights at clubs like the Lido and the Le Bantu.[79] In Munich too, Elvis spent most of his time at the local Moulin Rouge nightclub, where a certain "Marianne" had developed a strip routine wearing nothing but an Elvis record. He also made headlines by briefly dating the local actress Vera Tschechowa, although she later denied that they actually had an affair.[80]

There were some more explicit attempts to co-opt Elvis for public relations exercises. West German tabloids and entertainment magazines occasionally tried to use Elvis in order to push their own agenda of postwar liberalization and the promotion of American popular culture.[81] Immediately after Elvis's arrival, the youth magazine *BRAVO* even dashed out the headline "Elvis turns German," accompanied by numerous pictures of Elvis freely interacting with his German fans.[82] A few weeks later, the Hamburg *Star Revue* organized a competition for fans to win "teatime with Elvis,"

---

[79]Guralnick and Jorgensen, *Day by Day*, 138–9; Mansfield, *Elvis the Soldier*, 89–96.
[80]Elvis's visit to Munich is well-documented in Andreas Roth, *The Ultimate Elvis in Munich Book* (Munich: self-published, 2004). For local press coverage of Elvis's two visits to Munich (and Marianne), see *Abendzeitung*, March 4 and 5, 1958 and *Abendzeitung*, June 15, 1959.
[81]Bösch, *Mediengeschichte*, 200.
[82]*BRAVO*, 44/1958.

even though the winners afterward professed disappointment that their idol had served them cola rather than tea.[83] The army too enlisted Elvis in various PR activities, trying to foster closer bonds with the local population and forging the image of a Cold War community. In January 1959, for example, Elvis was pictured donating blood to the German Red Cross; a few months later, he helped resurrect a memorial statue for German veterans of the First World War.[84] All of these tasks were reported prominently in the West German press, including in prestigious daily newspapers like the *Frankfurter Allgemeine Zeitung*.[85] They also helped shape Elvis's new image as a dutiful and patriotic soldier in the German public imagination. "Since Elvis has arrived in Germany as an American soldier, everybody knows that he is a nice and almost shy boy, who is far away from any showing-off or arrogance," *BRAVO* wrote, not failing to add that "BRAVO has once again been proven right. BRAVO has always been Elvis's friend."[86]

Although still not everybody was Elvis's friend, his stationing in West Germany seems to have muted public criticism of the singer. On the eve of the Second Berlin Crisis, the public acceptance of the US Army as the key guarantor of West German security was still high, with 61 percent of West Germans apparently believing that the Americans would help defend them against a Russian attack.[87] While such support for the US military presence obviously did not automatically or necessarily translate into a broader acceptance of American cultural influences and lifestyles, Elvis's identification as a G.I. soldier clearly helped his public acceptability. When the riots at Bill Haley's concert tour of West Germany in October 1958 triggered yet another sweeping debate over the vices and virtues of rock 'n' roll, Elvis was largely exempt from such public criticism: *BRAVO* even published an open letter by Elvis in which he pleaded to his West German fans not take part in such riots.[88]

In East Germany, Elvis's deployment aroused surprisingly little official comment, even though the GDR's more general campaign against rock 'n' roll was in full swing.[89] The only major controversy that was directly connected to Elvis's military service appeared in November 1958, when a NATO general's claim that Elvis was part of the psychological warfare against the Soviet Union found its way into the press: the very next day, the GDR newspaper *Junge Welt* proclaimed that it could now finally be read "black on white" that the "whistle buoy Elvis Presley" was indeed part of

[83]Bloemeke, *Roll over Beethoven*, 93–5.
[84]Guralnick and Jorgensen, *Day by Day*, 131, 137; Höhn, *GIs and Fräuleins*, 58–60; *BRAVO* 3/1959; *BRAVO* 7/1959.
[85]*Frankfurter Allgemeine Zeitung*, January 17, 1959.
[86]*BRAVO* 7/1959.
[87]Peters and Reiche, *Elvis in Deutschland*, 22.
[88]*BRAVO*, 47/1958
[89]As discussed in Chapter 2.

the West's "Cold War cannonry."[90] It also claimed that "the Americans and their Adenauer" were to blame for the riots surrounding Bill Haley's concert tour, and mused darkly that "Bonn's psychological warfare works on all areas, with all possible means … The politics of NATO, the American way of life—those are the things that have to be abolished if young people are to be saved from decay."[91] Yet, Elvis's refusal to appear as anything else than an ordinary soldier gave the GDR little additional ammunition for such propaganda, and Elvis's stationing in West Germany was widely known among the GDR youth. The US Colonel Frank Athanason, for example, recalls how he once crashed with an army helicopter over East Germany and was then captured and interrogated by a group of Russian and East German officials: "The interpreter was interested to find out if I'd ever seen Elvis Presley because he was in our division," Athanason recalls. "I said, 'No, he's not in my town, he's in a different town'. I've never seen him. They liked Elvis Presley."[92]

# Act IV: The Home Front

Elvis Presley may have physically spent the period from October 1, 1958, to March 3, 1960, in West Germany, but he retained a continuous presence in the United States throughout. Already prior to his departure, he had hastily recorded five songs in a highly energetic one-night session, which were now released periodically during his absence. While most of them sold around one million copies, and one of them even became a number-one hit, the sales figures nonetheless failed to live up to Elvis's heyday in 1956–57.[93] The picture was similar in the album market: various LP and EP releases performed respectably but not great, mostly because they were often put together from previously released or leftover materials. There were almost constant battles between RCA executive Steve Sholes and Colonel Parker whether Elvis should schedule some sessions in Germany or even release some substandard recordings from previous sessions; Parker's warnings against an oversaturation of the market eventually prevailed.[94] Throughout Elvis's time in Germany, Parker kept the singer informed in regular telephone calls and letters, even though he never visited his protégé in person.

---

[90]*Junge Welt*, November 19, 1958. The article referred directly to *Berliner Zeitung*, November 18, 1958.

[91]*Junge Welt*, October 29 and 30, 1958.

[92]"Interview with Colonel Frank Athanason," June 10, 2005, Library of Congress, Washington, DC, Manuscript Division, Frontline Diplomacy, The Association for Diplomatic Studies and Training Foreign Affairs Oral History Project, www.loc.gov/item/mfdipbib001678 [last accessed September 4, 2019].

[93]Jorgensen, *A Life in Music*, 114.

[94]Guralnick, *Careless Love*, 25–9.

Apart from the constant flow of Elvis records, Parker's attempts to keep Elvis's name in the public interest centered on Elvis's personality, rather than on his musical output. One way of doing so was to ensure that stories about Elvis's soldiering life would regularly appear in newspapers and magazines. In December 1958, for example, *Life* magazine featured a picture of Elvis in full winter uniform playing guitar and singing to his fellow soldiers; a few months later, the *New York Herald Tribune* reported extensively on how "Corp Presley" was "Still Playing It Straight."[95] In 1959, the highly popular *This Week* magazine, a nationally syndicated weekly supplement to around forty Sunday newspapers, printed several long pieces on Elvis's military service, a promotion that had once again been initiated by Parker.[96] Such reports almost invariably pushed the by-now-familiar narrative of Elvis as an all-American patriotic soldier. "LOOK WHAT GERMANY'S DONE TO ELVIS!" *This Week* screamed, before going on to (erroneously) claim that Elvis had initially been "the most unwelcome American visitor since V-E Day," but was now "beyond all question the most popular G.I. in the country."[97] Parker frequently advertised upcoming features on Elvis to fan clubs in regular newsletters, and he continued to shower them with all sorts of other news and promotion materials throughout Elvis's time in the army.[98]

Although Elvis spent a total of sixteen months in West Germany, he never disappeared entirely from the public eye in the United States. Once Elvis's time in the army was coming to an end, Parker accelerated his promotional efforts. In December 1959, *This Week* ran another major article dwelling extensively on what Elvis had allegedly learned from the army. "If you take a bored, feet-dragging attitude you've got two miserable years in front of you," Elvis told the reporter George Riemer, but "[i]f you just try, that's all the Army likes to see. The best medal they can pin on you is to say, 'He's a good soldier. That guy really tries!'"[99] This set the tone for the jubilant press coverage of Elvis's return. In early 1960, the journalist Alan Levy even published a short book on the singer's military service, which was serialized in the *Chicago Tribune*.[100] "Soldiering above and beyond the call of peacetime duty," Levy concluded, Elvis had won "a badge of respectability that he had been unable to buy as a civilian millionaire ... By pretending that he was just like anybody else, the Army had demonstrated to the world The Importance of Being Elvis."[101] In spite of such hyperbole,

---

[95]*Life*, December 22, 1958; *New York Herald Tribune*, July 12, 1959. The *Life* photoshoot was criticized internally by the army, but no follow-up action was taken, since it had apparently taken place while Elvis was off-duty. See Levy, *Operation Elvis*, 88.
[96]For Parker's involvement, see Nash, *Colonel*, 188.
[97]*This Week*, July 19, 1959.
[98]Guralnick, *Careless Love*, 26–9.
[99]*This Week*, December 6, 1959.
[100]Levy, *Operation Elvis*; *Chicago Tribune*, April 24, May 1, May 8 and May 15, 1960.
[101]Levy, *Operation Elvis*, 113–14.

the book did not go down entirely well with the fans, who complained that Levy had misrepresented them as "gawdy and frantic" by focusing only on the "crackpot fringe" of Elvis followers.[102]

The decision to focus the advertising and press coverage primarily on Elvis's personality constituted an important part of Parker's strategy to transform Elvis into an accepted US establishment figure. It matched the wider changes in the popular music field that were taking place at the same time. Almost from the date of Elvis's induction, the rock 'n' roll hype of the mid-1950s had slowly but surely started to fade out. On February 3, 1959, Buddy Holly, Ritchie Valens, and "The Big Bopper" all died tragically in a plane crash, while Jerry Lee Lewis fell into disgrace by marrying his 13-year-old once-removed cousin. The Payola scandal around the disc jockeys Alan Freed and Dick Clark, which exposed their illegal practice of taking payments in return for airplay, dealt a further blow to the popularity of rock 'n' roll. By the end of the 1950s, the charts were dominated by balladeers like Bobby Darin, Paul Anka, or Frankie Avalon, and even Bing Crosby excitedly told the LA Times how his "kind of music" was finally "coming back."[103]

Not only did it make sense for post-army Elvis to move in similar directions; it also matched his personal ambitions and taste. As seen earlier, Elvis had never regarded himself solely as a rock 'n' roller, but rather as an eclectic singer able to perform all sorts of material, and one of his biggest idols was Mario Lanza. During his time in Germany, Elvis worked hard on improving his vocal technique with Charlie Hodge, a new army friend who was also a professional singer. Together, they tackled various gospel and rhythm 'n' blues standards as well as more demanding materials like Tony Martin's operettic "There's No Tomorrow," an English version of the Italian "O Sole Mio." Elvis was so excited by the tune that he asked his music publisher Freddy Bienstock to commission new lyrics so he could record it back in the United States.[104] The result, of course, was "It's Now or Never."

Apart from the change in musical direction, Elvis and Parker had their eyes firmly set on Hollywood. In Elvis's absence, Parker had set in stone a number of highly lucrative deals that were designed to secure Elvis's post-army movie career for the foreseeable future. Already in October 1958, he had managed to improve Elvis's original Paramount contract with Hal Wallis for the singer's first post-army movie, raising Elvis's fee from the original $25,000 to $175,000 plus 7.5 percent of gross receipts. The contract also included provisions for three additional movies at $125,000, $150,000, and $175,000 respectively.[105] A few days later, Parker concluded

[102]Elvis Monthly 8, September 1960.
[103]Los Angeles Times, April 24, 1960.
[104]Guralnick and Jorgensen, Day by Day, 136–7.
[105]Ibid., 127.

a similarly improved deal with 20th Century Fox for two pictures at $200,000 and $250,000, including a 50–50 split of profit after expenses had been recouped.[106] As early as January 1959, plans for Elvis's first post-army movie with Paramount were well under way: a comedic take on Elvis's military experience provisionally entitled *Christmas in Berlin*. Not only did these deals give Elvis three movies for 1960 with a guaranteed minimum income of over half a million dollars, but they also reflected his personal ambitions to become a serious actor.[107]

# Act V: Return and Transfiguration

Elvis's return from West Germany on March 2, 1960, was depicted almost universally as the culmination of his transformation from youthful rebel into a decent and patriotic all-American boy. Upon his arrival at Fort Dix in New Jersey (this time by airplane), Nancy Sinatra welcomed Elvis with a message from her father, who thanked Elvis for having done "a tremendous job during the past two years."[108] She was joined by 200 fans and roughly the same number of journalists, who all awaited Elvis's arrival amid a massive snow storm.[109] In a quick press conference, Elvis appeared characteristically humble, professing how glad he was to have served his term "rather than have something thrown in my face the rest of my life."[110] He seemed honestly proud of having served his country well, and he would frequently refer to his time in the army in later years.

Just how widely accepted military service and the draft still were in early 1960s America can be seen in how unanimously positively Elvis's return was celebrated in the press.[111] All major newspapers ran stories on the event, celebrating him "for doing his duty cheerfully and not behaving like a spoiled young man."[112] The local Memphis newspaper *Commercial Appeal* printed a statement by some of Elvis's neighbors, who claimed that their initial unease over the singer had turned into "genuine respect."[113] The Tennessean Democratic Senator Estes Kefauver, who had after all chaired the Subcommittee on Juvenile Delinquency in the early 1950s, delivered an emotional eulogy to Elvis in Congress:

---

[106]Ibid.

[107]For further details on Elvis's acting ambitions, see the next chapter.

[108]*Commercial Appeal*, March 4, 1960.

[109]*Hartford Courant*, March 4, 1960; *Boston Globe*, March 4, 1960; *Chicago Tribune*, March 4, 1960.

[110]*Commercial Appeal*, March 4, 1960.

[111]Flynn, *The Draft*, 161.

[112]*Baltimore Sun*, March 2, 1960.

[113]*Commercial Appeal*, March 8, 1960.

It may have been a temptation for him to have asked for special privileges because of his civilian fame as an entertainer. To his great credit, this young American became just another GI Joe. He went through recruit training with one intent and that was to become a good soldier ... Some of my generation may ridicule the antics of rock and rollers, but none of them will find fault with Sgt. Elvis Presley or millions of other young Americans who have served and will continue to serve their country in both peace and war with courage and patriotic zeal. Sergeant Presley will return to his home town of Memphis to be greeted by thousands of his neighbors in a well-deserved homecoming ceremony. I, for one, would like to say to him: "Yours was a job well done, soldier."[114]

Elvis's fans too appeared almost uniformly proud of their idol's achievements. "By entering the army like any other young American El gained great respect from fans and troops alike as he could have got off his National Service by entertaining troops," a fan from Glasgow wrote in *Elvis Monthly*; "Elvis soon proved that he was as good at soldiering as at singing and his shining career in the army made the critics, who had sneeringly predicted an inglorious career for Elvis, think again."[115] Some even believed that Elvis had made a sizeable contribution to the bigger Cold War struggle. One US-based fan, for example, claimed that the numerous denunciations of Elvis in East German newspapers only revealed the regime's "deadly fear of his influence on their young people. Elvis has fans who love him in every country of the world, and the word that the Communists hate most is the word 'LOVE'."[116] Such was the pride in Elvis's military service that some fans feared that their idol might be recalled to active service at the height of the Second Berlin Crisis.[117] "Elvis can be replaced as a soldier," a fan from West Berlin protested in *Elvis Monthly*, "but he can *never* be replaced as a singer and entertainer!"[118]

Elvis's newly found credibility was the essential prerequisite for his desired transformation into a mainstream entertainer. The first demonstration of the new public image came with the ABC television special *Welcome Home Elvis*, which aired on May 12, 1960. It was pointedly hosted by Frank Sinatra, who had viciously denounced rock 'n' roll in the 1950s.[119] Elvis, who received the unprecedented fee of $125,000 for little more than ten minutes' total screen time, appeared in a black tuxedo with a white-collar shirt and heavily greased pompadour but no sideburns, and performed his first post-army single release

---

[114]"4 March 1960," *Congressional Record: Proceedings of Congress and General Congressional Publications,* 85th Congress, 2nd Season, 106/4 (Washington DC, 1960), 4151–2.
[115]*Elvis Monthly* 3, April 1960.
[116]*Elvis Monthly* 9, October 1960.
[117]*Elvis Monthly* 2/10, October 1961.
[118]*Elvis Monthly* 2/11, November 1961.
[119]Wiener, *Channeling Elvis*, 103–24.

"Stuck on You," the ballad "Fame and Fortune," as well as a somewhat uneasy duet with Sinatra. His movements seemed restrained and at times subdued, projecting a more mature and almost choreographed stage personality. Although the show scored a 67.7 percent audience share, its reviews were mixed: while the *Chicago Daily Tribune* proclaimed that Elvis had reclaimed "his Crown," the *New York Times* found it "merely awful."[120] Most of the fans, however, were jubilant, and did not seem to mind their idol's new image. "Our King was now debonair and impeccably attired in a tuxedo ... a curious combination of the poised sophisticated and shy, unsure little boy," two American viewers reported in *Elvis Monthly*; "[h]e was all things to us at that moment ... a flower, a flame, a peaceful mountain stream, a raging wind tossed sea. He was 'ours.' Every fibre of him belonging to the masses who love him."[121] Many fans also reacted strongly to a characteristically slanting review of the show by the *Washington Post*'s Lawrence Laurent, whose mailbox was once again flocked with angry complaints about his treatment of Elvis: "Your obvious jealousy of his hair is probably because you are wearing a wig at your age," one of the letters read.[122]

The new maturity in Elvis's public personality soon became reflected in his musical output. His first post-army recording session, which was recorded on a three-track machine for the first time and featured top-level studio musicians like Floyd Cramer, resulted in an eclectic output of six songs that ranged from the sentimental "Soldier Boy" to the raunchy "A Mess of Blues."[123] It was followed up by two of Elvis's finest recordings of all time: "Are You Lonesome Tonight?" and "It's Now or Never." Both records not only demonstrated Elvis's development as a vocalist, but they also performed very well in commercial terms. While the first post-army single had somewhat failed to live up to expectations, "Are You Lonesome Tonight?" and "It's Now or Never" became two of Elvis's best-selling single releases of all time.[124] Indeed, most fans embraced Elvis's attempt to branch out. "Elvis is going to be bigger than ever," the US-based fan Louise Spencer wrote about the *Elvis Is Back* album; "he can adapt, he has adapted to changing conditions" and his material was "completely different from what he has done in the past."[125] A few months later, *Elvis Monthly* editor Albert Hand described "It's Now or Never" as "a surprise move that has left even his own admirers breathless ... a successful attempt to capture the almost untrodden fields of mums and dads."[126]

---

[120]*Chicago Daily Tribune*, May 13, 1960; *New York Times*, May 13, 1960.
[121]*Elvis Monthly* 6, 1960.
[122]Lawrence quoted some of the letters in a subsequent column. See *Washington Post*, May 19, 1960.
[123]Jorgensen, *A Life in Music*, 120–1.
[124]Ibid., 135, 142.
[125]*Elvis Monthly* 5, June 1960.
[126]*Elvis Monthly* 9, October 1960.

**Figure 3.4** *Frank Sinatra welcomes Elvis back to the United States in an ABC television special, March 1960.*

Elvis's new musical style was embraced not only at home, but also far beyond. Outside the United States, Elvis's sales figures frequently surpassed 1950s levels, and "It's Now or Never" reached number one in Australia, Austria, Belgium, Norway, the UK, and the Netherlands.[127] Apart from generally rising postwar affluence and the growing professionalization of the popular music industry outside the United States, it also seems like

---

[127]Jorgensen, *A Life in Music*, 1.

Elvis's post-army material better reflected European tastes than his previous rock 'n' roll numbers.[128] Occasionally, Elvis even mimicked the common European practice of re-recording American hits in native language by simply turning the issue around: quite a few of Elvis's recordings, like "It's Now or Never," "Surrender," "Wooden Heart," or "Tonight's All Right For Love," were based on old European standards whose copyright had run out. These recordings were often more successful in Western Europe than in the United States, where some of them were not even released as a single. "[A] ll over Europe, fans were buying the single Wooden Heart, backed with the elusive Tonight's All Right For Love, in their thousands. No. 1 in the charts everywhere one looked!," Albert Hand exclaimed in *Elvis Monthly*. "U.S.A. fans marvelled from a great distance."[129] Yet some American fans loved the songs too: Tom Petty, for example, claimed to have become an Elvis fan because of "Wooden Heart," and a cover version of the song reached number one in the *Billboard* charts the following year.[130]

What shaped the legacy of Elvis's military service most was its subsequent transfiguration in his first post-army movie *G.I. Blues* (1960). It was designed as a somewhat comedic take on Elvis's army experiences that would also showcase the change in Elvis's image, as well as daily life in the US Army, to the wider world.[131] The Department of Defense cooperated closely with Paramount during the movie's production, even allowing Wallis to shoot some footage in West Germany while Elvis was stationed there.[132] It also seemed reasonably happy with the pre-circulated script, having "no objection ... other than [it] being a harmless but pathetic type comedy."[133] A pre-screening revealed an "unanimously favorable" reaction, apparently turning *G.I. Blues* into "one of the very few films produced with military cooperation that we have screened that escaped any criticism at all."[134]

*G.I. Blues* opened to great fanfare on November 4, 1960. Joe Hazen, one of Wallis's partners at Paramount, had apparently spent a budget of around $500,000 on "an intensive and no-cost-spared campaign, with an all-out sales drive for the Thanksgiving and Christmas playing time," making him "most optimistic about the success of G.I. Blues and the enlarged and

---

[128]Burzik, "Musik der fünfziger Jahre," 257–8.

[129]The Fabulous Wooden Heart, *Elvis Monthly* 2/5, May 1961.

[130]Petty later recorded his own version of the song at Sun Studios. For more details, see Simpson, *Elvis Films FAQ*, 370.

[131]Linn, *Elvis's Army*, 231.

[132]Although Elvis himself did not take part in any shooting. See Denton to Captain Wallace (Pentagon), June 26, 1959, [G]eorgetown [U]niversity [L]ibrary, Booth Family Center for Special Collections, [D]epartment of [D]efense [F]ilm [C]ollection 1, Box 22, Folder 6, G.I. Blues.

[133]McPheron, "Memorandum: Paramount Pictures, Café Europa," July 7, 1959, GUL, DDFC 1, Box 22, Folder 6, G.I. Blues.

[134]Ellington to Denton, July 19, 1960, GUL, DDFC 1, Box 22, Folder 6, G.I. Blues.

growing public for Elvis."[135] Colonel Parker too was targeting such new audiences, rejoicing that the movie's soundtrack was doing "especially well in the supermarkets and retail stores ... which may be some indication of a new group of customers in addition to the old one's."[136] Elvis's new image was clearly reflected in the movie's promotion materials as well. "The idol of the teenagers is now the idol of the family!" one poster declared, and the change in Elvis's on-screen personality was plain for everybody to see. "Whatever else the Army has done for Elvis Presley," the New York Times wrote, "it has taken that indecent swivel out of his hips and turned him into a good, clean, trustworthy, upstanding American young man."[137] Yet some feared that the attempt to attract new audiences might alienate some older ones. The LA Times, for example, wondered whether Elvis's "squealing teen-age fans" would ultimately "go along with the metamorphosis," and the Boston Globe was not at all sure whether Elvis as an "amiable, gentlemanly, courteous, likeable, honorable, well-mannered" hero was "what his fans want of him. They'll feel the Army has ruined their boy."[138]

On the surface, such fears proved unfounded: G.I. Blues turned out to be the expected box office success, ending up as the fourteenth biggest grossing film of the year. The soundtrack album too sold over 700,000 copies, turning it one of Elvis's best-selling LPs during his lifetime and far surpassing the artistically more ambitious Elvis Is Back, which had only sold a disappointing 200,000 copies.[139] Fans too were overwhelmingly positive. The newsletter of the Memphis fan club Tancaster, which had been founded by the local superfan Gary Pepper in September 1958, described it as "a humdinger of a picture ... ELVIS in and under tanks, and jeeps in Germany with his pals are mighty fine, and a baby sitting job of scene with Juliet [Prowse] are hilarious."[140] But there were some dissenting voices too. A twenty-one-year-old secretary for the air force at Colorado Springs, for example, complained angrily about Elvis's new screen personality in a letter to Hal Wallis:

> Did you have a girdle on him? Did he have polio recently? There must be an explanation somewhere for all that lost motion. Not one, NOT ONE wiggle, stiffning [sic] out or pointed finger action in the entire movie. DO YOU WANT TO RUIN HIM? ... There is nothing left that is different because he sang just like any other NUT would: LIFELESS with NO ENERGY ... AND THAT GOOFY HAIR CUT DIDN'T HELP

[135]Hazen to Parker, October 18, 1960, MHL, HW, Presley, Elvis—correspondence, f.2115.
[136]Parker to Diskin, October 19, 1960, MHL, HW, Presley, Elvis—correspondence, f.2115.
[137]New York Times, November 5, 1960.
[138]Los Angeles Times, November 16, 1960; Boston Globe, November 24, 1960.
[139]Jorgensen, A Life in Music, 147.
[140]MHL, HW, Presley, Elvis correspondence, f.2116, "The Tancaster," November 15, 1960. Hal Wallis was an honorary member of the Tancaster, and kept a copy of the newsletter in his files.

MATTERS BY ANY MEANS. Without his hair in his eyes, his hands stiffened out, and his legs appearing like butter, he ain't worth watchin' while singing. JUST WHO DO YOU THINK BUYS 99.9 % OF HIS RECORDS? IT AIN'T MY MOTHER.[141]

In West Germany, by contrast, the reception of *G.I. Blues* (released as *Café Europa* [1960]) was rather more ambivalent, which again sheds light on some of the wider debates surrounding the country's alleged "Americanization" at the time. Although the movie seemed to fit West German tastes for escapist musical comedies, many reviewers were less than impressed by Hollywood's bland depiction of postwar Germany. The left-wing magazine *Der Spiegel*, for example, described it as a "post-card movie ... full of heart-warming clichés about frolleins, Punch and Judy shows and pumpernickel."[142] Elvis's on-screen performance of "Wooden Heart," a version of the German folk song "Muss I Denn ..." in which he alternated between English and German lyrics, was received in similarly ambivalent ways. Although the scene usually triggered applause, with some audiences allegedly even singing along and clapping their hands, it was also criticized harshly as an exploitation of traditional German music for quick commercial gains. Although the single sold over 400,000 copies within a week, it was immediately banned by radio stations in West Berlin and Bavaria.[143] Even after his army duty, then, Elvis and his brand of American popular culture were by no means accepted uncritically in postwar Germany.

# Conclusions

Elvis's time in the US Army marked a crucial caesura of his career, transforming the erstwhile youth rebel into an all-American boy. Both Elvis's management and the army turned the singer's military service into a giant marketing coup, consciously staging Elvis's humble and dutiful service for public consumption. As the rock 'n' roll wave slowly faded, it helped him overcome his former image of a teenage rebel, and provided the necessary precondition for his post-army role as a more mainstream entertainer and Hollywood star. Elvis's army service thus gave him the widespread public acceptance he had previously lacked, and in so doing opened up new audiences and manifested his image as an all-American superstar that would be crucial to his 1960s career.

---

[141]Fan letter to Wallis, October 31, 1960. MHL, HW, Presley, Elvis correspondence, f.2116.
[142]*Der Spiegel*, 3/1961.
[143]*Der Spiegel*, 9/1961.

Elvis's army stint also sheds light on some bigger themes of 1950s America's role in the world. Within the United States, the heated debates over Elvis's induction reveal how intensely larger societal issues over the principle of universal military service or the inequity of the draft were negotiated through Elvis's public image. Yet the fact that Elvis's dutiful service was depicted almost universally positive by critics and fans alike also shows the degree of acceptance that the principle of military service still enjoyed at the time. Outside the United States, Elvis's stationing on the Cold War frontline offers a fascinating early case study of an emerging transatlantic celebrity culture: in West Germany, Elvis not only served as a G.I. soldier, but he also constituted an informal ambassador for the everyday affluence, individual consumerism, and upward mobility allegedly at the heart of American-style capitalism. The Hollywood career that he was about to embark upon for much of the following decade would do much to further cement that image.

# 4

# Shining Elvis: The Hollywood Movies

In the wacky 1965 movie *Harum Scarum* (1965), Elvis Presley plays an American-singer-cum-movie star traveling the Middle East on a promotional tour. Upon arrival at "Babelstan," he is welcomed by the local US ambassador. "You have no idea how important this occasion is," the ambassador remarks, "Your goodwill tour of this part of the world will be most helpful to the State Department." Although the assertion is certainly not borne out by the subsequent ninety minutes—the turban-wearing Elvis sings to sultans, plays with slave-girls, and fights a leopard with his bare hands—the scene suggests that popular culture had by the mid-1960s come to be widely recognized as a powerful tool for projecting positive images of the United States at home and abroad.

Following his post-army comeback, Elvis Presley concentrated firmly on his acting career, abandoning live performances and increasingly neglecting non-soundtrack music recordings as well.[1] Until 1969, he starred in twenty-seven feature films, averaging three productions a year as one of Hollywood's highest-paid actors of the decade.[2] These so-called Elvis movies not only

---

[1] With the exception of three charity concerts in Memphis (2x) and Honolulu (1x) in 1961, Elvis did not perform live between November 11, 1957, and July 31, 1969. The decline in his non-soundtrack recordings in the mid-1960s will be discussed in later parts of the chapter.

[2] There have been comparatively few works on Elvis's movie career. Simpson, *Elvis Films FAQ* offers a comprehensive overview; as does Neibaur, *Elvis Movies*. Douglas Brode's *Elvis Cinema* also provides some fascinating interpretations, although these tend to suffer from occasional psychological overinterpretations based on Albert Goldman's problematic Elvis biography. James, *Rock "N" Film* includes two excellent chapters on Elvis, 73–122; and Julie Lobalzo Wright, *Crossover Stardom: Popular Male Music Stars in American Cinema* (London: Bloomsbury, 2017) also devotes a whole chapter to the singer's movies, 45–72.

transformed the singer's image from his erstwhile rebel figure into a more mature family entertainer, but they also reveal a lot about the underlying self-perceptions of American society at the time, as well as about the images it sought to project to the wider world. Designed to appeal to the broadest possible audience at home and abroad, the Elvis movies unabashedly celebrated consumerism and confirmed traditional self-understandings of 1960s middle America while also reaffirming highly conservative gender roles and all but ignoring the major upheavals of the decade. As the 1960s went on, not only did the movies thus seem increasingly anachronistic but they made Elvis too appear dejected and far removed from a rapidly changing social and cultural landscape.

## Finding the Elvis Formula

In the 1950s, Elvis Presley had become a movie star almost as soon as he had found fame as a singer and musician. The rapid move to Hollywood had been due not least to the initiative of Paramount producer Hal Wallis, who had become fascinated by Elvis's charisma on television within weeks of his arrival on the national stage.[3] Having already worked successfully with earlier crossover stars like Jerry Lewis or Dean Martin, Wallis saw in Elvis an ideal opportunity to transform his established studio-era production techniques to target the rapidly growing teenage market.[4] During the 1950s, Elvis's four pre-army films—two for Paramount, one for Metro-Goldwyn-Mayer (MGM), and one for 20th Century Fox—were usually, if not always accurately, perceived as part of the rock 'n' roll film genre so popular with teenagers at the time.[5] Given the singer's post-army re-invention as a mainstream entertainer, as well as the more general decline of rock 'n' roll during the late 1950s, Elvis's movie image had to be adjusted accordingly. As Elvis himself told journalists at a press conference in March 1960, he believed his future movies would no longer "be rock and roll pictures 'cause I have made four already and you can only get away with that for so long."[6]

The fact that Elvis would focus his future career on Hollywood seemed out of question. Elvis himself was keen to pursue his strong passion for acting further, telling journalists at the Graceland press conference on March 7, 1960, that his ultimate goal was to become a serious actor.[7] During his youth, he had worked several years as an usher at Loew's State

---

[3]Wallis and Higham, *Starmaker*, 147–8.
[4]Landon Palmer, "King Creole: Michael Curtiz and the Great Elvis Presley Industry," in Barton Palmer and Murray Pomerance (eds.), *The Many Cinemas of Michael Curtiz* (Austin, TX: University of Texas Press, 2018), 173, 182.
[5]For an overview, see James, *Rock 'n' Film*, 73–91.
[6]Osborne, *Word for Word*, 158.
[7]Ibid., 123.

Movie Theatre, where he admired Tony Curtis, Rudolph Valentino, and James Dean; he had watched *Rebel without a Cause* (1955) so many times that he could recite almost the entire script from memory. He regularly booked entire cinemas for all-night movie screenings with friends, and his taste remained highly eclectic: lifetime favorites were, among countless others, Mario Lanza's *The Student Prince* (1954), *Dr. Strangelove* (1964), *Patton* (1970), and *Monty Python and the Holy Grail* (1975).[8] In 1962, he appeared deeply disappointed that the Oscar for Best Picture went to *Lawrence of Arabia* rather than to *To Kill a Mockingbird*, telling a local Memphis newspaper that *Lawrence* would win "because it's had more money spent on it but Mockingbird was really better – that was a wonderful movie."[9]

Apart from Elvis's personal ambitions, Hollywood was still where most money could be made in the early 1960s.[10] Colonel Parker was clearly attracted by the financial rewards of exploiting Elvis in Hollywood, as well as perhaps by the degree of personal control he was able to exercise as a gatekeeper between Elvis and film producers.[11] He also hoped to capitalize further on the strong synergies between Elvis's acting and musical career, marketing Elvis's films in tandem with simultaneously released soundtracks.[12] At the time, Elvis's income from a single movie was far higher than the total annual royalties from his music recordings, and the soundtracks helped fulfil contractual obligations to his record label while generating additional royalties and publishing revenue with minimal effort.[13] After Elvis's return from the army, Parker therefore lost no time in setting up long-term contracts for his client. On November 2, 1960, he negotiated a deal for two films with United Artists with a salary of $500,000 each for Elvis (plus 50 percent of profits); on January 6, 1961, he extended the existing Paramount contract to five films with salaries between $175,000 and $200,000; and the same month, he also concluded a deal with MGM for four pictures at $500,000 each (plus 50 percent of the profits).[14] Taken together, these eleven films committed Elvis for much of the first half of the 1960s.[15] Importantly, neither Elvis nor Parker had any explicit contractual influence over the movies' scripts or songs: once contracts were signed, the

---

[8]Simpson, *Elvis Films FAQ*, 224–6.
[9]Ibid., 226.
[10]Duffett, *Understanding Fandom*, 7; Marcus, *Drama of Celebrity*, 12–14.
[11]Nash, *The Colonel*, 200.
[12]Palmer, "Introducing Elvis Presley," 177–90; Wright, *Crossover Stardom*, 55.
[13]Simpson, *Elvis Films FAQ*, 335.
[14]The deal with Paramount was subsequently re-negotiated and improved several times on Parker's insistence. See Guralnick and Jorgensen, *Day by Day*, 159, 163.
[15]The films covered by these agreements were *Follow That Dream* and *Kid Galahad* (both United Artists); *Blue Hawaii, Girls! Girls! Girls!, Fun in Acapulco, Roustabout,* and *Paradise Hawaiian Style* (all Paramount); *It Happened at the World's Fair, Viva Las Vegas, Kissin' Cousins,* and *Girl Happy* (all MGM).

studios took complete charge and responsibility. "Give me a million dollars and you can have him and shoot the phone book, if you're crazy enough," Parker once told the director Norman Taurog.[16]

At first, the various studios differed quite significantly over how they wanted to utilize Elvis. At Paramount, Hal Wallis was determined to market Elvis as an all-round celebrity, utilizing the movies as merely one of several vehicles in the promotion of the superstar.[17] He thus sought to develop a formula that would showcase Elvis not only as an actor, but also as a singer and performer. As he later reflected rather candidly, his main goal was "to show him [Elvis] off to best advantage in a plot framed around the twelve songs necessary for a simultaneous album release."[18] Parker had similar goals. In December 1958, for example, he wrote to Wallis with the suggestion of using Hawaii as a potential movie location: not only would the picturesque islands make for an ideal setting, but there was also growing evidence that Hawaiian-style music was getting ever more popular and might fit Elvis's post-army musical identity.[19] The eventual result of Parker's suggestion, *Blue Hawaii* (1961), epitomized Wallis's formula like few others: it featured Elvis as a returning soldier who refuses to work for his wealthy parents' pineapple business and instead sets up his own tourism company. In between, he enjoys lush Hawaiian beaches, is chased by various girls in bikinis or bathing suits, and sings a total of fourteen songs. The *New York Times* accurately described it as an "amiable, synthetic and blandly uneventful movie."[20]

20th Century Fox, by contrast, opted for a completely different strategy. Rather than mimicking Wallis's light-touch, musical-style comedies, producer David Weisbart, who had also been responsible for James Dean's *Rebel without a Cause* (1955) and Elvis's first movie *Love Me Tender* (1956), hoped to develop Elvis into a serious dramatic actor. The first such attempt was *Flaming Star* (1960), a sophisticated western that featured Elvis as a half-native American cowboy becoming entangled in a racial conflict between the Kiowa tribe and white settlers. In a role that had originally been designed for Marlon Brando, Elvis delivered a generally convincing performance, singing only one song throughout the film. Already at production stage, however, there were several disputes over whether a dramatic role such as *Flaming Star* really constituted a suitable vehicle for Elvis's, as well as over the apparent lack of music. Indeed, Parker continuously pushed 20th Century Fox to include additional songs to please the singer's fan base and to accrue enough materials for a potential soundtrack, whereas Weisbart

---

[16]Simpson, *Elvis Films FAQ*, 135, 135–40.

[17]Palmer, "Introducing Elvis Presley," 177–90.

[18]Wallis and Higham, *Starmaker*, 149.

[19]Parker to Wallis, December 18, 1958, MHL, Hal Wallis Papers, Presley, Elvis—correspondence f.2115.

[20]*New York Times*, February 22, 1962.

insisted that having Elvis randomly burst into song would inevitably destroy what he regarded as a very good script.[21]

Such tensions ultimately reflected confusion about Elvis's post-army target audience. Don Siegel, the director of *Flaming Star*, highlighted the issue in an internal memorandum just prior to its release. Elvis fans might "possibly be disappointed in seeing their hero in a serious picture about a minority, Indians, being mistreated," he wrote, whereas "people who want to see a picture about a minority might stay away from the picture thinking that it was a rock-and-roll musical."[22] A similar problem occurred over 20th Century Fox's follow-up production *Wild in the Country* (1961), which again constituted a serious dramatic performance rather than lighthearted musical entertainment.[23] Reviewing draft promotion materials that showcased Elvis as a singer rather than as an actor, the movie's director Philip Dunne complained furiously about such mixed marketing messages. He was "all in favor of nailing down the Presley fans," Dunne protested, but they would "like the picture whatever we say about it. So why deliberately set out to alienate the millions in our potential audience who are <u>not</u> Presley fans but will play their money to see a great love story on the screen?"[24]

The market, however, soon gave a rather unequivocal answer. Paramount's *Blue Hawaii* was a massive hit, making more than $5 million at the box office and becoming the eleventh-highest-grossing film of 1961 (and fourteenth in 1962).[25] By contrast, *Flaming Star* and *Wild in the Country* both disappointed heavily, the latter reportedly even losing some money.[26] The sales pattern was mirrored in the respective soundtracks, or lack thereof. Whereas the *Blue Hawaii* LP spent an incredible twenty weeks at number one, selling two million in its first year and becoming Elvis's best-selling album during his lifetime, neither *Flaming Star* nor *Wild in the Country* was even accompanied by a soundtrack—much to the annoyance of Weisbart, who estimated that the lack of such cross-channel promotion had cost several hundred thousand dollars of exploitation.[27] Back at Paramount, people felt that their strategy had been vindicated. "[Y]ou are the only one who knows how to treat Presley's personality," a jubilant adviser wrote to Wallis on December 1, 1961. "Where

---

[21]Weisbart to Adler, June 2, 1960; Weisbart to Adler, June 6, 1960, [U]niversity of [S]outhern [C]alifornia, Cinematic Arts Library (Los Angeles, CA), David Weisbart Collection, Flaming Star.

[22]Siegel to Brand, October 13, 1960, USC, David Weisbart Collection, Flaming Star, Siegel to Brand.

[23]It also suffered from serious overlength and a still unfinished script at the start of filming.

[24]Dunne to Wald, February 6, 1961. USC, Philip Dunne Collection (41): Correspondence.

[25]Simpson, *Elvis Films FAQ*, xix, xxiii.

[26]Neibaur, *Elvis Movies*, 72.

[27]For Blue Hawaii, see Simpson, *Elvis Films FAQ*, 336; for Weisbart, Weisbart to Cain, August 10, 1960; Einfeld to Weisbart, November 10, 1960. USC, David Weisbart Collection, Flaming Star.

you emphasize Elvis the entertainer over Elvis the actor, which invariably seems to work because apparently this is what Elvis' public wants, everybody else does the reverse—and invariably falls on his face."[28]

Journalists and film critics agreed, interpreting the success of *Blue Hawaii* as a reflection of Elvis's new post-army audience that seemed to look primarily for good, harmless family entertainment.[29] The *Chicago Defender,* for example, suggested that *Blue Hawaii* had "something for every member of the family to enjoy," and the *Boston Globe* even claimed to have discovered "men and women of mature age" in the audience.[30] It also attributed the particular success of *Blue Hawaii* to the sense of optimism and lightheartedness hanging over the movie, as well as over early 1960s America: "the joy, the carefree fun and the refusal to compromise with adult standards which characterize the younger generation today."[31] It was a far cry from the rebellious image Elvis had cultivated in his 1950s movies like *Jailhouse Rock* (1957) or *King Creole* (1958).

**Figure 4.1** *Elvis Presley on the set of* Blue Hawaii *(1961).*

---

[28]Sokolove to Wallis, December 1, 1961. MHL, Hal Wallis Papers, Presley, Elvis, contract correspondence f.2113.
[29]James, *Rock "N" Film,* 95.
[30]*The Chicago Defender*, November 18, 1961; *Boston Globe*, November 23, 1961.
[31]*Boston Globe*, November 23, 1961.

*Blue Hawaii* indeed seems to have reflected what the majority of Elvis's fan base wanted at the time. The fan magazine *Elvis Monthly* lauded it as a movie that simply "could not have been bettered. Just imagine! A film that runs more or less for 100 minutes, and containing fourteen Elvis songs and three Hawaiian production numbers!" Given Elvis's "effervescent showmanship, delightful songs, and beautiful girls," the rather shallow storyline seemed like a minor shortcoming.[32] By contrast, *Flaming Star* received mixed evaluations, with one fan claiming that it did not really attract fans "due to its morose subject, lack of songs ... and depressing conclusion."[33] The numerous fan letters Wallis received offer similar impressions: one of them praised *Blue Hawaii* because it was "gay, it was happy, it was beautiful, and (thank God!) it was clean!," and urged Wallis to "keep Elvis under control" and not "lend him out to any more Jerry Walds or the like. Because <u>you</u> apparently are the fellow who puts him in musicals, and musicals are all I want to see him in."[34] For Paramount's next Elvis movie *Girls! Girls! Girls!* (1962), Wallis received similar praise. "Thanks again Mr. Wallis for a very entertaining movie with our RED-BLOODED Boy – ELVIS!," a fan club member wrote,

> We've seen the movie so far 15 times and all agree OUR GREAT STAR-ELVIS! NEVER so: UTTERLY CHARMING, BEAUTIFUL, APPEALING, BOYISH, CUTE, GORGEOUS, SEXY, SWEET, INCREDIBLY HANDSOME! as he is in "Girls!Girls!Girls!" Elvis' acting is smooth as silk, his voice and delivery of all the songs were fabulous. The clothes he wore were "THE MOST!" What a DOLL especially in the numbers in which he wore black. MAN O MAN! May we say, Mr. Wallis for the first time the camera-man (LOVE HIM) almost captured the true-to-life masculine handsomeness of ELVIS – we said ALMOST![35]

The success of the early 1960s movies eventually pushed Elvis's non-Hollywood career to the side-lines, and soon came to dominate the singer's public image.[36] The process was accelerated by the fact that Elvis's musical output too increasingly concentrated on soundtracks, rather than on the more ambitious material he had recorded after his return from Germany. From a purely commercial perspective, it was the obvious path to take: the sales figures of soundtrack albums usually exceeded those of his non-soundtrack

---

[32]*Elvis Monthly*, 3/1, January 1962.

[33]*Elvis Monthly*, 2/3, March 1961.

[34]Fan letter to Wallis, December 29, 1961. MHL, Hal Wallis Papers, Presley, Elvis correspondence f.2116.

[35]The "RED-BLOODED Boy" was an explicit reference to the lyrics of the movie's title song "Girls, Girls, Girls." Fan letter to Wallis, December 1962, MHL, Hal Wallis Papers, Presley, Elvis correspondence f.2116.

[36]Doll, *Understanding Elvis,* 141.

recordings by three or four times, and his personal income from a single movie was substantially higher than his recording royalties for an entire year.[37] For example, whereas the *Elvis Is Back!* album had only sold around 200,000 copies, the almost simultaneously released *G.I. Blues* soundtrack came in at over 700,000 copies.[38] In due course, Elvis's highly elaborate soundtrack production machinery took over the musical repertoire almost entirely, with publisher Freddy Bienstock ensuring that Elvis only recorded songs for which copyright could be controlled by his two publishing companies—Elvis Presley Music and Gladys Music. While such exploitative mechanisms inevitably compromised the artistic quality of the soundtracks, it ensured an additional income for Elvis of around $400,000 per year in royalties alone.[39] It was a highly lucrative effort for many composers as well, and Bienstock received up to 300 demo tapes for one soundtrack.[40]

By 1961, then, the magic key to Elvis's post-army success had apparently been found. Reinventing Elvis as an all-round family entertainer, the movies and soundtracks soon came to follow highly formulaic production patterns, creating a unique genre that became known as the so-called "Elvis movie" with almost complete consistency in style and iconography.[41] Being targeted at the widest possible mainstream audiences, they reveal a lot about Hollywood's self-understandings of early 1960s America, as well as about the wider images of American lifestyles and society it hoped to project to the world.

# Elvis Movies and Early 1960s America

Although Hollywood had been one of the US' biggest success stories during the first half of the twentieth century, its predominance of the entertainment field slowly began to wane after 1945. Facing rising production costs, anti-cartel legislation, and the powerful competition of television, Hollywood seemed in deep crisis by the 1950s. In response, it not only looked at revitalizing its domestic product, but it also hoped to expand its reach of foreign markets by lobbying for reductions in tax barriers and quotas as part of the US' wider economic expansion during the early Cold War.[42] The State Department willingly co-operated in this quest, not least because it believed in Hollywood's power to positively influence images of the United States abroad.[43] Indeed, American movies were highly popular outside the

---

[37]Jorgensen, *A Life in Music*, 190.
[38]Simpson, *Elvis Films FAQ*, 336.
[39]Jorgensen, *A Life in Music*, 165, 198.
[40]Ibid., 163.
[41]Doll, *Understanding Elvis*, 143.
[42]Nolan, *Transatlantic Century*, 241–2.
[43]Tony Shaw and Denise J. Youngblood, *Cinematic Cold War: The American and Soviet Struggle for Hearts and Minds* (Lawrence: University Press of Kansas, 2010), 27, 99, 107.

United States: in the early 1960s, the USIA estimated that over 150 million tickets for Hollywood movies were bought outside the United States each week; in Western Europe alone, American films constituted between one-half (UK) and one-third (France, West Germany) of all films shown.[44] Although Hollywood movies rarely constituted overt propaganda, they nonetheless popularized countless images of US-style affluence, consumerism, and social harmony on a mass scale, infusing rather abstract notions of the so-called American Way of Life with concrete images and meanings.[45]

Given their massive commercial successes, the so-called Elvis movies constituted an integral part of Hollywood visions of early 1960s America, and their highly formulaic nature offers some clues about the more general sort of images they hoped to project.[46] They are almost always held together by a plot constructed around Elvis's character, who displays much more conventional looks compared to the 1950s: the hair is now well groomed and the sideburns are gone.[47] The plots rarely contain explicit biographical references; rather, Elvis plays some happy-go-lucky chap with an exciting occupation like race car driver, aircraft pilot, or carnival worker.[48] Elvis—I will simply refer to him as Elvis, as most promotional materials did at the time—then usually faces some sort of challenge, for example, hunting for a treasure or winning a motor-car race. He succeeds admirably, and in so doing also tends to effortlessly win the hearts of the countless women who invariably surround him. In short, the Elvis movies often present a quintessential Hollywood success story; a Horatio Alger–like tale of individual achievement in a land of unlimited opportunities.[49]

These highly formulaic plots were usually set against a colorful background that illustrates the natural beauty of America, something that was frequently picked up by reviewers and fans alike at the time. In *Blue Hawaii,* Elvis actually becomes a tourist guide, showcasing the natural beauty as well as highly idealized images of multiracial harmony in the youngest US state to millions of audiences around the world.[50] The technological advantages Hollywood productions still enjoyed at the time became evident in Paramount's use of Panavision Technicolor, which was commented upon

---

[44]"The Impact of Hollywood Films Abroad," July 1961, NARA, RG306, Series A1/1011, Program and Media Studies, 1956–62, Box 2, PMS-50; "Posts' Assessment of the Impact of Hollywood Films Abroad," September 1961; Program and Media Studies, Box 2, PMS-54.
[45]Shaw and Youngblood, *Cinematic Cold War,* 26; Tony Shaw, *Hollywood's Cold War* (Edinburgh: Edinburgh University Press, 2007), 301, 304; Bryan Upton, *Hollywood and the End of the Cold War: Signs of Cinematic Change* (Lanham: Rowman & Littlefield, 2014), 14.
[46]For a much more detailed and highly entertaining plot analysis of the so-called "Elvis movies" in the 1960s, see James, *Rock "N" Film,* esp. 96–102. It also includes a very amusing chart.
[47]Doll, *Understanding Elvis,* 138.
[48]Ibid., 140.
[49]Shaw and Youngblood, *Cinematic Cold War,* 26.
[50]Sarah Miller-Davenport, *Gateway State: Hawai'i and the Cultural Transformation of American Empire* (Lawrenceville, NJ: Princeton University Press, 2019), 68–9.

widely by fans and reviewers. The *Chicago Defender* proclaimed that "the 50th State has never been seen to a more eye-catching advantage,"[51] and the *Boston Globe* thought that one of the movie's main pleasures was "the scenery – so vivid in color the picture turns into a series of travel posters, each more gorgeous than the one before."[52] Many fans agreed. "Describe it what you will ... a travel folder ... a picture book ... it all comes down to one word: BEAUTY," one of them wrote in *Elvis Monthly*. "Beauty in the breathtaking scenery (including girls), beauty in the form of a soundtrack full to overflowing with THE golden voice, and certainly an artist's conception of beauty in tall, tanned and handsome Chad Gates [Elvis's screen name]."[53]

Most Elvis movies not only projected the natural beauty of the American continent, but they also portrayed the United States as a technologically highly advanced country of consumerist abundance whose benefits could be enjoyed by all citizens. The movies regularly featured high-end gadgets like water skis or helicopters, as well as comfortable apartments, and

**Figure 4.2** *Elvis's 1960s movies often offered unabashed celebrations of the so-called American Way of Life.*

[51]*The Chicago Defender*, November 18, 1961.
[52]*Boston Globe*, November 23, 1961.
[53]*Elvis Monthly*, 3/2, February 1962.

modern office buildings. Cars, perhaps the quintessential symbol of postwar American-style freedom, featured particularly prominently, with Elvis often playing race car drivers or motorcyclists.[54] In 1962, *It Happened at the World's Fair* was even shot on location at the world fair in Seattle. It included numerous panorama shots of the fair's futurist buildings and had Elvis riding the newly constructed Monorail and going on a date in the Space Needle restaurant—in the final scene, he signs up for NASA's space program. A few years later, the highly successful *Viva Las Vegas* (1964) similarly included frequent shots of lush hotels and swimming pools, and featured Elvis motor-racing, water-skiing, and taking a helicopter-ride over the Hoover Dam.

Such displays of American wealth and technological advancement reflected the undisputed lead the United States still enjoyed in mass consumption, both producing and consuming most of the world's appliances at the time.[55] In the aftermath of Nixon's infamous "Kitchen Debate" with the Soviet leader Khrushchev at the 1959 American National Exhibition, the Elvis movies thus matched the US' more general propaganda messages of prosperity and everyday affluence under a mass consumerist society. Indeed, the common display of everyday symbols of modernity and prosperity clearly struck a chord with many external audiences. A major USIA survey of the impact of US commercial movies in Western Europe noted how audiences usually gained the impression that the United States were a country "where even the common people live comfortably."[56] One participant from the United Kingdom, for example, recorded his impression that Americans seemed to "live much better" and enjoyed a "higher standard of living": "Plenty of good things. Seem well-off, rich, plenty of money, prosperous, well-dressed. Conditions of houses are good, luxury flats, kitchens, labor-saving devices."[57]

The Elvis movies are just as notable for what they tend to leave out about life in the United States of the 1960s. Elvis's own personal background as a marginalized Southern poor white, for example, was usually trivialized or ignored altogether.[58] Although some of the movies were still set in the South, they generally did really reflect anything of the hardship and ongoing racial violence at the time; if anything, films like *Kissin' Cousins* (1964) depicted the South in a patronizing and occasionally insulting manner.[59] Female characters were commonly objectified and portrayed in conservative

[54]Brode, *Elvis Culture*, 188–204; Simpson, *Elvis Films FAQ*, 282–3.

[55]Nolan, *Transatlantic Century*, 260.

[56]"A Brief Overview of recent survey findings on the economic image of America abroad," November 1958. NARA, RG306, Series A1/1011: Program and Media Studies, 1956–62, PMS-33.

[57]"The Impact of American Commercial movies in Western Europe," December 1962. NARA, RG306, Series P142: Research Reports, Box 12, R-166–62.

[58]James, *Rock "N" Film*, 96, 103–4.

[59]Simpson, *Elvis Films FAQ*, 289–91.

and antiquated ways, often featuring as little more than props for Elvis's pursuits.[60] As the pressbook for *Fun in Acapulco* (1963) put it rather bluntly, Elvis "has a girl Friday (called Elsa) and a girl (called Ursula) for every other day of his very tropic weeks."[61] While the common sight of short dresses or bikinis might reflect a somewhat more liberal attitude toward sexuality in the early 1960s, the movies retain a fairly prudish flair: until *Live a Little, Love a Little* (1968), kissing (and marriage) is as far as Elvis's character tends to go.[62] Perhaps the only exception is Ann-Margaret's character in *Viva Las Vegas* (1964), who does display some sort of female agency, even though it gets somewhat diminished once she asserts that all she really wants to do is to get married and live in a little suburban house.[63]

Most striking is the glaring omission of race. Whereas some of Elvis's 1950s films like *King Creole* (1958) at least vaguely alluded to rock 'n' roll complex relationship with African American culture, such references were completely removed in the 1960s movies; if people of color featured at all, it was usually in cliché-like allusions to an American "melting pot" or in seemingly exotic settings like Mexico or the Middle East that were very obviously set on a Hollywood soundstage. While several Asian Americans feature in Elvis's movies throughout the years, they are usually confined to being girlfriends or children. From today's perspective, some movies also include chauvinistic or demeaning stereotypes, not least in the form of exaggerated accents like in *It Happened at the World's Fair* (1962) or *Fun in Acapulco* (1963).[64] Only Elvis's final dramatic movie *Change of Habit* (1969) features a black character with a major part, the well-known Barbara McNair. Overall, however, the movies' main thrust as regards race and gender is best illustrated by the final scene of *Girls! Girls! Girls!* (1962): Elvis's character proudly proclaims in song that he is just a red-blooded boy who cannot stop thinking about girls from all around the world, but above all the good ol' United States.

The Elvis movies therefore created as well as reinforced one-dimensional, idealized, and at times highly utopian images of early 1960s America. They presented the United States as a country of capitalist abundance and individual opportunity, untroubled by any racial tensions, and held together by a socially conservative and highly patriarchal value system. In so doing, they not only shaped Elvis's post-army image, but they also reconfigured his cultural legacy. By reducing the singer to a banal and somewhat folkloristic character, the movies marginalized the African American roots of Elvis's music and all but ignored the major racial,

---

[60]Brode, *Elvis Culture*, 59.
[61]"Paramount Merchandising Manual and Press Book: Fun in Acapulco," preserved at USC, Elvis Presley press books.
[62]Brode, *Elvis Culture*, 104–5; James, *Rock "N" Film*, 105.
[63]Brode, *Elvis Culture*, 157.
[64]James, *Rock "N" Film*, 105–6.

sexual, and generational tensions at the very heart of his 1950s appeal.[65] Elvis thus became re-framed for a predominantly white, middle-aged, and socially disengaged family audience, which the film historian Douglas Brode described as a mixture of "farming folk in the rural South and blue collar workers in the industrial North."[66]

Elvis himself appeared somewhat uneasy about some of the movies, as well as about the apparent change in his public image. As early as 1960, he told friends or co-stars about his embarrassment with some plotlines and soundtracks, occasionally even requesting that certain numbers would not be released on record.[67] Contractually, however, he had no influence over the movies' content, and the nature of the deals—where Elvis received a high advance fee whatever the movies' costs—made producers less likely to experiment with more artistic scripts or deviate from the established formula of a light plot and twelve musical numbers for a soundtrack.[68] Elvis's highly eccentric lifestyle also meant that he himself relied on continuous income from the movies. As his then girlfriend and future wife Priscilla Beaulieu recalls, "whenever he complained to the Colonel, Colonel reminded him that they were making millions, that the fact that his last two serious films, *Flaming Star* and *Wild in the Country*, were box-office failures proved that his fans wanted to see him only in musicals."[69] Elvis's personal insecurities about his acting skills did not help, making him almost deferential toward Parker's arguments. In a rare candid interview with Lloyd Shearer in 1962, he mused that one could not "go out of your capabilities ... your limitations ... if you goof a few times, you don't get many more chances in this business. That's the sad part about it. So, you're better off if what you're doing is doing okay, you're better off stickin' with it until time itself changes things."[70]

Yet one cannot argue about the overwhelming commercial success of the Elvis movies at the time. Even by the mid-1960s, films like *Viva Las Vegas* (1964), *Roustabout* (1964), and *Girl Happy* (1965) still performed well at the box office, and the soundtrack albums of the latter two sold around 400,000 to 500,000.[71] In November 1964, the *New York Times* reported that Elvis's movies were making "profits with a consistency that continues to astonish Hollywood's money men," and had turned Elvis into the "by far [...] highest paid movie star in Hollywood history."[72] In light of such numbers, Parker, for one, certainly did not mind the movies' lack of artistic quality. As early as 1960, he had bluntly told the press that the movies would

---

[65]Ibid., 111.
[66]Brode, *Elvis Culture*, 279.
[67]Guralnick and Jorgensen, *Day by Day*, 156; Jorgensen, *A Life in Music*, 175.
[68]Simpson, *Elvis Films FAQ*, 137.
[69]Presley, *Elvis and Me*, 188.
[70]Osborne, *Word for Word*, 191.
[71]Simpson, *Elvis Films FAQ*, 242, 336.
[72]*New York Times*, November 22, 1964.

never win any Academy Awards and were only good for making money;[73] in April 1964, producer Hal Wallis added insult to injury when he was quoted in the press that Elvis's "commercially successful" films helped him finance more artistic productions like the recently released *Becket* (1964).[74] Elvis was deeply hurt by these remarks, but his Hollywood career continued unabatedly.

## Elvis Abroad: Transnational Fan Activism and East–West Contacts

Although Elvis had become known in almost all corners of the world during the 1950s, it was only in the early 1960s that he truly achieved widespread acceptance. Ballads like "It's Now or Never" or "Are You Lonesome Tonight" turned Elvis into an entertainer who was popular far beyond his erstwhile teenage fan base. This was particularly true in Western Europe, where Elvis's pop ballads became far more popular than his earlier rock 'n' roll numbers.[75] Yet, such widespread acceptance also eradicated many of the bigger debates that had previously surrounded Elvis. By the early 1960s, Elvis was no longer discussed controversially outside the United States, and the more extensive reporting on the singer was usually confined to music or youth magazines.

Elvis movies were highly successful outside the United States, where they often retained their popularity longer than at home. While this was partly due to the fact that the movies constituted the only possibility for non-US fans to get a glimpse at their idol, they also seem to have exerted an additional fascination as idyllic dream worlds of American-style modernity. In the Asia-Pacific, for example, the Elvis movies were embraced partly for their projections of consumerist abundance and everyday affluence, as well as for their colorful and gaudy entertainment that was popular in many parts of Asia, such as Thailand. "His kind of movies fit the idea of Thai entertainment," the head of Thailand's major Elvis fan club reflected; "[p]eople were happy when they left the theatre. The Thais love to see 'beautiful things' and listen to 'beautiful sounds'."[76] In a similar vein, an MGM representative in Hong Kong predicted in 1963 that *Viva Las Vegas* hit just the right spot with its colorful depictions of US nightlife, and would therefore be a massive success during the Chinese New Year holidays.[77] Elvis

---

[73]Guralnick, *Careless Love*, 75.
[74]Guralnick and Jorgensen, *Day by Day*, 195.
[75]Jorgensen, *A Life in Music*, 1, 181.
[76]Quoted in Simpson, *Elvis Films FAQ*, 293.
[77]MGM Hong Kong to Cummings, December 28, 1963. MHL, Jack Cummings Papers, Viva Las Vegas—miscellaneous, f.91.

also remained highly popular in Australia. In 1965, the low-budget flick *Tickle Me* (1965) entirely sold out for eight weeks at Sydney's 2,5000-seat State Theater; in 1968, even a touring exhibition of one of Elvis's golden Cadillacs attracted spectators in over forty cities and towns in Australia and New Zealand.[78] Clearly, Elvis was not merely popular for his music or songs; he also functioned as a pop-cultural symbol for American consumerism and capitalist luxury.

The extent of Elvis's 1960s popularity outside the United States can also be gauged by the professionalization of his fan scene at the time. In January 1960, the British fan and printer Albert Hand published the first edition of *Elvis Monthly,* a professionally produced journal dedicated exclusively to Elvis. It quickly turned into one of the major organs of the Elvis fan scene: less than a year after its first edition, Hand already claimed to receive more than 500 readers' letters each week from all around the world.[79] The magazine also included several features from US-based fans, such as regular "American Reports" by Lou Hohn or insider updates by the local Memphis superfan Gary Pepper.[80] Most importantly, it provided networking opportunities for fans all around the world: there were regular contributions from international fans who looked for pen pals, described Elvis's popularity in their home countries, or simply wanted to share their personal musings. By 1962, *Elvis Monthly* had become a major news hub for Elvis fans, featuring contributions from all over Western Europe (e.g., France, West Germany, Sweden, Norway, Malta) and far beyond (e.g., Israel, South Africa, Thailand, Hong Kong, Malaya, Chile, the Philippines).[81] In 1965, the magazine helped organize the first European Elvis fan convention in London; it was followed up by a similar event in Brussels the following year.[82] One organizer of the Brussels convention wrote to Hal Wallis afterward how Elvis fans were like a "big world-wide fraternity" based on common tastes and common admiration without borders of nationality, religion, or race.[83]

As Cold War tensions relaxed with the slow onset of détente in the mid-1960s, fan networks occasionally even stretched beyond the Iron Curtain. Again, *Elvis Monthly* was a major facilitator of such cross-border contacts,

---

[78]Simpson, *Elvis Films FAQ*, xx; "Elvis Presley's GOLD Cadillac Tour of AUSTRALASIA 1968–69 (book review)," www.elvisinfonet.com/bookreview_goldcaddy_2011edition.htm [last accessed May 3, 2020].

[79]*Elvis Monthly* 11, December 1960.

[80]At the time, Pepper was also running his own US-based fan magazine *The Tancaster*. Pepper's first story for *Elvis Monthly* already appeared in the magazine's third edition; see *Elvis Monthly* 3, March 1960.

[81]Examples of countries taken from the "Around The World" sections in *Elvis Monthly* 2/2 and *Elvis Monthly* 3/7, February 1961 and July 1962.

[82]*Elvis Monthly* 69, October 1965.

[83]Letter to Wallis, August 2, 1966. MHL, Hal Wallis Papers, Presley Elvis correspondence f.2116.

printing letters by fans from Czechoslovakia or Hungary who wanted to get in touch with Elvis fans from non-socialist countries.[84] Some American and West European fans also started to send letters and records to their East European counterparts. In October 1962, for example, a member of an Elvis fan club in Cincinnati wrote to the Hollywood columnist Hedda Hopper about her penpalship with an East European boy, proclaiming how wonderful it was to bring a part of the free world behind the Iron Curtain.[85] In April 1968, *Elvis Monthly* launched "Vikki's Iron Curtain Mission," an initiative for East–West exchanges drawn up by a Leicester-based fan:

> All you have to do is write to me at the fan club address and I'll send you the name and address of a fellow fan in one of the Communist countries. From then on it's up to you to correspond with him/her, but you must be prepared to buy two copies of Elvis Monthly each month – one for yourself and one for your Iron Curtain fan.[86]

Some East European fans also published their own fan stories in *Elvis Monthly*. Interestingly, a lot of them had become fascinated by Elvis as a mainstream entertainer only during the 1960s, rather than by his 1950s rock 'n' roll persona. In April 1968, for example, a West Hungarian fan from Kószeg described vividly how she had first been introduced to Elvis by letters from her brother in Switzerland. Since she was unable to purchase Elvis's records or watch his movies herself, she asked another friend from Switzerland to supply her with copies of the West German youth magazine *BRAVO*, whose colorful celebrity stories caused a minor sensation among her peers at school. "Before that we did not see such magazines with stars of singing and cinemas," she recalled. "Our whole class read them during the lessons. So I could get news about Elvis films, records and private life."[87] A fan from the Czechoslovakian town of Horka told a similar story: he got into Elvis by listening to "It's Now or Never" on Radio Luxembourg, and then found rather creative ways of getting hold of new Elvis materials over the years. "I asked my West German pen-pal if he could give me any information on this singer and his records," he recalled, and promptly received "a big package with the 'Now or Never' platter, German Pop Magazine cuttings and glossy pictures of Elvis." He then decided to learn English, and started corresponding with Elvis fans in the West with the help of *Elvis Monthly*. He even managed to visit some of his British pen pals in the mid-1960s, where he could finally watch an actual Elvis movie for the very first time: "To see Elvis on pictures is fabulous, but to watch him

---

[84]*Elvis Monthly* 69, October 1965; *Elvis Monthly* 72, January 1962.
[85]Fan letter to Hopper, October 8, 1962, MHL, Hedda Hopper Papers, Presley, Elvis, f.2664.
[86]*Elvis Monthly* 99, April 1968.
[87]Ibid.

'life-like' on the screen can't be described in words! I'm sure every Elvis fan knows this feeling inside, when watching an Elvis movie. Great! Great! Great!"[88] Elvis Presley may have become mainstream in the United States and Western Europe by the mid-1960s, but he remained as exciting as ever as a major American celebrity and quintessential embodiment of US popular culture behind the Iron Curtain.

# The Times They Are a-Changin' ...

In the United States, Elvis Presley's predominance over the entertainment field ended on February 7, 1964, when a four-piece band from Liverpool landed on PanAm flight 101 at New York's John F. Kennedy airport. For the past few months, The Beatles had already enjoyed colossal success in Britain; achievements that had quickly fed over the Atlantic by an ever-expanding network of internationally operating newspapers, magazines, and agencies. Now, they set out to conquer the entertainment scene of the United States in person, closely following the carefully laid-out plans of their manager Brian Epstein. Two days after their arrival, The Beatles performed on *The Ed Sullivan Show* to an estimated audience of seventy-four million, at the time the largest audience ever recorded and roughly twenty million more than Elvis's viewing figures in the 1950s. Sullivan read out a telegram by Elvis who congratulated them on their appearance, even though it had been sent by the Colonel unbeknownst to Elvis.[89] What followed was an unprecedented hype that even surpassed the excitement that had surrounded Elvis in the 1950s: in the first three months of 1964, The Beatles alone accounted for around 60 percent of all music singles sold in the United States.[90]

The connections between Elvis and The Beatles, of course, went back a lot longer than Elvis's congratulatory telegram. Most of the group members had been avid fans of rock 'n' roll in 1950s Britain, and they frequently cited Elvis as one of their major influences. "I heard Elvis Presley," John Lennon recalled in the *Rolling Stone*. "There were a lot of other things going on, but that was the conversion. I kind of dropped everything."[91] Indeed, The Beatles had spent much of their first few touring years covering rock 'n' roll standards by Elvis, Buddy Holly, and others in the clubs of Liverpool and Hamburg.[92] They eventually started writing their own songs that added new creative influences to 1950s rock 'n' roll, which differentiated them from their former idol Elvis, who saw himself strictly as a performing artist rather

---

[88]Ibid.
[89]Jonathan Gould, *Can't Buy Me Love: The Beatles, Britain, and America* (New York: Harmony Books, 2007), 1–5.
[90]Ibid., 6.
[91]As quoted in ibid., 22.
[92]Ibid., 58; Sneeringer, *Social History of Early Rock 'n' Roll*, 78–82.

than as a songwriter. In due course, The Beatles created a completely new
type of rock band that soon became a role model for many other aspiring
musicians around the world. While bands like The Beatles and The Rolling
Stones were often depicted as signs of a "British invasion" at the time, then,
it is evident that they rather were the product of highly complex transatlantic
pop-cultural transfers that far transcended national borders.[93]

The public contrast between Elvis and The Beatles was accentuated
further by the band's experimental and new-waveish movies like *A Hard
Day's Night* (1964) and *Help!* (1965), which were a far cry from Elvis's light
and somewhat prudish musical comedies.[94] Indeed, The Beatles had by that
stage become disappointed by their former idol's post-army career. As early as
July 1963, John Lennon proclaimed that he was "off" Elvis because he "just
doesn't seem to bother any more," claiming that his music was no longer "the
sound that myself and people of my age group want."[95] Elvis, in turn, may
privately have perceived The Beatles as a threat, but he remained cordial in
public. "[I]f these young people can come over here and do well, regardless
of what crowd they impress, well more power to them, really," he told the
interviewer Danny Thomas shortly after the band's *Sullivan* appearance in
February 1964; "I'm only glad of the success that I have had. And I couldn't
be envious of some other young, or new, guy that's trying to make it too.
Because as the old saying goes, I been [sic] down that road before."[96]

On August 27, 1965, Elvis Presley and The Beatles met for the first
and only time at Elvis's Bel Air home in Los Angeles. It turned out to be a
somewhat anti-climactic encounter.[97] After some awkward silence and a bit
of small talk, Elvis started to jam on his Fender bass to the tune of Charlie
Rich's "Mohair Sam" with Paul McCartney, and then spent some time
chatting with John Lennon about their favorite Peter Sellers movies. George
Harrison smoked weed with Elvis's hairstylist and spiritual adviser Larry
Geller.[98] The atmosphere seems to have been pleasant enough, although
Elvis politely declined The Beatles' return invitation for the following day.
Elvis's friend and bodyguard Jerry Schilling, however, followed it up, and

---

[93]Egbert Klautke, "Die 'britische Invasion': britische Pop- und Rockmusik in den USA," in
Dietmar Hüser (ed.), *Populärkultur—transnational: Sehen, Hören, Lesen, Erleben im Europa
der langen 1960er Jahre* (Bielefeld: Transcript, 2017), 107–25.
[94]Brode, *Elvis Culture*, 162, 165; for a comparative analysis of *A Hard Day's Night* and *Viva
Las Vegas*, see David E. James, "Rock 'n' Film: Generic Permutations in Three Feature Films
from 1964," *Grey Room* 49 (2012), 16–22.
[95]*Disc*, July 6, 1963.
[96]Osborne, *Word for Word*, 197–8.
[97]There are numerous recollections of the meeting, and they differ quite significantly. See, for
example, Schilling, *Me and A Guy Named Elvis*, 129–34; Geller and Spector, *If I Can Dream*,
119–25. For an excellent summary with some rare pictures, see Elvis Australia, "Elvis Presley
Meets The Beatles," www.elvis.com.au/presley/elvis-meets-the-beatles.shtml [last accessed
January 5, 2020].
[98]Geller, *If I Can Dream*, 122.

was taken aside by John Lennon. "I couldn't say this to Elvis last night, but you see these sideburns?" Lennon told him; "I almost got kicked out of high school trying to be like Elvis. Tell Elvis that if it hadn't been for him, I would have been nothing."[99] Clearly, though, Lennon was talking about the Elvis he had imagined and admired in the 1950s, not about the actual person he had met the night before.

Like McCartney and Lennon, Bob Dylan had been an avid Elvis fan from the earliest days in the mid-1950s. "When I first heard Elvis' voice I just knew that I wasn't going to work for anybody; and nobody was going to be my boss", he famously reflected; "Hearing him for the first time was like busting out of jail."[100] He remained fascinated by Elvis throughout his career, evident not least in his cover versions of "A Fool Such as I" and "Can't Help Falling in Love." During the late 1960s, he even claimed in a *Rolling Stone* interview that Elvis's version of "Tomorrow Is a Long Time" was the one recording he treasured the most, even if some readers took his remark as a joke.[101] Just like The Beatles, however, Dylan had by the mid-1960s developed into a very different type of artist. In marked contrast to Elvis, Dylan was a prolific singer-songwriter, and used his lyrical skills to transport bigger political and social messages.[102] He was also an early advocate of the burgeoning civil rights movement, and in May 1963 famously refused to appear on *The Ed Sullivan Show* because CBS tried to ban him from performing the "Talking John Birch Society Blues."[103] Elvis, by contrast, retained a completely apolitical stance in public for much of the 1960s, regarding himself strictly as an entertainer.

If Elvis seemed indifferent or apathetic toward some new cultural developments in public, he appeared curious about them behind closed doors. He appreciated many of The Beatles' recordings and songs by Bob Dylan, even if he tended to prefer the latter in the cover versions on the *Odetta Sings Dylan* album.[104] Around 1966–67, he even taped his own version "Blowin' in the Wind" on a private home recorder.[105] Elvis also kept close track of The Beatles' movie career. When the British journalist Ray Connolly randomly mentioned the name of one of the Beatles' assistants during a conversation, Elvis exclaimed, "Yeah, he's the guy in *Help!* that kept swimming."[106] Elvis was also intrigued by some of the

---

[99]Quoted in Schilling, *Me and A Guy Named Elvis,* 133.

[100]As quoted in Michael Gray, *The Bob Dylan Encyclopedia* (New York and London: continuum, 2006), 546.

[101]Ibid., 549.

[102]David Boucher, *Dylan and Cohen: Poets of Rock and Roll* (London: Bloomsbury, 2004).

[103]Sean Wilentz, *Bob Dylan in America* (New York: Anchor Books, 2010 [2011]), 92–3.

[104]Guralnick and Jorgensen, *Day by Day,* 215.

[105]This recording was discovered in only the 1990s, and subsequently released by RCA. See Jorgensen, *A Life in Music,* 206.

[106]Quoted in Simpson, *Elvis Films FAQ,* xxi.

emerging counter-culture's experimental lifestyles. He began to read widely about religion and spirituality, absorbing works like Joseph Benner's *The Impersonal Life*, Kahlil Gibran's *The Prophet*, or Paramahansa Yogananda's *Autobiography of a Yogi*. He also established a strong relationship with Sri Daya Mata of the *Self-Realization Fellowship* in Pacific Heights, and initiated the construction of his own Meditation Garden at Graceland.[107] Inspired by the writings of Timothy Leary and Aldous Huxley, Elvis even conducted a onetime experiment with LSD for spiritual enlightenment. Not much enlightenment seems to have come out of it, however, as Elvis and his friends eventually ended up eating pizza and watching science-fiction on television.[108]

Yet, these important dimensions of Elvis's personality were not at all reflected in his artistic output. In the eyes of the wider public, it seemed like times had moved on, and Elvis had not quite moved along with them. By the mid-1960s, the well-worn movie formula started to show some strains, particularly since most productions now lacked the consistency and professionalism of his earlier efforts. Quality took a further nosedive once Colonel Parker enlisted the services of Sam Katzman, a Hollywood B-movie veteran who boasted to have shot Bill Haley's *Rock Around the Clock* in only thirteen days.[109] Katzman's two Elvis movies surely count among the singer's worst efforts: in *Kissin Cousins* (1964), Elvis plays two lookalike cousins in the Smoky Mountains simply by wearing a strawberry blonde wig for one of the parts; in the above-mentioned *Harum Scarum* (1965), he is a turban-wearing American singer captured by assassins during a tour of the Middle East. In 1967, Elvis was performing "Old MacDonald" on the back of a farmer's truck in *Double Trouble* while films like *Bonnie and Clyde* or *The Graduate* attracted critical acclaim as well as mass audiences.

By the mid-1960s, reviews became ever more damning, perhaps reflecting such wider changes in the cultural landscape. "[E]ven compared to some previous Presley turkeys," the *New York Times* wrote about *Frankie and Johnny* in 1966, "this one sheds feathers almost from the start. Never has his vehicle formula seemed so feeble and so obvious."[110] *Clambake* (1967) was similarly derided by the *LA Times* for its "synthetic appearance. The starlets look lacquered, the sets plasticized and there's much reliance on process work. ... Elvis' songs are as forgettable as ever, and the whole picture has a garish, cluttered look."[111] Fans started to complain that Elvis's new movies were no longer released in major theaters, but only in off-beat locations or drive-ins.[112] In 1966, a British fan from Aldershot even wrote a personal

---

[107]Guralnick, *Careless Love*, 215–16.

[108]Schilling, *Me and A Guy Named Elvis*, 137–40; Ibid., 217.

[109]Dawson, *Rock Around the Clock*, 144–5; Nash, *Colonel*, 210.

[110]*New York Times*, July 21, 1966.

[111]*Los Angeles Times*, July 1, 1967.

[112]See, for example, Fan letter to Small, January 27, 1966. USC, Frankie And Johnny Files.

letter to Hal Wallis complaining that *Frankie and Johnny* had not premiered at the city's major Odeon cinema but only at the much smaller Alexandra.[113] "Presley has had his day with the youngster," the *Boston Globe* concluded in November 1967. "There was a time when every theater showing a Presley film was as crowded with screaming girls and yelling boys as now happens with the Beatles or the Rolling Stones. But earlier fans have now married and are bringing up babies, while younger sisters and brothers have quite different ideas about entertainers."[114]

There were also no new musical releases to counterbalance the increasingly poor movie output, since the initially much higher sales figures of the soundtrack albums had made Parker and RCA focus their release strategy almost solely on them. Elvis too appeared somewhat lethargic about proper recording sessions, frequently cutting them short or canceling them altogether.[115] Between January 1964 and May 1966, he recorded no

**Figure 4.3** *Elvis Presley on the set of* Paradise, Hawaiian Style *in 1966.*

[113]White to Wallis, undated but likely mid-1966, MHL, Hal Wallis Papers, King Creole f.720.
[114]*Boston Globe*, November 24, 1967.
[115]Jorgensen, *A Life in Music*, 190.

non-soundtrack music at all; his only notable chart success in the period was the re-release of the five-year-old recording of "Crying in the Chapel" during Easter 1965.[116] Instead, he sought escape in his private life, continuing to explore New Age spiritualism or purchasing an entire horse ranch at the cost of almost a million dollars.[117] By the late 1960s, Elvis seemed increasingly removed from the realities of life in a rapidly changing America.

# Changes in Elvis's Public Image During the Late 1960s

The 1960s were not only a decade of massive cultural change; they were also a decade of profound political, economic, and societal transitions. The burgeoning civil rights movement, widespread opposition against the Vietnam War, and the activism of groups like the SDS or the peace movement all sought to challenge the very foundations of the 1960s United States. In 1968, the dual assassinations of the Democratic soon-to-be presidential candidate Robert Kennedy in Los Angeles and Martin Luther King in Memphis seemed to mark the tragic climax of the decade; both were followed by protests, turmoil, and upheavals.

Set against that background, Elvis's movies seemed not merely out of touch; they had become anachronistic relics of a bygone age.[118] Reviewers frequently put their finger on the apparent disconnect between the ahistorical world of Elvis movies and the harsh realities of everyday life in the 1960s United States. Reviewing *Harum Scarum,* for example, the *Boston Globe* complained that it reeked "from the cigars of middle-aged Hollywood gag writers";[119] the *Christian Science Monitor* denounced *Clambake* as "a low-budget Hollywood musical from the '50's or perhaps even the '40's."[120] Such impressions were reinforced by the almost complete ignorance of new cultural developments in Elvis movies. The only explicit engagement with 1960s counterculture came in the form of a completely misguided attempt at parody in *Easy Come, Easy Go* (1967), which has Elvis observing an artistic "happening" of a couple getting drenched in spaghetti and making awkward twists at a yoga class. The follow-up production *Speedway* (1968), which features him as a stock car driver alongside Nancy Sinatra, seemed similarly anachronistic to many observers. "Music, youth and customs were much changed by Elvis Presley twelve years ago," the *New York Times* remarked; "from the twenty-six movies he has made since he sang

---

[116]Ibid., 200.
[117]Presley, *Elvis and Me,* 227–9; Schilling, *Me and A Guy Named Elvis,* 165–70.
[118]James, *Rock "N" Film,* 110–11; Brode, *Elvis Culture,* 9.
[119]*Boston Globe,* November 11, 1965.
[120]*The Christian Science Monitor,* November 27, 1967.

'Heartbreak Hotel,' you would never guess it."[121] If future audiences would not be able to gauge from Elvis's movies "what American society was like in the summer of 1968," the film critic Roger Ebert commented, then "at least they will discover what it was not like."[122]

By the late 1960s, the Elvis movies were suffering from a rapidly dwindling market. In 1965, *Girl Happy* had been the last Elvis's film to make it into the weekly top ten list of best-grossing films; most subsequent efforts disappointed commercially. In April 1966, Hal Wallis concluded a deal for one further Elvis movie, but then displayed absolutely no interest in negotiating another one.[123] The sales figures of the soundtracks also plummeted, rarely selling more than two hundred thousand copies by 1966.[124] Even Elvis himself seemed alienated from his career, frequently complaining about scripts, showing up late on sets, or canceling recording sessions. For the production of *Clambake* (1967), he arrived so overweight that the costumes had to be readjusted to his new measurements.[125] While there were some signs of a possible musical rejuvenation on the horizon— in May 1966, Elvis made his first non-soundtrack recordings in over two years, which included several of his all-time gospel favorites as well as cover versions of The Clovers' "Down in the Alley" and Bob Dylan's "Tomorrow Is a Long Time"—such minor efforts did not have any noticeable impact on Elvis's public image. The resulting gospel album failed to make an impact on the charts, although it won a Grammy for Best Sacred Performance.[126]

The anachronism of Elvis's movie persona, as well as his commercial failures, combined to form widespread impressions that Elvis was massively out of touch with the realities of his place and time. In the eyes of the public, Elvis had become a Gatsby-like symbol of the US entertainment industry, as well as of the exploitation mechanisms at its heart. "As any mature multi-millionaire should," the *Evening Times Glasgow* wrote condescendingly on the eve of Elvis's thirtieth birthday, the singer would celebrate "quietly on his 14-acre estate" after a year in which he had allegedly made "about $4,000,000" and even temporarily purchased the Potomac presidential yacht (albeit for charity). There were no longer any signs of sideburns or flashy clothes; Elvis had turned into "a well-groomed, quietly dressed man, who never drinks, smokes only because he doesn't know what to do with his hands, never gets arrested, seldom visits a nightspot, is unfailing courteous to autograph hunters and fellow performers and always calls his elders 'sir'

---

[121]Quoted in Brode, *Elvis Culture*, 7.

[122]Roger Ebert, "Speedway," June 28, 1968. Published on www.rogerebert.com/reviews/speedway-1968 [last accessed December 31, 2019].

[123]Guralnick and Jorgensen, *Day by Day*, 215.

[124]Jorgensen, *A Life in Music*, 222.

[125]Ibid., 201, 227.

[126]Ibid., 208–17, 244.

and 'ma'am'."[127] If Elvis still made occasional headlines, they were usually concerned with his private life, such as his marriage to Priscilla Beaulieu in May 1967, or the birth of his daughter Lisa Marie nine months later, which both added to his increasingly conservative image.[128] But he was no longer seen as a major cultural force. To the *LA Times*, he had become a symbol of "fame of brutal dimensions; a prodigious amount of money; a success as solid as the Statue of Liberty, as unsinkable as J. Edgar Hoover."[129]

Even some of Elvis's most hardcore fans had become disillusioned by the evident stalling of Elvis's career. In 1968, two British fans who had just moved to the United States reported in *Elvis Monthly* that Elvis's popularity was "practically down to nil" there: "We listen to all the pop stations on the radio here in New York from 8 a.m. to 8 p.m. every day and if we have heard them play twenty records we have been extremely lucky. All of his films released in the past two years have had bad reviews and get second billing in the movie shows."[130] Some European fans even started a mailing campaign for a re-release of *King Creole* (1958), so that Elvis's new fans could witness the singer's 1950s persona rather than the caricature he had allegedly become since.[131] In January 1968, the British fan Gordon Minto wrote a damning piece on the singer's recent output, and closed with a heartfelt plea: "Please, Elvis, if you have any regard to your career and fans get out of this rut and establish yourself right back at the top where you really belong."[132]

It is not like Elvis did not notice the decline in his reputation. As he reflected a few years later in a rare candid interview for the *Elvis on Tour* (1972) documentary,

> I don't think anyone was trying to harm me. It's just Hollywood's image of me was wrong. I knew it and couldn't do anything about it. I had thought they would give me a chance to show my acting ability or do an interesting story, but it never changed. They couldn't have paid me no amount of money to make me feel some sort of self-satisfaction inside.[133]

To be sure, some of the final films tried to break with the worn-out formula: in *Charro* (1969), Elvis played the role of a cowboy outlaw that had originally been offered to Clint Eastwood, and he did not perform a

---

[127]*Evening Times Glasgow*, January 7, 1965.
[128]Doll, *Understanding Elvis*, 143.
[129]*Los Angeles Times*, February 18, 1968.
[130]*Elvis Monthly* 108, January 1969.
[131]They collected an impressive number of 6,608 signatures. See the several letters and files in MHL, Hal Wallis Papers, King Creole f.720.
[132]*Elvis Monthly* 96, January 1968. Minto is still a well-regarded Elvis expert today.
[133]Quoted in Paul Simpson, *Elvis Films FAQ*, xvii.

single song during the entire ninety minutes. In *Change of Habit* (1969), he was cast as a physician working in a rough Harlem ghetto who then falls in love with a nun played by Mary Tyler Moore. Like his 1966–67 recordings, however, such small adjustments in Elvis's artistic output were little noticed outside the by-now-fairly-small circle of die-hard Elvis fans. It would take much more drastic changes to reinstate Elvis as a major cultural force in the eyes of the wider public.

# Conclusions

Although usually dismissed or belittled by fans and critics alike, Elvis's 1960s movie career was instrumental in reshaping Elvis's public image as a major American pop-cultural icon. Marking a clear departure from Elvis's pre-army image as a teenage rebel, the movies transformed Elvis into an all-round American entertainer appealing to the widest possible audiences at home and abroad. They also communicated powerful, if one-dimensional, images of the United States as a country of natural beauty, everyday affluence, technological advancement, and self-fulfillment, thereby showcasing the alleged virtues of US-style capitalism and the so-called American Way of Life around the world. The Hollywood years therefore completed Elvis's transformation into a widely accepted figure of American public life, even if he was perhaps still not universally liked. At the Expo '67 at Montreal, the US pavilion even featured one of Elvis's guitars as an exhibit—perhaps the ultimate sign of Elvis's by-now-almost-complete endorsement by the US establishment.[134]

Yet, Elvis's dominance of the entertainment field was not there to stay. As exciting new performers and erstwhile Elvis admirers like The Beatles, The Rolling Stones, or Bob Dylan went into new directions to revolutionize the field of popular music yet again, Elvis rapidly declined in popularity; a decline undoubtedly intensified by the abysmal quality of some of his artistic output at the time. Yet the change in Elvis's public image also reflected bigger shifts in the political, social, and cultural landscape in 1960s America. As artists like The Beatles or Bob Dylan became key reference points for the burgeoning student and civil rights movements, the lighthearted and seemingly apolitical Elvis movies increasingly felt like historical anachronisms from a bygone era; perceptions that contributed to the more general change in Elvis's public image from an erstwhile rebel figure into a mainstream and somewhat conservative entertainer far removed from the realities of the decade.

---

[134]*Boston Globe*, April 25, 1967.

# 5

# Iconic Elvis: The 1970s Comeback

At 9:15, Elvis appeared, materialized, in a white suit of lights, shining with golden appliques, the shirt front slashed to show his chest. Around his shoulders was a cape lined in cloth of gold, its collar faced with scarlet. It was anything you wanted to call it, gaudy, vulgar, magnificent. He looked like a prince from another planet, narrow-eyed, with high Indian cheekbones and a smooth brown skin untouched by his 37 years. He was girdled by a great golden belt, a present from the International Hotel in Las Vegas for breaking all attendance records ... and when he started to work with the mike, his right hand flailing air, his left leg moving as though it had a life of its own, time stopped, and everyone in the place was 17 again ... He used the stage, he worked to the people. The ones in front, in the best seats, the ones in back, and up in the peanut galleries. He turned, he moved, and when a girl threw a handkerchief on the stage, he wiped his forehead with it and threw it back, a gift of sweat from an earthy god ... He stood there at the end, his arms stretched out, the great gold cloak giving him wings, a champion, the only one in his class.—*The New York Times*, June 18, 1972.

In the late 1960s, Elvis Presley emerged out of the ashes. Abandoning a movie career that had evidently run out of steam, he reinvented himself as a prolific recording artist and charismatic live performer. Many of the iconic images of Elvis that circulate in public memory today—flashy jumpsuits, golden capes, silver sunglasses—can be traced back to that final period of his career, as the *New York Times* review of his Madison Square Garden concert shows. Between 1969 and 1977, Elvis sold out 646 Las Vegas shows, as well as several engagements at Lake Tahoe and around 200 on-tour appearances all around the United States. It was also during this period that he achieved some of his biggest hit records, including "In the Ghetto" and "Suspicious Minds." The comeback was crucial in securing Elvis's status as American's biggest pop-cultural icon of the twentieth century, elevating him into a larger-than-life figure in the public eye. On January 14, 1973, his superstardom found its ultimate expression in the megalomaniac *Aloha From Hawaii* concert, which was broadcasted live via satellite from Honolulu to a worldwide audience purported to be around one billion at the time.[1]

The comeback was in itself an important event that shaped Elvis's public image; but it also led to a profound reconfiguration of his 1950s legacy. In spite of Elvis's attempts to reinvent himself as a contemporary artist, audiences and critics alike tended to perceive him through lenses of the past. Coinciding with the bigger rock revival in the late 1960s, Elvis's reception became inextricably interwoven with popular (and often highly idealized) reconstructions of the 1950s. As the decade's prime pop-cultural symbol, Elvis's public image became a key reference point through which bigger questions of US history and identity were renegotiated by his fans and critics alike. At a time of economic uncertainty and political upheaval, Elvis was seen to embody the very incarnation of an idealized, bygone era of alleged prosperity and innocence that many Americans were desperate to recapture. The 1970s thus played a crucial role in the canonization of Elvis Presley, and in so doing reshaped his 1950s legacy profoundly: whereas the young Elvis had seemingly emerged as a threat to the social, racial, and moral order of the times, he now seemed to have embodied almost the contrary.

Yet, the 1970s are also at the heart of many unflattering clichés and stereotypes associated with Elvis today. As the decade went on, Elvis's struggles with his private life, health problems, and a growing dependence on prescription drugs all started to take a toll on him. By the mid-1970s, his concerts had become sloppy, his recording sessions sporadic, and rumors about his health and weight problems had begun to circulate widely in the media. The public perceptions of Elvis's concerts also changed markedly: whereas his comeback had been received enthusiastically, they were now depicted as having dissolved into a mere personality cult surrounded by unabashed commercialism. At a time of widespread talk about US decline, many observers thus came to depict Elvis as a prime victim of the country's consumerist ideology—impressions seemingly vindicated by his tragic death on August 16, 1977. It is impossible to understand Elvis without taking the 1970s into account.

---

[1] The actual number of viewers, of course, was much lower, as will be discussed in later parts of the chapter.

# Resurrecting Elvis: The 1968 Comeback

The first time the wider American public took note of Elvis Presley again after his lengthy movie hiatus was through the NBC television special *Singer Presents Elvis* … on December 3, 1968. Most viewers probably expected an hour of mellow Christmas entertainment, but what they saw had little to do with the upcoming holiday: a slim, sun-tanned Elvis belted out old hits like "Hound Dog" or "Jailhouse Rock," wearing a custom-made full-body leather suit while sweating and gyrating in front of a small, intimate audience. The television special also featured an informal jam session with his old band mates Scotty Moore and D.J. Fontana, as well as two elaborate production numbers that put Elvis in a larger trajectory of American popular music. The show's climax was the song "If I Can Dream," which had been especially written for the TV special and constituted a surprisingly political statement by Elvis's standards, with lyrics about peace and brotherhood that loosely echoed Martin Luther King. For the finale, Elvis performed it in an all-white suit, standing in front of a gigantic "ELVIS" sign made out of red lightbulbs.[2] It was a game-changer that signified nothing less than the resurrection of Elvis's image almost overnight. It reached a 42 percent market share, thereby becoming NBC's most successful program of the year; the accompanying single "If I Can Dream" climbed to number 12 in the charts, which constituted became Elvis's biggest musical success since 1965.[3]

Although Elvis's return to US television screens after an eight-year absence had caught most viewers by surprise, the origins of the special can be traced back over a year. Confronted with the fact that Elvis's movie career had slowly but surely run out of steam, Colonel Parker had sounded out the possibilities of an Elvis television appearance with NBC President David Sarnoff as early as October 1967. They ultimately agreed to a package deal: $250,000 for the special, tied to a one-off $850,000 movie contract for a NBC co-production with Universal Pictures.[4] While Parker had originally envisaged a conventional Christmas special, the choice of producer Bob Finkel and director Steve Binder triggered a change in artistic direction. Binder in particular was determined to reinstate Elvis as a serious artist in the public imagination, having earned praise for his previous productions of the innovative *Hullabaloo* music television series and the *T.A.M.I. Show* concert documentary.[5] "I felt very, very strongly that the television special was Elvis's moment of truth," he reflected a few years later;

---

[2]Duffett, *Counting Down Elvis*, 218–23; Guralnick, *Careless Love*, 323.
[3]Ibid. For general accounts of the special, see Steve Binder, *Comeback '68/Elvis: The Story of the Elvis Special* (Los Angeles, CA: Meteor 17 Books, 2018); Wiener, *Channeling Elvis*, 131–82; Guralnick, *Careless Love*, 293–317.
[4]Nash, *The Colonel*, 232.
[5]Guralnick, *Careless Love*, 294.

**Figure 5.1** *Elvis performing on the Elvis comeback TV special on June 27, 1968 in Burbank, California*

If he did another M-G-M movie on the special, he would wipe out his career and he would be known only as that phenomenon who came along in the fifties, shook his hips and had a great manager. On the reverse side, if he could do a special and prove he was still number one, he could have a whole rejuvenation thing going.[6]

Significantly, Elvis played along. His personal frustration with the movies had by that stage become evident to everybody, and he told Finkel early on how he wanted the special to be different from anything he had done

---

[6]Quoted in Hopkins, *Elvis*, 335.

before.[7] Binder, who initially could not have cared less about Elvis, was impressed by the singer's honesty and thus decided to turn the special into an homage to Elvis's musical roots and contributions to American culture. He was also determined to give the public a rare glimpse of Elvis's personality. During the rehearsals, he had witnessed Elvis's emotional reaction to the assassination of Robert Kennedy, after which he had spent the entire evening talking about conspiracies and how ashamed he was that Martin Luther King's assassination had taken place in his hometown Memphis two months earlier.[8] As Binder later reflected, "I wanted to let the world know that here was a guy who was not prejudiced, who was raised in the heart of prejudice, but who was really above all that."[9] The closing of the show with "If I Can Dream" served exactly that purpose, in effect taking Elvis full circle from his 1950s roots to the present day.[10]

The fusion of old and new was at the heart of the special's content; but it also shaped its receptions by fans and critics alike. While many reviewers applauded Elvis's musical prowess, they almost inevitably compared his performance to his 1950s legacy. Robert Shelton at the New York Times, for example, thought that "Mr. Presley still knows more about basic rock than most inheritors of his style," and the countercultural music magazine The Great Speckled Bird even declared Elvis to be the "big daddy of rock and roll."[11] Many of Elvis's fans too perceived the special primarily through lenses of the past. One fan who had actually been in the audience told Elvis Monthly readers that Elvis had performed "Heartbreak Hotel" "in the early 1956 style, Baby," and that he had "lost none of the early zing that rock this old world wild-eyed"; another one agreed that "Elvis looked exactly as he looked some 12 year ago ... in fact I found it hard to believe it wasn't a film of an earlier stage performance back in 1956."[12] Some fans also reminisced about their own experiences back in the 1950s. A few months later, one of them recalled his thoughts while watching the special:

I'm a kid. I must be. No, no, they are running "Jailhouse Rock" on Tuesday Night at the movies ... My head reels. Black leather, old guitar, 1956. Has someone really discovered the fountain of youth? No, there are no Beatles, and Bob Dylan is Robert Zimmerman. He's watching too, out there in the gulf of the Mid-West. No, it's almost 1969. But I know Dylan is watching, for one hour I know what Dylan is doing ... I curse the darkness for the loss of Alan Freed, and thank whatever god there may be for Elvis Presley. Still THE KING.[13]

---

[7]Wiener, Channeling Elvis, 133–4.
[8]Guralnick, Careless Love, 297.
[9]Quoted in ibid., 298.
[10]Wiener, Chaneling Elvis, 167.
[11]New York Times, December 4, 1968; The Great Speckled Bird, December 13, 1968.
[12]Elvis Monthly, 107, November 1968; Elvis Monthly 109, January 1969.
[13]Elvis Monthly 114, July 1969.

The response to the television special was not unanimously positive, however. In spite of the mythology that came to surround it almost immediately, there were several voices who regarded it as a largely unsuccessful attempt to recapture bygone glories, and often took it as a cue to reflect over the wider changes that had swept the landscape of popular culture since the 1950s. The *Boston Globe*, for example, claimed that the special had ultimately proven that "[y]ou never can go back" in time, and the *Washington Post*'s Lawrence Laurent, who had written some contemptuous columns on Elvis in the 1950s, now looked back almost nostalgically on the singer's past.[14] "Nothing indicates the changing morality of the times better than an appearance on television of someone who was controversial a decade earlier," he wrote; "The pelvis swinging that once caused mothers to worry about teen-aged daughters was quite tame. And where once the pompadour and sideburns were symbols of wickedness, Elvis now looks like a barber's best friend."[15] Such nostalgic reminiscences fitted the wider cultural climate of the times.

# Reinventing Elvis: The 1970s Nostalgia Wave

"The Good Old Days: Our Growing Love For Yesterday," a headline in the *Chicago Tribune* claimed on November 8, 1970. The article went on to describe how the "Soaring Sixties" had made way for the "Secondhand Seventies ... The midi is back, and the Gibson Girl hairdos. And Elvis Presley is breaking his own records in Las Vegas and on one-night concert tours." Why was it now "more than at any other time in our country's history," it asked, that Americans were "more concerned with moving backward than with moving ahead?"[16]

The *Chicago Tribune* was not the only one asking such questions at the time. From the late 1960s onward, the onset of what was soon called the "nostalgia wave" became hotly debated in major newspapers and magazines.[17] Historically, "nostalgia" has been used as a mainly medical term to describe feelings of homesickness; it was only in the early 1970s that its meaning changed to denote a sentimental yearning for the past.[18] At the time, commentators tried to explain the phenomenon as a reaction against the political radicalism and social permissiveness of the 1960s, or as

---

[14]*Boston Globe*, December 4, 1968.
[15]*Washington Post*, December 5, 1968.
[16]*Chicago Tribune*, November 8, 1970.
[17]*Life Magazine*, February 19, 1971 and June 16, 1972; *Time*, May 3, 1971; *Newsweek*, December 29, 1970.
[18]For the semantic shifts and the emergence of nostalgia in the 1970s, see in particular Tobias Becker, "The Meanings of Nostalgia: Genealogy and Critique," *History and Theory* 57/2 (2018), 234–50.

a sort of escapism from the political and economic woes of the early 1970s, whereas historians now tend to interpret the phenomenon as part of a more general self-referential cycle always inherent in popular culture.[19]

Indeed, the 1970s nostalgia wave centered first and foremost on 1950s pop culture, rather than on the decade's political divisiveness. Popular reconstructions portrayed the 1950s as a highly idealized age of affluence, prosperity, innocence, and teenage fun.[20] Such renewed interest in the 1950s was driven not only by an older generation clinging onto the memories of their youth, but also by a new generation of teenagers and young adults. As *Life* magazine put it, "Kids barely old enough to remember what a fallout shelter was are digging the hand jive and the Bunny Hop, circle skirts and cinch belts, penny loafers, saddle shoes, white books and shirts with cigarette packs tucked into rolled-up sleeves."[21] Petticoats, leather jackets, and ducktails were back in vogue, former rock 'n' roll stars like Chuck Berry or Bill Haley suddenly became popular again, and the doo-wop group Sha Na Na celebrated massive successes with cover versions of 1950s hits.[22] In February 1972, the musical *Grease* started its hugely successful seven-year Broadway run; in 1973, *American Graffiti* was released with a soundtrack full of 1950s rock 'n' roll classics; and in January 1974, ABC aired the first of what would become a total of 255 episodes of the sitcom *Happy Days*. The "nostalgia wave" therefore served to resurrect the 1950s as a central epoch in the public memory, and in so doing turned it into an important reference point for constructions of American identities.[23]

Elvis Presley was anything but a nostalgia act. Whereas former rock 'n' roll stars like Bill Haley or Chuck Berry merely recycled their old hits, Elvis set out to completely redefine himself as a contemporary artist.[24] The first manifestation of Elvis's ambitions can be detected in his music. In January and February 1969, Elvis completed extensive recording sessions at the American Sound Studios in Memphis, a trendy venue where owner Chips Moman had recently produced hits for artists like Dusty Springfield, Dionne Warwick, and the Box Tops.[25] The recordings that came out of the session were testimony to a new and much more mature sound, including

---

[19]Ibid.; Tobias Becker, "Rückkehr der Geschichte? Die „Nostalgie-Welle" in den 1970er und 1980er Jahren," in Fernando Esposito (ed.), *Zeitenwandel: Transformationen geschichtlicher Zeitlichkeit nach dem Boom* (Göttingen: Vandenhoeck & Ruprecht, 2017), 93–117.

[21]*Life Magazine*, June 16, 1972.

[22]Marcus, *Happy Days*, 13–14.

[20]Daniel Marcus, *Happy Days and Wonder Years: The Fifties and the Sixties in Contemporary Cultural Politics* (New Brunswick, NJ: Rutgers University Press, 2004), 9–35; Michael D. Dwyer, *Back to the Fifties: Nostalgia, Hollywood Film, and Popular Music of the Seventies and Eighties* (New York, NY: Oxford University Press, 2015).

[23]Dwyer, *Back to the Fifties*, 5.

[24]Although Chuck Berry did score an original number one hit with *"My Ding-a-Ling"* in 1972.

[25]Guralnick, *Careless Love*, 328.

raunchy reinterpretations of country songs like "Long Black Limousine" or "After Loving You" as well as blues numbers like "I'll Hold You in My Heart" or "Stranger in My Own Home Town." Elvis's new style matched the rediscovery of early country and roots rock by groups like Creedence Clearwater Revival that was taking place at the same time, and it was commercially successful as well: "In the Ghetto," a socially critical song that Elvis had been warned against recording by his manager and friends because of its political lyrics, sold more than a million copies and peaked at number three in the *Billboard* charts; the follow-up single "Suspicious Minds" became Elvis's first number one hit in the United States since 1962.[26]

Even more important for Elvis's artistic rejuvenation was his abandonment of Hollywood and return to live performances. Immediately after the airing of the 1968 television special, the *New York Times* reported that Elvis was planning a return to live performances.[27] The decision first and foremost reflected Elvis's personal wishes, who had told Colonel Parker that he would like to perform live again immediately after the taping of the final television special concert, but it also made commercial sense:[28] not only were there no attractive new movie contracts in sight, but megalomaniac live shows were also becoming the next big thing in the music, and it was clearly where most money could be made.[29] As Parker's sidekick Tom Diskin told the *New York Times*, it took Elvis fifteen weeks to make a movie, and if he appeared "for 10 weeks, one concert a week, at $100,000 each" he could "do much better."[30]

On July 31, 1969, Elvis Presley took the stage at the 2,000-seat showroom at the International Hotel in Las Vegas. Built by the billionaire Kirk Kerkorian for $60 million, the International Hotel constituted the by far biggest Vegas hotel resort at the time, and with its thirty floors and 1,512 rooms seemed an exercise in pure megalomania.[31] The terms of Elvis's engagement too were record-breaking. Between July 31 and August 28, 1969, Elvis performed a total of fifty-seven concerts with two shows a night, drawing a total audience of 101,500 people with gross ticket receipts around $1.5 million.[32] It was a hugely successful engagement that not only set the path for the transformation of Las Vegas entertainment away from fairly intimate night-club venues to lavish mega-star residencies, but that also served to attract a new, middle-America family crowd to a city previously known mainly for adult entertainment. In due course, Elvis thus became part of the city's rejuvenation, and Las Vegas in turn a crucial part of the myth surrounding Elvis's own resurrection.[33]

[26]Ibid., 331–2.
[27]*New York Times*, December 4, 1968.
[28]Guralnick, *Careless Love*, 317.
[29]Weinstein, *Rock'n America*, 129–30.
[30]*New York Times*, December 4, 1968.
[31]Guralnick, *Careless Love*, 325.
[32]Zoglin, *Elvis in Vegas*, 215.
[33]Ibid., 18–19.

If the decision to set the comeback in Las Vegas had astounded observers given the city's image of raunchy nightclub entertainment,[34] Elvis's shows too went completely against the grain of established Vegas routines. Elvis was determined to create a new musical identity for himself. As he told his friend Charlie Hodge at the time, his ambition was nothing less than to showcase "the full spectrum of American music ... everything that he had ever admired in music," and he went at great lengths to achieve it.[35] He put together a new band that, among others, featured lead guitarist James Burton and bassist Jerry Scheff, who at the time also recorded with The Doors and Bob Dylan. Many band members were surprised by Elvis's musical prowess. "I didn't think I wanted to play watered-down white rockabilly music," Scheff later reflected on his audition; "I was expecting some vanilla approximation of the blues, but when James [Burton] started with a low, growly blues-guitar riff I began to realize that this was not going to be a rehash of 50s rockabilly."[36] The band was backed up by two gospel groups and a showroom orchestra, and while the setlists always included plenty of Elvis's old hits, they also featured lots of his new material and contemporary songs by Del Shannon, Neil Diamond, or Simon & Garfunkel. Elvis's former producer Sam Phillips, who was present at the opening night on the personal invitation of Elvis, afterward described the sound as "some raunchy-ass shit," and declared that he had "never heard a better rhythm section in [his] life."[37]

Yet there was a striking discrepancy between the content of Elvis's show and the way it was perceived by critics and the wider public. Whatever the novelty in Elvis's act, many reviewers portrayed it overwhelmingly through lenses of the past. "At a time when pop is infused with nostalgia," Richard Goldstein wrote in the *New York Times*, "what better way to summon up the immediate past than by resurrecting its most genuine artefact. A white boy with black hips ... It was enough to watch him move: that hip action still powerful, not because it was obscene but because it seemed so innocent, so traditional."[38] *Newsweek* too described how the crowd "roared and squealed in nostalgic appreciation" as they observed him "shaking, gyrating and quivering ... oozing the sullen sexuality that threw America into a state of shock in the 50's," and the music magazine *Billboard* claimed that Elvis's crowd "found itself reliving the 1950's when Elvis was king of rock and soul was something on a shoe."[39] In February 1970, David Dalton, one of the founding editors of *Rolling Stone* magazine, wrote a particularly poignant feature on "Elvis doing his imitation Elvis" at his second Las Vegas engagement:

---

[34]Ibid., 16–17.
[35]Quoted in Guralnick, *Careless Love*, 343–4.
[36]Jerry Scheff, *Way Down: Playing Bass with Elvis, Dylan, the Doors, and More* (Milwaukee, WI: Backbeat Books, 2012), 14.
[37]Guralnick, *Sam Phillips*, 489–90.
[38]*New York Times*, August 10, 1969.
[39]*Newsweek*, August 11, 1969; *Billboard*, August 16, 1969.

Figure 5.2 *Elvis on stage at the International Hotel in Las Vegas, August 1970*

He is very good at it; he looks like he's been rehearsing the part for 13 years ... Elvis singing "All Shook Up" is a put-on too, of course, but it's a serious put-on; he's putting on a whole era, he's putting on the '50s. He's the medium and this ritual is so drenched in memory, time and remoteness that his act is a violent manipulation of the audience's heads. The memory floats back to the first time everyone heard "Hound Dog" and the details of that day, that afternoon, come flashing up like a rainy windshield. And Elvis is the man who knocked out a whole generation, a whole civilization. See, in this corner there was Ike "Nukeler" Eisenhower, and over in that corner was Elvis the Pelvis. Man, it was a massacre.[40]

---

[40]*Rolling Stone*, February 21, 1970.

Dalton's description provides a vivid example of the delicate relationship between Elvis and 1960s counterculture. While the comeback resurrected Elvis as a major pioneer and key icon of rock music, he remained curiously anchored in an altogether different era—it is important to recall that roughly 400,000 people gathered at Woodstock the very month that Elvis was conquering the stage in Las Vegas. The tensions between rock's imagined past and present became also evident in the way Dalton reacted to the somewhat bizarre settings of the International Hotel. "Presiding over the gigantic dining room and its 2,000 paying guests are a giant 20-foot pair of *papier maché* statues representing Marie Antoinette and Louis XIV, holding a lace handkerchief the size of a tablecloth," he described the scenery afterward; "from the ceiling hang a pair of gargantuan cherubs exchanging a length of cream satin material. Above the stage there's a dumpy coat of arms, strictly from Walt Disney. Funky."[41] Elvis's audience too hardly resembled typical *Rolling Stone* readers; they were "super-straight, mostly middle-aged people with children and affluent old Elvis fans in their late thirties, their ducktails trimmed into neat executive crewcuts, their leather jackets turned in for seersucker suits. The silicone couples in their After-Six tuxedos and dynel wigs would not admit it but what they were paying $15 a plate for is a Resurrection. They have embalmed him like the queen bee – with love, money, energy, and in return he performs the precious ritual."[42]

For Elvis's fans, of course, it was an altogether different experience. The International Hotel almost seemed to resemble an Elvis festival at times, becoming a major meeting point for Elvis fans from all around the world who often stayed for entire weeks. At the time, it was estimated that around 10 percent of Elvis's Vegas audiences were fan club members.[43] Yet, even for some of the most loyal fans, the experience of seeing Elvis on stage resembled a trip to their past. "For thirteen years I had waited for the chance just to get a glimpse of this dynamic performer," one of them wrote in *Elvis Monthly*; "he looked like the Elvis of '57 only much more slick and very much more mature … The movements are still there and the excitement projected by this colossal phenomenon called Elvis is unbelievable until you have witnessed it."[44] Memphis superfan Gary Pepper, who attended the August 7, 1969, dinner show, reflected afterward how Elvis had not only "recapture[d] his old fans who grew up with him with these performances," but had also "been able to show the fans who were only six or seven years old in 1956 what he was really like when he first started his career … Believe me, it really brought back memories of yesteryear."[45]

---

[41]Ibid.
[42]Ibid.
[43]Zoglin, *Elvis in Vegas*, 216.
[44]*Elvis Monthly* 117, October 1969.
[45]*Elvis Monthly* 118, November 1969.

The experience of an Elvis concert on tour was rather different. In marked contrast to the prolonged Vegas residencies, Elvis's shows often constituted major local events, since they were often the very first time that Elvis had set foot in a particular city or town. In February 1970, Elvis tested the waters with a one-off gig at the Houston Astrodome; it was followed by two major tours in September (Phoenix, St Louis, Detroit, Miami, Tampa, and Mobile) and November (Oakland, Portland, Seattle, San Francisco, Los Angeles, San Diego, Oklahoma City, and Denver) the same year. At a time where megalomaniac arena shows were becoming the norm, Elvis was at the very top of the game, and his tours were organized by a highly professional entertainment machine. In November 1970, he broke the Rolling Stones' attendance record at the L.A. Inglewood Forum with a gross of $313,000; in 1972, he was the first artist to sell out four consecutive shows at New York's Madison Square Garden.[46]

In the bigger coastal cities in particular, Elvis attracted not only the usual hordes of fans, but also many spectators who were simply curious to see the Elvis phenomenon in person, and people of all age groups tended to flock into Elvis's shows.[47] At the Inglewood Forum, the LA Times described the crowd as a fusion between "what one would find at an adult, middle America, dominated Tom Jones concert and a younger typical rock concert."[48] By contrast, the crowds tended to resemble Las Vegas audiences more closely in more remote areas. Reviewing a November 1971 concert in Tuscaloosa, Alabama, for example, the music magazine Great Speckled Bird thought it to be "a strange mixture of people" with a "good percentage of young people, but mostly older folks"; in Tampa, Florida, people apparently looked "as though they had dressed for a church social or a state fair."[49]

The demographic of Elvis's audiences added to the general sense of nostalgia that often hung over the 1970s tours. "The teen-agers of the 1950s are today's pushing-40 adults," the Arizona Republic reflected in October 1970. "They sat on comfortable chairs in the refrigerated Coliseum in contrast to the 1956 outdoors show on a hot, dusty night. The women streamed into the coliseum in miniskirts, pants suits, dark hosiery, high heels, plunging necklines ... Their men walked beside them wearing ties, white shirts, dress trousers and sport coats."[50] For a journalist covering Elvis's appearance in Detroit, "[o]ne of the strangest things about the audience was the parents of 25-year-old people sitting there, whether they liked it or not. I guess it was, once again, the 'in' thing to do. Anyway, 10 or 15 years ago

[46]Los Angeles Times, November 16, 1970; Nash, The Colonel, 274.
[47]San Diego Evening Tribune, November 16, 1970.
[48]Los Angeles Times, November 16, 1970.
[49]Great Speckled Bird, November 4, 1971; St. Petersburg Times, September 14, 1970.
[50]Arizona Republic, October 18, 1970.

these same parents were refusing to allow their children to go and hear 'that crazy, obscene, dirty rock 'n roll singer.' Now the children were too busy to go and the parents couldn't be kept away."[51]

Many people who flocked Elvis's concerts in the early 1970s were as interested in the myth as in the performer. "For me, up until Friday night there was a legend centering around a man named Elvis Presley," the music journalist Mike Gormley reflected in the *Detroit Free Press*; "When Elvis appeared off at stage-left wearing a white jump suit, orange scarf and jet black hair, two things happened to me. I immediately thought 'Don't say, don't say it'. The second thing that happened was — I said it. 'There he is. There he is.' The legend had become flesh and appeared before us."[52] Gormley's experience seems to have mirrored the experience of many others at the time. In St. Louis, MO, the local press claimed that the fans had cheered "for the myth, if not the man"; in San Francisco, the *Stanford Daily* mused that the 15,000-strong crowd "hadn't paid to hear music" but to witness a "figure from their past [that] had returned and dared them to ride with him just one more time."[53] Even the *New York Times* could not resist embedding its review of Elvis's 1972 Madison Square Garden appearance in a wider cultural panorama of the 1950s:

> In Pepsi-drinking Elvis' heyday, the world was more innocent, or people were more willing to pretend it was. On the Ed Sullivan show, they used to shoot Elvis from the waist up, so the grinding of his hips wouldn't drive little girls wild, and mothers bemoaned their daughters' infatuation. Almost 20 years later, those daughters brought their own teen-agers to hear the man whose appeal bridges a generation gap.[54]

Elvis's comeback, then, constituted a highly successful, if somewhat uneasy, fusion between old and new. Although Elvis went at great lengths to reinvent himself as a contemporary artist and performer, his reception remained inexorably bound up with his past. As part of an already ongoing 1950s revival, Elvis re-emerged as the quintessential icon of a bygone era, enabling his audiences to project and occasionally re-live their seemingly distant and often highly idealized memories of the decade. Such nostalgia-infused projections paved the way for Elvis's subsequent public canonization, and transfiguration into a figure through which even bigger questions of American identity could be negotiated.

[51]*Detroit Free Press*, September 15, 1970.
[52]Ibid.
[53]*St. Louis Post-Dispatch*, September 11, 1970; *Stanford Daily*, November 18, 1970.
[54]*New York Times*, June 18, 1972.

# Rediscovering Elvis: The Canonization of an American Icon

On the eve of the 1970s, Elvis Presley was back at the very top of the game, scoring hit records and breaking records with extensive hotel and on-tour engagements. Given such phenomenal success, Elvis's management started to consciously foster his status as a larger-than-life public figure. Superstardom, rather than the singer's music or performances, increasingly became the center of his image. In the early 1970s, two full-length movies documented the cult that surrounded Elvis's performances at the time. In 1970, MGM's *That's the Way It Is* documented Elvis's August 1970 Las Vegas engagement, featuring not only Elvis's concerts but also numerous shots of giant Elvis posters and wallpapers, as well as of several fans confessing their love of Elvis. It was as much a documentary as it was an exercise in myth-making. "Nothing is explained; the dynamics of the cult phenomenon remain as much a mystery as ever," one reviewer reflected. "But it's there for our examination; and when the subject is as extraordinary a show-business personality as Mr. Presley, there is much to observe and contemplate."[55] In 1972, *Elvis on Tour* (also MGM) offered an even more powerful example of the iconography around Elvis: it featured countless close-ups of Elvis in rhinestone-studded jumpsuits and wearing luxurious jewelry, as well as numerous shots of screaming fans and Elvis boarding a private jet. Some historic footage of his 1950s television appearances and soundbites of Elvis looking back on his career completed the picture of eternal fame and celebrityhood. The trailer advertised it as "an unprecedented invitation to the past and present of the ultimate popular hero."[56]

Elvis's transformation into such a mythical public figure not only fitted a more general trend toward the megalomaniac in the early 1970s entertainment industry; it was also helped by the fact that Elvis himself did not shy away from self-aggrandizement either. During his concerts, he started to wear increasingly opulent jumpsuits and spent a lot of time handing out sweaty scarves to fans and kissing some of the girls in the front rows. In July 1971, he first entered the stage to the dramatic sounds of "Also Sprach Zarathustra," which became a regular feature of his shows; he usually finished them on his knees, at times with a cape stretched out like a superhero. It somewhat mirrored Elvis's self-elevation off-stage. When he received a Jaycee award as one of the "Ten Outstanding Young Men of the Nation" in January 1971, he transfigured his life-story as the quintessential American Dream story in a self-written acceptance speech:

---

[55]*The Christian Science Monitor*, November 16, 1970.
[56]MGM, "Elvis on Tour—Trailer." It can also be watched on YouTube: www.youtube.com/watch?v=4G1zC_l0-xA [last accessed May 2, 2020].

When I was a child, ladies and gentlemen, I was a dreamer. I read comic books, and I was the hero of the comic book. I saw movies, and I was the hero in the movie. So every dream I ever dreamed has come true a hundred times.[57]

By that time, Elvis's shows had not only become much more bombastic, but they had also come to reflect his personal patriotism, a process that perhaps linked to the more general rise of grassroots conservatism in the 1970s United States.[58] Although Elvis had always tried to keep his personal views out of the public ("Honey, I'd just sooner keep my own personal views about that to myself cause I'm just an entertainer and I'd rather not say," he replied to a question about war protesters at a press conference in 1972), the concerts now regularly featured allusion to bigger notions of American identity.[59] His jumpsuits, for example, often featured symbols like the American eagle or occasional Native American and Aztec influences. From January 1972, Elvis regularly included Mickey Newbury's "An American Trilogy" as a dramatic showstopper, a medley of "Dixie," "The Battle Hymn of the Republic," and "All My Trials." While such a pairing of Civil War hymns with an African American spiritual that had been popularized by the 1960s folk movement might well have been intended as a partly critical or ironic statement by Newbury, Elvis's version was sincere, heartfelt, and deeply patriotic.[60]

Elvis's self-stylization into a popular American folk hero fitted neatly into some of the bigger narratives that were constructed around him at the time. Whereas Elvis had commonly been belittled or dismissed by the establishment during the 1950s and much of the 1960s, the 1970s comeback led to the first serious investigations of Elvis's music, as well of his bigger historical and cultural importance. It mirrored the more general canonization of rock music since the late 1960s, which found its expression not least in the founding of specialized music journals like the *Great Speckled Bird* or the *Rolling Stone*. It was also a *Rolling Stone* writer who wrote the first serious biography of Elvis: in 1971, Jerry Hopkins published *Elvis*, a fairly

---

[57]Guralnick and Jorgensen, *Day by Day*, 290–1. An excellent summary of the award ceremony is provided by David English and David Troedson, "Elvis Presley | U.S. Jaycees | Ten Outstanding Young Men 1970," www.elvispresleyphotos.com/1971-january-16-jaycees-award.html [last accessed January 21, 2020].
[58]Bruce J. Schulman and Julian E. Zelizer (eds.), *Rightward Bound: Making America Conservative in the 1970s* (Cambridge, MA: Harvard University Press, 2008); Anna von der Goltz and Britta Waldschmidt-Nelson (eds.), *Inventing the Silent Majority in Western Europe and the United States: Conservatism in the 1960s and 1970s* (Cambridge: Cambridge University Press, 2017).
[59]"Transcript of Elvis' 1972 Madison Square Garden Press Conference, June 9, 1972", www. elvis.com.au/presley/interview-with-elvis-presley-the-1972-press-conference.shtml [last accessed August 25, 2019].
[60]Duffett, *Counting Down*, 216–18.

factual 450-page account based largely on interviews that became the main reference work on Elvis for several decades.[61] Interestingly, Hopkins had been inspired to write the Elvis biography by Jim Morrison, the front man of The Doors—which again shows Elvis's complex relationship with 1960s counterculture.

During the mid-1970s, Hopkins's biography was complemented by several other writings that endowed Elvis with a new cultural credibility by fitting him into the wider trajectories of popular music and even bigger narratives of American identity.[62] In *Mystery Train* (1975), for example, the music writer Greil Marcus depicted Elvis as a "supreme figure in American life, one whose presence, no matter how banal or predictable, brooks no real comparisons."[63] According to Marcus, Elvis's rise signified a "classically American (poor country boy makes good in the city)" story that illustrates powerful notions individual liberty and democratic egalitarianism allegedly inherent in US popular culture.[64] Around the same time, the music journalist Peter Guralnick followed similar lines, depicting Elvis's life as the quintessential American Dream based on Elvis's musical talent and "ferocious determination to escape the mold that had seemingly been set for him at birth."[65]

Both writings constitute powerful examples of how many of the myths and legacies surrounding Elvis today were already forged during his lifetime. Yet they also reflect a certain cultural pessimism that was prevalent in much of mid-1970s rock music writing. Marcus, for example, claimed that Elvis's contemporary performances, with his "superman cape and covered with jewels no one can be sure are fake," were illustrative of an "all-but-complete assimilation of a revolutionary musical style into the mainstream of American culture"; Guralnick too suggested that Elvis had ultimately been "converted to product" and "become part of the fabric of corporate America."[66] Both writings thus used Elvis as an articulation point for bigger projections of American identity, but such projections could have negative as well as positive connotations.

Yet the 1970s were not only a decade of public nostalgia and cultural pessimism, but also one of vibrancy, eccentricity, and renewal. Interestingly, many of the decade's most flamboyant stars can again be tracked back to Elvis. David Bowie, for example, had always been an avid Elvis fan with an almost encyclopedic knowledge of the singer: his first performance at the

---

[61]Hopkins, *Elvis.*

[62]Marcus, *Mystery Train*; Guralnick, *Lost Highway*, 118–40. The Guralnick chapter is a reprint of an article that originally appeared in 1976.

[63]Marcus, *Mystery Train*, 137.

[64]Ibid., 147.

[65]Guralnick, *Lost Highway*, 120.

[66]Marcus, *Mystery Train*, 139–40; Guralnick, *Lost Highway*, 4, 132.

age of eleven had been an Elvis impersonation at a Boy Scouts event, and his own music and performances were frequently infused with manifold Elvis references like the lightning bolt logo on the cover of *Aladdin Sane*, the song "Golden Years," or indeed the very title of his final album.[67] In June 1972, Bowie even flew to New York between two of his own UK shows to attend one of Elvis's Madison Square Garden appearances in full Ziggy Stardust outfit.[68] Numerous other glam rock artists also drew heavily on rock 'n' roll legacies, as well as perhaps on Elvis's flashy looks at the time. Rather than seeing Elvis's mid-1970s public persona as a culture that had reached its dead end, then, it might also have reflected the confused public and cultural mood of the mid-1970s United States.

## Elvis and the "Me Decade"

In August 1976, Tom Wolfe published his famous essay "The 'Me' Decade and the Third Great Awakening" in the *New York Magazine*. Depicting contemporary US society as one driven by radical self-fulfillment, vanity, and narcissism, Wolfe declared the 1970s to be "the greatest age of individualism in American history."[69] At the heart of such unrestrained individualism, however, often stood uncertainty, anxiety, and fear.[70] Politically, the assassinations of Robert Kennedy and Martin Luther King had exposed the country's bitter internal divisions, just as the Watergate scandal had evaporated trust in its political institutions. Economically too, millions of Americans were struggling with rising living costs, falling wages, and unemployment, the result of the multiple crises triggered by the oil shock and more general processes of deindustrialization.[71] As a result,

---

[67]The lightning bolt reflected Elvis's self-designed "Taking Care of Business" logo that Elvis often had engraved in jewelry for his partners and friends; *Golden Years* was allegedly written for Elvis; and the album title "Blackstar" might have been an allusion to Elvis's song "Black Star" that deals with cultural signs of impending death. Elvis recorded "Black Star," but the title and lyrics were eventually changed to "Flaming Star." See Jones, *Bowie*, 237–8; David Buckley, *Strange Fascination—David Bowie: The Definitive Story* (London: Virgin, 2005), 236–7; *The Guardian*, January 21, 2016.

[68]See Bowie's own recollection in *New York Mag*, September 18, 2003, http://nymag.com/nymetro/arts/music/features/music2003/n_9252/ [last accessed May 16, 2019].

[69]*New York Magazine*, August 23, 1976.

[70]Bruce J. Schulman, T*he Seventies: The Great Shift in American Culture, Society, and Politics* (New York: The Free Press, 2001), xv; Thomas W. Zeiler, "Historical Setting: The Age of Fear, Uncertainty, and Doubt," in Hallvard Notaker, Giles Scott-Smith and David J. Snyder (eds.), *Reasserting America in the 1970s: U.S. Public Diplomacy and the Rebuilding of America's Image Abroad* (Manchester: University Press, 2016), 9–24.

[71]Schulman, *The Seventies*; Beth Bailey and David Farber (eds.), *America in the Seventies* (Lawrence, Kansas: University Press of Kansas, 2004); Niall Ferguson et al. (eds.), *The Shock of the Global: The 1970s in Perspective* (Cambridge, MA and London: Harvard University Press, 2010).

the 1970s have since often been depicted as a period of widespread soul-searching; a time in which identities were renegotiated and reconfigured in the public discourse as well as in private life. It was against this wider cultural background of solipsism and dislocation that Elvis Presley too slowly seemed to lose his way.

First signs of Elvis's increasingly erratic behavior came in his private life. Although he had always led a highly eccentric lifestyle, things began to spiral out of control in the final months of 1970. Not for the first time, he went on a massive spending spree: he impulsively purchased countless Mercedeses, self-designed jewelry for his inner circle, and even entire houses for close friends or himself. When his father Vernon attempted to talk him out of such spending habits, Elvis tried to placate him with another Mercedes.[72] It was also during this time that Elvis's obsession with guns, police badges, and the FBI intensified considerably, perhaps in reaction to an assassination threat during his August 1970 Vegas engagement. In October 1970, Elvis managed to obtain an official deputy sheriff's badge for his Shelby home county that allowed him to legally carry a pistol; that December, he privately donated $7,000 to the Los Angeles Police community relations program and then spent $20,000 on guns and gun-related equipment at Kerr's Sporting Goods for himself and random passers-by.[73]

The most iconic image of Elvis during this period, however, goes back to his famous White House Meeting with President Nixon in December 1970.[74] Its fascinating background story is worth recalling at some length. Angered by yet another attempt of his father Vernon and wife Priscilla to confront him about his spending habits, Elvis escaped Graceland and flew to Washington DC, only to turn around immediately to Los Angeles where he met his friend Jerry Schilling. It was the first time that Elvis had traveled entirely on his own in over a decade. Elvis told Schilling about his intention to get an official badge from Federal Bureau of Narcotics and Dangerous Drugs (BNDD), which his private detective John O'Grady had shown him a few months earlier. Elvis and Schilling then flew back to Washington DC together, where Elvis randomly bumped into the Californian Senator George Murphy on board. Immediately taken by Murphy's suggestion to write a personal letter to Nixon, Elvis did so on the spot, scribbling a five-page letter to the President on an American Airlines notepad. In the letter,

---

[72]Guralnick and Jorgensen, *Day by Day*, 285.

[73]Ibid., 283.

[74]Countless factual and fictional takes have been published on this meeting. The following paragraphs build primarily on the official documents of the meeting published in their entirety by the US National Archives as an online exhibit. Files can be found at https://www.archives.gov/exhibits/nixon-met-elvis/ [last accessed August 22, 2019]. For some even more colorful recollections, see Guralnick, *Careless Love*, 414–22; Schilling, *Me and a Guy Named Elvis*, 208–22; Egil Krough, *The Day Elvis Met Nixon* (Bellevue, WA: Pejama Press, 1994).

Elvis professed to be deeply worried about his country. "I have no concerns or notives [sic] other than helping the country out," he wrote, adding that he had done "an in-depth study of drug abuse and the Communist brainwashing techniques" and was therefore "right in the middle of the whole thing." Yet, he did not want any official position or publicity: "I can and will do more good if I were made a Federal Agent at Large and I will help out by doing it my way through my communications with people of all ages. First and foremost, I am an entertainer, but all I need is the Federal credentials."[75] Elvis personally delivered the letter at the White House front gates right after landing around 6.30am.

Nixon's advisers were at loss over how to react. While the letter undoubtedly struck them as somewhat bizarre, they were also taken by the idea of using Elvis's celebrity for the administration's ongoing anti-drug campaign. Nixon's personal assistant Dwight Chapin thus suggested that the President should meet Elvis briefly, given that it would take little time and could be "extremely beneficial." Chapin also mused that Nixon might want to meet "some bright young people outside of the Government" in which case Elvis might be "a perfect one to start with"—next to which Chief of Staff H.R. Haldeman scribbled, "You must be kidding." Nonetheless, the meeting was approved, even if the White House was still unsure over what exactly they might do with the singer. The quickly drawn-up agenda recommended that Nixon should thank Elvis "for his offer to help in trying to stop the drug epidemic in the country, and to ask him to work with us in bringing a more positive attitude to young people throughout the country." It also suggested a one-hour television special "in which Presley narrates as stars such as himself sing popular songs and interpret them for parents in order to show drug and other anti-establishment themes in rock music," or that Elvis might record "an album with the theme 'Get High on Life'."[76]

According to the official record of the meeting, Elvis Presley promptly entered the Oval Office at 12.30pm, and "immediately" started showing his numerous law enforcement badges to Nixon. He "was just a poor boy from Tennessee who had gotten a lot from his country, which in some way he wanted to repay," Elvis declared, going on to proclaim that his aim was purely "to restore some respect for the flag which was being lost." He also professed that "the Beatles had been a real force for anti-American spirit," who had "[come] to this country, made their money, and then returned to England where they promoted an anti-American theme." Yet, Elvis seems to have had little idea about how exactly he could help Nixon's anti-drug campaign. He

---

[75]Presley to Nixon, undated [but in flight December 20–21, 1970]. Full document reproduced in ibid.

[76]Chapin to Haldeman, December 21, 1970; Memorandum: Meeting with Elvis Presley, December 21, 1970. Full documents reproduced in ibid.

"did his thing by 'just singing'," he explained, and that he simply would not be able to "get to the kids" if he "made a speech on the stage." Rather, he could be of most help if he was made a federal agent at large without any publicity. Nixon eventually gave in, asking his aide Bud Krogh to get Elvis a BNDD badge. According to the official record, Elvis responded by telling Nixon again "how much he supported him, and then, in a surprising, spontaneous gesture, put his left arm around the President and hugged him."[77]

While Elvis's meeting with Nixon has often been interpreted as a sign of Elvis's alleged drift toward 1970s conservatism, such a reading is too simplistic. Rather, the meeting signified an uneasy collision of two very different worlds. Already the photographs of Elvis and Nixon reveal some tensions and contradictions, as Elvis's flamboyant appearance with cape, sunglasses, and golden belt contrasted starkly with Nixon's conformist grey suit and tie. And Elvis certainly did not see himself as part of American conservatism either. Already in his letter, he had claimed that "[t]he drug culture, the hippie elements, the SDS, Black Panthers, etc. do not consider me as their enemy or as they call it the establishment"; in the Oval Office, he similarly told Nixon that he "could go right into a group of young people or hippies and be accepted."[78] And when Bud Krogh showed Elvis

**Figure 5.3** *Elvis Presley showing off his cuff links to President Nixon, December 21, 1970.*

---

[77]Meeting Notes, December 21, 1970. Full document reproduced in ibid.
[78]Ibid.

the White House Situation Room, the singer could not resist bursting out his favorite line from *Dr. Strangelove*: "No fighting in the War Room."[79] Indeed, it is impossible to pin down Elvis's multifaceted personality to any simple political denominator. As his bass player Jerry Scheff later reflected, "in some ways Elvis was more conservative, and in other ways he was very liberal."[80] In that sense, Elvis was not unlike his fellow Southerner Johnny Cash, who was well known for his prison concerts and strong support of numerous other social causes, but who also visited American troops in Vietnam and played for Richard Nixon at the White House soon afterward.[81]

# Personal Troubles and American Decline

By the mid-1970s, there were clear indications that Elvis's career, but even more so his personal life, were slowly taking a turn for the worse. While Elvis's physical appearance and the quality of his performances had been nothing short of phenomenal in the immediate comeback period, the demanding touring schedule, as well as his eccentric lifestyle and eventual split from his wife Priscilla, had taken a toll on him. Such personal problems were undoubtedly aggravated by a long-standing abuse of prescription pills that now began to spiral out of control.[82] Rumors about Elvis's health and weight problems were ripe in the national press as well: on January 8, 1975, several newspapers reported that Elvis had spent his fortieth birthday locked in his bedroom, worried about being "fat and forty."[83] The singer's eccentric lifestyle reinforced perceptions that his life was getting out of control: stories of Elvis handing out Cadillacs to strangers, spontaneously flying to Denver just to eat a sandwich, or shooting impulsively at television sets in his hotel suite have since become integral parts of Elvis mythology.

Such personal struggles inevitably had an impact the quality of Elvis's performances. On January 14, 1973, the *Aloha From Hawaii* television special showed the singer once again at the peak of his artistic prowess, but things went downhill shortly afterward. By the mid-1973, reviewers frequently commented on Elvis's lackluster performances, slurry speech, or moody outbursts on stage. "Old songs, new scarves, the usual gimmicks, and more overweight than he's ever appeared in Las Vegas," the *Hollywood Reporter*

---

[79]Schilling, *Me and a Guy Named Elvis*, 221.

[80]Arjan Deelen, "Interview with Jerry Scheff," *Elvis Australia: Official Elvis Presley Fan Club*, January 1, 2016, www.elvis.com.au/presley/interview-jerryscheff.shtml [last accessed August 21, 2019.]

[81]Jonathan Silverman, "A 'Dove with Claws'? Johnny Cash as Radical," *Journal for the Study of Radicalism* 1/2 (2007), 91–106.

[82]Guralnick, *Careless Love*, 487–518.

[83]*Los Angeles Times*, January 8, 1975; *Boston Globe*, January 9, 1975; *The Baltimore Sun*, January 9, 1975.

wrote in August 1973, Elvis had been "at his most indifferent, uninterested, and unappealing." The singer was "not just a little out of shape, not just a bit chubbier than usual, the Living Legend is fat and ludicrously aping his former self; what used to be considered sexy gyrations and surprise karate chops are now sluggish and gross parodies."[84] While the hotel engagements and other concerts still sold out regularly, the tours now tended to focus on the South and Midwest rather than on the big coastal cities: Cincinnati, Tulsa, and Tampa rather than Boston, New York, or Los Angeles. Postponements and cancellations became more frequent, as Elvis spent days and weeks in hospitals for various illnesses or vain attempts by doctors to get him off the pills. On September 2, 1974, he astounded a Las Vegas audience when he went into a lengthy, rambling monologue about tabloid rumors that he had been "strung out" on heroine. "If I find or hear the individual that has said that about me," he busted out, "I'm gonna break your goddamn neck you son of a bitch."[85] Things only got worse as time went on. In July 1975, Elvis insulted his background singers so harshly that they walked out; at a New Year's Eve show in Michigan that same year, he ripped his pants on stage.[86]

Such changes inevitably came to affect Elvis's public image. The concerts in particular were singled out by critics, who often depicted them as having dissolved into a mere personality cult, or compared them to royal visits or religious ceremonies. "The 'king' was escorted to his throne by a trio of palace guards who were there to protect him from the power of his own charisma," the *Detroit News* condescendingly wrote in October 1974; "[t]he stadium erupted with screaming sights of recognition as he reviewed his subjects with a patronizing hand raised above his head."[87] The *Tucson Daily Citizen* reported in a similarly deriding tone how the "Elvis Presley worship service started around 7 p.m. when the congregation began gathering at the doors of the Community Center Arena." Elvis's fans, it claimed, "weren't there to listen, they weren't there to be critical. They were there to adulate."[88] Such reviews were often accompanied by patronizing descriptions of fans and audiences. "The 8,000 mostly white, middle-aged fans didn't mind a bit that their idol just stood there clutching the microphone and crooning most of the time, or that his belly bulged out at times making him look something like a chubby penguin," the Florida *St. Petersburg Times* wrote in April 1975; "They too have grown older, and they understand."[89] More sympathetic authors, like Robert Hilburn at the *LA Times,* painted the picture of an artist trapped in his own legacy:

---

[84]*The Hollywood Reporter*, August 18, 1973.
[85]The incident can be listened to on several bootlegs, including Fort Baxter's *Desert Storm,* as well as of course on YouTube.
[86]Guralnick and Jorgensen, *Elvis Day by Day*, 341, 350–1, 355.
[87]*Detroit News*, October 5, 1974.
[88]*Tucson Daily Citizen*, June 2, 1976.
[89]*St Petersburg Times*, April 28, 1975. For some of the countless other examples, see *Tulsa Daily World*, March 2, 1974; *Charlotte Observer*, March 10, 1974; *Lakeland Ledger*, April 28, 1975.

At 40, his records are increasingly uneven, his choice of material sometimes ludicrous and his concert performances often sloppy. Worst of all, there is no purpose or personal vision in his music any more ... The lesson, I'm afraid, he learned in those months after his comeback was that nostalgia – coupled with even a modest display of his talent – was enough after all. The quality of his show didn't seem to have a noticeable impact on the reaction of the audience. They wanted, most of all, to see Elvis, the idol of their youth ... Even if he mostly disappoints us now, he remains a symbol of what much of a generation once believed possible. If he, at 40, is no longer perfect, he is no different from the rest of us who also have fallen short of what we once hoped.[90]

The personality cult that had become the center of Elvis's concerts was only reinforced by Colonel Parker's aggressive marketing machinery, which at times gave them the feel of a fun fair rather than a rock event. Already in July 1969, many observers had expressed bewilderment over the tens of thousands of Elvis posters, banners, balloons, and booklets that Parker had showered upon the International Hotel; by the mid-1970s, overzealous salesmen selling trashy gimmicks like $1 buttons, $3 photo books, or $7 scarves were a key part of any Elvis experience.[91] In June 1972, the *New York Times* commented how an "air of shabby carnival" had hung over Elvis's Madison Square appearance; four years later, the *Dallas Morning-News* felt that even Elvis himself had been reduced to just another "piece of merchandise – another one of the 'super souvenirs' that were hawked throughout his show."[92] At the same time, however, such unabashed commercialism also reinforced notions of Elvis as an essential American icon. In November 1976, for example, the *Nevada State Journal* suggested that the marketing machinery surrounding Elvis somehow reflected the very essence of the United States:

Perhaps it was the commercial, carnival machine surrounding the aura of the rock 'n' roll star who, at age 41, can deserve to slow down the pace and bask in the worship of millions of followers. The man's magic - with a little slick sales savvy - was nicely distilled into buttons, photo albums, programs, $8 posters and mini-binoculars hawked by roving vendors and at "Elvis Super-Souvenir" concession stands ... The whole scene seemed suited more to football or basketball, not a music concert. Ahhhh – but this is Elvis. And Elvis – like baseball, hot dogs and apple pie – is all-American. What better way to celebrate him than with the commercial trappings of all-American hucksterism?[93]

---

[90]*Los Angeles Times*, January 19, 1975.
[91]Guralnick, *Careless Love*, 346; *Memphis Press-Scimitar*, March 18, 1974; *The Times Herald*, March 12, 1974; *Chicago Daily News*, October 16, 1976.
[92]*New York Times*, June 18, 1972; *Dallas Morning-News*, June 4, 1976.
[93]*Nevada State Journal*, November 26, 1976.

It was no coincidence that the *Nevada State Journal* published these musings in 1976, the year of the American Bicentennial. Festivities of the US' two hundredth anniversary were subdued at best, following Vietnam and Watergate.[94] Elvis spent the year playing a total of 127 concerts spread across several tours and two Las Vegas and Lake Tahoe engagements. The concerts largely followed the predictable pattern of previous years, apart from Elvis's opulent Bicentennial suits and the inclusion of the patriotic anthem "America The Beautiful". "Fat, Puffy, Has-Been Elvis Is Outshone By His Custome," a headline in the Syracuse *Post-Standard* ran on July 26, 1976—to many Americans, it also appeared like an accurate reflection on their country at its two-hundred-year anniversary.[95] Elvis seemed to reflect a country that had lost its way, musings that tied well into the cultural pessimism and wider declinist panoramas so prevalent at the time.[96] It was also during this period that Elton John, who was about to perform his own Bicentennial gig dressed up as the Statue of Liberty, attended his first ever Elvis concert at the Landover Capital Center in Largo, MD. He was shocked by what he saw. "There was something desperately, visibly wrong with him," he later recalled; "[o]ccasionally, you would see something spark, a flash of the incredible artist he had been. It would last for a couple of lines of a song and vanish again. My main memory is of him handing out scarves to women in the audience."[97]

Many fans, by contrast, took the Bicentennial as a cue to reflect on Elvis's relationship with the United States in more positive terms. "Where but only in America can a poor country boy from Tupelo, Mississippi, practically overnight, have fame and fortune at his command?" a fan who had attended Elvis's 4 July concert in Tulsa reflected in *Elvis Monthly*; the singer had "lived up to his image and gave the people what they paid for ... this Fourth of July was as American as hot dogs, baseball, apple pie and Elvis Presley."[98] Indeed, most fans still defended their idol against what they regarded as ill-fated rumors and mean-spirited press campaigns. Having traveled especially from the UK to witness Elvis's December 1976 Las Vegas residence, one fan struck an almost defiant tone afterward. "The myth that told the whole of England that he was fat was dissolved from my mind there and then as I witnessed for myself that HE WAS NOT FAT!" she claimed. "Gee, I cannot find the right words to describe my first live look at Elvis Presley ... I cannot remember what he sang, nor do I care. I remember that amidst all the pain he still found the energy to joke and prank around. I loved him all the more."[99]

---

[94]Christopher Capozzola, "'It Makes You Want to Believe in the Country': Celebrating the Bicentennial in an Age of Limits," in Beth Bailey and David Farber (eds.), *America in the Seventies* (Lawrence, KS: University Press of Kansas, 2004), 29–49.

[95]*The Post-Standard*, July 26, 1976.

[96]For the mood of "declinism" in mid-1970s US public debate, see Zeiler, "Age of Fear, Uncertainty, and Doubt," 9–24.

[97]John, *Me*, 139–40.

[98]*Elvis Monthly* 201, October 1976.

[99]Viva Las Vegas, *Elvis Monthly* 208, May 1977.

**Figure 5.4** *Elvis at the Philadelphia Spectrum during his Bicentennial tour in June 1976.*

Not all fans shared such enthusiasm, however. The constant rumors about Elvis's health, as well as the evident decline in the quality of his performances and records, had made some of them conspicuous. Todd Slaughter, the editor of *Elvis Monthly,* wondered why Elvis had seemingly "ignored his own country's bi-centennial celebrations and why his country has ignored him in this very special year," and professed puzzlement over "why Elvis doesn't become involved with the outside world."[100] Only days before Elvis's passing, he published another emotional editorial in the August 1977 edition of the magazine. "I am a fan who cares, cares about him gaining respect, recording quality material, losing weight and being admired not only by

---

[100]*Elvis Monthly* 201, October 1976.

his fans," he wrote. "In the last two weeks I have received 200 letters from Elvis fans and 178 of you are dissatisfied with Elvis' career at the moment, so please let's not pretend that everything is alright."[101]

## Absent Elvis: The 1970s outside the United States

On January 14, 1973, Elvis Presley's global superstardom was demonstrated in a novel and unprecedented way: Elvis's *Aloha From Hawaii* concert at the Honolulu International Center was broadcasted live via satellite around the world, to an audience purported at the time to be around one billion.[102] Allegedly inspired by the recent broadcast of Nixon's China visit in 1972, the show was designed to showcase Elvis's global popularity, evoking a powerful iconography that consciously projected Elvis as an all-American superhero.[103] The broadcast started with Morse signals stating, "Elvis Presley Aloha from Hawaii via Satellite," Elvis's name then flashed up in various languages including in Cyrillic and Arabic script, and the subsequent album's cover photo showed Elvis being "beamed" from satellite to the Earth. The bombastic stage was set up with colorful lightbulbs, huge mirrors, and even a flashing LED-Elvis, which his pianist later memorably described as "a damn Christmas tree with blinking lights."[104] Elvis himself was dressed in an exorbitant white jumpsuit embroidered with 6,500 rhinestones that featured an American eagle on its front, back, and cape. It was clearly intended as an unabashed statement of the globalization of US popular culture over the past few decades: The special was watched live by 37.8 percent of viewers in Japan, 70 percent in Hong Kong, around 70 to 80 percent in South Korea, and an alleged 91.8 per cent in the Philippines; the accompanying album LP was the first record in RCA's history that was released throughout the world at the same time.[105]

On closer inspection, however, *Aloha From Hawaii* also reveals some of the limitations of Elvis's allegedly global popularity. First, the show's

---

[101]*Elvis Monthly* 211, August 1977.

[102]The actual number, of course, was much lower, and probably around 150–200 million. For a detailed investigation, see Michael Werner and Bianca Weber, "Aloha from Hawaii via Satellite: Fact&Fancy," *Elvis Australia*, March 11, 2018, www.elvis.com.au/presley/aloha-from-hawaii-via-satellite-fact-fancy.shtml [last accessed May 13, 2019].

[103]For a colorful take on the utopian imagery evoked by the special, see most recently Jens Balzer, *Das Entfesselte Jahrzehnt: Sound und Geist der 70er* (Berlin: Rowohlt, 2019), 188–206.

[104]Wiener, *Channeling Elvis*, 207.

[105]Ibid., 198, 230. In the United States, the television special was aired months later because the concert date clashed with the 1973 Super Bowl. It reached a 51 percent audience share; the accompanying LP became Elvis's last album to reach number one in the Billboard charts during his lifetime.

international reach was of course far less than what his management claimed at the time. Given the Intelsat IV F-4's satellite limited reach, it was broadcasted live only in Australia, Japan, South Vietnam, South Korea, the Philippines, and Hong Kong; the imperatives of the Cold War also meant that it was not shown at all in China and the Soviet Union. Even in Western Europe, where Elvis remained popular, most stations aired the special days or even weeks later, depending on their particular agreements with NBC; it was not shown at all in the UK until after Elvis's death.[106] The British fan Pennie Sayer even flew to Copenhagen where she could watch the show twice, first on Danish television and then an hour later on Swedish television.[107] Yet those fans in South East Asia who had been able to watch the special live were jubilant. "It looked like this day was almost Elvis Presley Day in the Philippines, what with all those El-activities that went on," one of them reported in *Elvis Monthly*, thanking "El himself, for giving us, his fans in the Far East, especially here in the Philippines, the chance to see him perform live via satellite. We may be a small country, but we're many (population about 40 million) and that's plenty of people-power for you, El."[108]

The fact that Elvis and his management opted for a worldwide television special, rather than a worldwide concert tour, highlights an even more fundamental particularity of Elvis's superstardom during the 1970s: at a time when major international tours by artists like Bob Dylan, Elton John, or the Rolling Stones had become the norm, Elvis never performed outside the United States throughout his entire lifetime.[109] It is striking not least because there was a clear demand, particularly in Western Europe: as early as May 1956, the British *New Musical Express* had speculated over a UK tour, and many fans continued to lobby strongly for it throughout the 1950s and 1960s.[110] "If you were in Presley's shoes would you want to stay in the U.S.A. and never visit any other countries in the world?" *Elvis Monthly* editor Todd Slaughter asked rhetorically in January 1969. "Why commute between Hollywood and Memphis, and go nowhere else. Elvis only works for three months each year, so he has plenty of time available."[111] There were also frequent rumors floating around, including proposals of a one-off appearance at Wembley Stadium, $1 million a night for Germany and Japan, and allegedly even a $5 million offer to play at the Giza pyramids.[112] While rumors about an imminent world tour continued to surface throughout the

---

[106]Werner and Weber, "Aloha From Hawaii"; Guralnick and Jorgensen, *Day by Day*, 324.
[107]*Elvis Monthly* 159, April 1973.
[108]Aloha From Hawaii in the Philippines, *Elvis Monthly* 159, April 1973.
[109]Except for the five concerts in Canada in April–August 1957 and three performances in Honolulu in November 1957, as mentioned in chapter one.
[110]See, for example, *New Musical Express*, May 4 and October 5, 1956.
[111]*Elvis Monthly* 109, January 1969.
[112]Nash, *The Colonel*, 271, 289–90.

1970s, most non-US fans eventually retorted to the second-best option of organizing trips to the United States.[113]

The fact that Elvis did not embark upon a worldwide tour during the 1970s caused considerable irritation, not least with the singer himself. He had repeatedly articulated his desire for international appearances from the earliest days of his career, and continued to do so after his comeback. At the press conference following his 1969 Las Vegas opening night, for example, he professed without hesitation that he would definitely like to appear in Britain and that such a date would be fixed "soon."[114] Privately too, Elvis often talked about such plans, at one point telling his friend Jerry Schilling how his European fans had "a certain image of me" and that he did not "want to wait until I'm forty goddamn years old to get over there."[115] Colonel Parker, however, continued to turn down all sorts of offers. Parker's ultimate motives have since aroused lots of speculation: while some point to Parker's uncertain immigration status or lack of US passport, others claim that he wanted to protect his client from problems that might arise out of his obsession with weapons and his increasing dependence on prescription drugs.[116] Although Elvis rarely pushed the issue with Parker, it had by the mid-1970s become a highly contentious issue between Elvis and his manager, and it was one of the reasons behind Elvis's rather short-lived decision to fire Parker in September 1973.[117]

Although Elvis's plans for an international tour came to nothing, his 1970s comeback benefited enormously from the expansion and professionalization of the popular culture industry that had taken place since the 1950s. The popular music industry in particular had moved from its erstwhile outsider status into a vibrant, transnationally linked scene that occupied a central role in the societies of many countries; many artists and trends circulated seamlessly between the United States, Western Europe, and other parts of the world.[118] Elvis's 1968 television special, for example, was widely reported in the international press, even if it was not broadcasted outside the United

[113]In June 1977, for example, around 250 members of the British fan club flew to the United States to attend what would become Elvis's last-ever concert tour. Some of them can be seen in the CBS *Elvis In Concert* television documentary, released posthumously in October 1977. *Elvis Monthly* 210, July 1977.

[114]Guralnick, *Careless Love*, 353.

[115]Schilling, *Me and a Guy Named Elvis*, 239.

[116]Nash, *The Colonel*, 289–90.

[117]Guralnick, *Careless Love*, 506–10; Schilling, *Me and a Guy Named Elvis*, 261–2.

[118]Pells, *Not Like Us*, 319; Dietmar Hüser, "Einleitung: Transnationale Populärkultur im Europa der langen 1960er Jahre: Forschungsstand und Forschungspisten," in Dietmar Hüser (ed.), *Populärkultur Transnational* (Bielefeld: transcript, 2017), 10–13; Stefan Schwarzkopf, "Transatlantic Invasions or Common Culture? Modes of Cultural and Economic Exchange between the American and the British Advertising Industries, 1945–2000," in Joel H. Wiener and Mark Hampton (eds.), *Anglo-American Media Interactions, 1850–2000* (Basingstoke: Palgrave Macmillan, 2007), 254–74.

States until many months later: the British *NME* writer Anne Moses had actually been in the audience, and wrote several ecstatic features afterward.[119] In West Germany, the youth magazine *BRAVO* and the tabloid *Bild am Sonntag* even started petitions to get it aired on German television.[120] Elvis's global record sales also improved markedly, as the *From Elvis in Memphis* album climbed to the top of the British and Norwegian charts. He scored some international hit records too: "In the Ghetto" reached number one in Ireland, Norway, Australia, and New Zealand, and became Elvis's first (and only lifetime) number one hit in West Germany. The follow-up single "Suspicious Minds" climbed to the top of the charts in Australia, Belgium, Canada, and South Africa, and in the UK, "The Wonder of You" achieved a surprise success where it topped the charts for six weeks.[121]

The fact that Elvis remained an abstract medial construction outside the United States throughout his lifetime also meant that he offered an ideal platform onto which some bigger images of the United States could be projected. Just like in the 1950s, Elvis again came to serve as symbol of the alleged excesses of American-style consumerism. In 1972, for example, the British rock critic Geoffrey Cannon's review of Elvis's Madison Square Garden concert in the left-wing newspaper *The Guardian* offered snotty takes on the alleged materialism and social conservatism of the early 1970s United States. "Elvis walked on, and for quite some time to come appeared to be a cartoon of himself, dressed in white, gold-studded trousers, flared to a foot wide," Cannon wrote; it was a style apparently "still designed for an impoverished audience. It said: I am inaccessibly rich and famous. You think you want me, but you cannot touch me."[122] Indeed, the flashy gaudiness of Elvis's 1970s appearance was a dominant feature in much of the press coverage outside the United States. "Elvis Presley loves luxury, and he admits that candidly," the West German youth magazine *BRAVO* wrote in 1972; "He presents himself to his fans in a white silk suit with diamond knobs, matter of expense: 15,000 Deutschmark."[123] It also published several other features focusing mainly on Elvis's wealth, including home stories with pictures of Elvis's Beverly Hills residence or Las Vegas hotel suite.[124]

Such journalistic emphasis on Elvis's exhibited wealth made him an ideal target for more general cultural criticisms of contemporary US society, particularly in Western Europe. In West Germany, for example,

---

[119] *NME*, July 20, 1968; *NME*, July 27, 1968; *NME*, December 14, 1968.

[120] The television special finally aired in West Germany in May 1970. For evidence of the campaign, see *BRAVO* 16/1969 and *SPIEGEL* 20/1970.

[121] Duffett, *Counting Down Elvis*, 176–8.

[122] *The Guardian*, June 17, 1972.

[123] *BRAVO* 30/1972.

[124] *BRAVO* 13/1970; *BRAVO* 51/1969.

the *Frankfurter Allgemeine Zeitung* dismissed the *That's the Way It Is* (1970) documentary as a piece of trashy "mythology" that presented only the "publicity façade" of Elvis; *Der Spiegel* regarded it as evidence that Elvis had become reduced to a "mere commodity" of the US entertainment industry.[125] Contemporary notions of the US' alleged cultural imperialism were never far away. In 1973, *Der Spiegel* even dismissed the entire 1970s nostalgia wave as an artificial construct of US capitalism. "Just like with ketchup and Coca-Cola," it claimed, "the US' consumerist imperialism has again infected the old continent with its new disease, the relished homesickness for a lost paradise with its supposed innocence."[126] Occasionally, Elvis also served as an example of the appropriation and exploitation processes allegedly inherent in US popular culture. "Nobody outside black ghettos and their black radio stations had ever heard songs like 'Hound Dog' or 'That's Alright Mama' in the early 1950s," *Der Spiegel* wrote in 1975, but when

> a cleverly-managed former truck driver called Elvis Presley came along and marketed such songs with twitching hips and internationally-selling vinyl records, they became signals of the rock revolution from Toronto to Tokyo ... Elvis "The Pelvis" Presley had himself drive on stage in a golden Cadillac with a pearl roof and declared on the cover of a LP "50 million Elvis fans can't be wrong".[127]

As Elvis's personal problems became more evident, his public image took a turn for the worse outside the United States as well. Indeed, it matched a more general decline of US popularity during the 1970s.[128] "Poll in West Europe Finds U.S. Prestige Lowest in 22 Years," a *New York Times* headline screamed on October 21, 1976, quoting a leaked USIA survey that West European attitudes toward the United States were apparently at the lowest level ever recorded.[129] While the report pointed mainly to familiar economic and political tensions in the transatlantic relationship, it also identified the US' allegedly materialistic nature and consumerist culture as a major factor behind such West European discontent.[130] To many, Elvis again seemed like the perfect example. In 1976, the UK's *New Musical Express* described the singer as "a strange archaic figure ... the last surviving dinosaur, whose rampages through the Las Vegas hotel lounges

---

[125]*Frankfurter Allgemeine Zeitung*, September 28, 1971; *Der Spiegel* 36/1971.
[126]*Der Spiegel*, 05/1973.
[127]*Der Spiegel*, 48/1975.
[128]Hallvard Notaker, Giles Scott-Smith, and David Snyder, "Introduction: Reasserting America in the 1970s," in Notaker, Scott-Smith, and Snyder (eds.), *Reasserting America*, 3–4.
[129]*New York Times*, October 21, 1976.
[130]"S-14–76, Some Indications of Trends and Current Opinions about US and NATO in Western Europe," November 1976, RIAS, Records of the US Information Agency, Part 1: Cold War Era Special Reports, Series B: 1964–82.

were entertaining spectacles, social curiosities, but hardly works of art."[131] Even sympathetic publications like *BRAVO* reported at length on Elvis's personal troubles, reports that often tied into more general critiques of mass consumerism.[132] "Elvis: The Lonely King" was the headline of one of its major features, claiming that the singer had "millions of dollars, houses, luxury limousines" but wondering whether "all his fame and money" had "really made him happy."[133]

Yet Elvis retained a highly active and devoted fan scene around the globe throughout his lifetime. The Official Elvis Presley Fan Club of Great Britain remained the key hub for many European fans, boasting over 12,000 members at the time of Elvis's passing, and there were countless other clubs that were often transnationally linked and met up regularly.[134] In 1970, for example, some West European fan clubs organized an eight-day international fan convention that stretched from Belgium to Holland, West Germany, and Luxemburg, parts of which were filmed for the *That's the Way It Is* documentary.[135] While such a devoted and active fan scene kept Elvis's name in the public domain, it occasionally also invited ridicule and condescension. In January 1976 the British punk musician Mick Farren decided to "infiltrate" the annual fan club convention at a North London *Holiday Inn* for the *NME*. "The hallmark of the Elvis fan is a kind of clear-eyed, absolute devotion," he wrote afterward; "It's a devotion that believes that Elvis can do no wrong ... When you talk to some of the fans you start to get the impression that for many of them Elvis Presley is the essential core of their whole lives."[136] Such cliché-ridden denouncements would become infinitely more pronounced after Elvis's death.

# Death and Transfiguration

"A Lonely Life Ends on Elvis Presley Boulevard," the headline of the *Memphis Press-Scimitar* ran on August 17, 1977.[137] The day before, the forty-two-year-old Elvis Presley had been found unconscious on his Graceland bathroom floor by his girlfriend Ginger Alden. Although an ambulance immediately rushed Elvis to the Baptist Memorial Hospital, all attempts to revive his body failed. Elvis Presley was pronounced dead at 3.30 pm, the cause of death being attributed to "cardiac arrhythmia

---

[131]*New Musical Express*, May 22, 1976.
[132]*BRAVO*, 31/1975; *BRAVO*, 10/1976.
[133]*BRAVO* 39/1976.
[134]The World's Most Successful Fan Club, *Elvis Monthly* 208, May 1977.
[135]Hopkins, *Elvis*, 408.
[136]*NME*, January 24, 1976.
[137]*Memphis Press Scimitar*, August 17, 1977.

due to undetermined heartbeat." Laboratory reports subsequently claimed polypharmacy as the most probable underlying cause, having found fourteen different drugs, including codeine ten times the therapeutic level, in his system.[138]

The death of Elvis constituted a global media event that transcended national boundaries, not unlike the assassination of John F. Kennedy.[139] Radio and television stations from Peru to Australia interrupted their programs for special reports: in Chile, radio stations compiled special features on "El Rey de Rock 'n' roll"; in Western Europe, Radio Luxembourg canceled all its commercials to play Elvis songs non-stop; and in Japan, television anchors shed tears over Elvis's death. The sale figures of Elvis's records skyrocketed, with the RCA plant in Indianapolis working twenty-four-hour shifts to press 250,000 Elvis albums a day. In Manila, fans organized a special two-hour radio tribute; in Brussels, crying fans assembled outside record stores, and in the North London borough of Cockfosters, a church performed a special memorial service. Over the next few days, more than 250 journalists from all around the world descended onto Memphis, transforming the local Chamber of Commerce into a global news hub. An estimated number of 80,000 fans held wake at Graceland, and more than 30,000 of them took part in the public viewing of Elvis's body, who was laid out in his coffin dressed in a white suit with a pale blue shirt and white tie. A gigantic flower arrangement from the British singer Elton John was put on display, while the *Beef and Liberty* fast-food restaurant across the street changed its billboard sign to "Rest in Peace, Elvis." Tragedy hit when a severely drunk man drove into the group of mourners outside Graceland, killing two people and severely injuring a third.[140]

As the immediate shock of Elvis's passing faded, countless obituaries and eulogies tried to investigate why his death caused such strong emotions. They offer a condensed view of the countless myths and narratives that had been constructed around the singer during his lifetime. The first wave of writings inevitably centered on Elvis's contribution to popular music. "Elvis Presley didn't invent rock 'n' roll," Robert Hilburn wrote in the *LA Times*, "but he was its most important figure and its primary symbol."[141] The *New York Times* too declared that Elvis would "remain the founder of rock-and-roll in most people's minds, and every rock singer owes something to him in

[138]Guralnick and Jorgensen, *Day by Day*, 379.

[139]Christian Morgner, "Zeitlichkeiten globaler Medienereignisse: Am Beispiel der Ermordung John F. Kennedys," in Friedrich Lenger and Ansgar Nünning (eds.), *Medienereignisse der Moderne* (Darmstadt: Wissenschaftliche Buchgesellschaft, 2008), 130–49.

[140]This section is based on the numerous reports, including *Memphis Press Scimitar*, August 17, 18, 19, and 20, 1977; *Hartford Courant*, August 18, 1977; *Chicago Tribune*, August 18, 1977; *Newsweek*, August 29, 1977.

[141]*Los Angeles Times*, August 17, 1977.

matters of inflection and visual style"; in the eyes of the *Boston Globe*, Elvis had "almost singlehandedly changed the profile of popular music."[142] The rock critic Lester Bangs articulated Elvis's cultural impact in rather more explicit language.[143] "Elvis Presley was the man who brought overt blatant vulgar sexual frenzy to the popular arts in America," he wrote in the *Village Voice*; "when Elvis started wiggling his hips and Ed Sullivan refused to show it, the entire country went into a paroxysm of sexual frustration leading to abiding discontent which culminated in the explosion of psychedelic-militant folklore which was the sixties."[144]

Such notions already suggest that the strong emotions aroused by Elvis's passing could not be explained by his contributions to the field of popular music alone. Rather than seeing Elvis merely as an innovative musician, most commentators depicted him as a generational icon, reflecting the nostalgic reconfigurations of the 1950s that were taking place in public memory at the time. In the *Washington Post*, for example, Marion Clark claimed to be "All Shook Up on the Day the '50s Died", and described at length her memories of "the way it felt, the way it smelled – Old Spice, sweatsox, too-sweet perfume – the way it sounded when we danced ... at a Teen-High."[145] She was not the only one who mourned "the passing of a generation as well as of a pop-culture idol."[146] In many such readings, Elvis was transfigured into an allegedly unifying generational experience. "There were a lot of dinner table debates that Sunday night in 1956," a writer at the *Hartford Courant* reminisced. "Would parents let their children watch a sneering, long-haired, swivel-hipped Mississippi country boy croon his suggestive rock 'n' roll on Ed Sullivan's television show? ... Tuesday night in Memphis, Elvis died. A generation of people cared."[147]

If Elvis's contributions to the field of popular music and historical importance were widely acknowledged, the finer aspects of his cultural legacy were debated more controversially. This applies in particular to questions of race, as questions of cultural appropriation came to feature prominently during the days following Elvis's funeral. The African American newspaper *New York Amsterdam News*, for example, wondered whether Elvis had been "'Nothing' But a Black Imitator," arguing that his success ultimately represented "the questionable, dual standards used today that combat or attempt to stifle the idea of equal opportunity."[148] Others were more ambivalent in their judgements. Several other African American newspapers

---

[142]*New York Times*, August 17, 1977; *Boston Globe*, August 17, 1977.
[143]*The Village Voice*, August 29, 1977.
[144]Ibid.
[145]*Washington Post*, August 17, 1977.
[146]Ibid.
[147]*The Hartford Courant*, August 17, 1977.
[148]*New York Amsterdam News*, August 27, 1977.

stressed the genuine originality of Elvis as a crossover artist, and depicted rock 'n' roll as a genuinely new fusion of musical styles. Others pointed to his initial popularity with black audiences, and his function as a door-opener for many black rock 'n' roll artists that followed.[149] Yet even those who judged his impact positively compared the hype surrounding his death with the public indifference toward many of his black contemporaries. To the *Los Angeles Sentinel,* for example, it seemed "more than a little strange that the names of Bill Broonzy and Jimmy Reed will soon be forgotten by the mass of the American public ... while the name of Elvis Presley will become a legendary figure to be talked about for decades and perhaps even centuries to come."[150]

Many commentators could not resist taking Elvis's death as a cue to reflect more widely on bigger questions of American identity. The familiar rags-to-riches narrative again featured prominently. In the eyes of the *Boston Globe,* Elvis's life had above all been "an American life," the "Horatio Alger story of a $35-a-week truck driver who made millions."[151] Whatever resistances Elvis may have faced in the 1950s, he was now re-interpreted as a shining example of social mobility and a popular egalitarianism allegedly inherent in US popular culture. "Elvis was and remains a working-class hero," the *New York Times* wrote, "a man who rose from obscurity and transformed American popular art in answer to his own needs – and who may possibly have been destroyed by the isolation that being an American celebrity sometimes entails. He was as much a metaphor as a maker of music, and one of telling power and poignancy."[152] The *Chicago Tribune* offered even more hyperbole:

> The death of Elvis reminds us of a lot of things. It reminds us that a meagerly educated former truck driver from a little Mississippi town could have more influence on the popular culture and popular music of America and of foreign lands than politicians and conservatory musicians. It reminds us that we are a society of incredibly upward mobility, where cultural democracy instead of cultural czars determines who shall be successful and influential. On his way to riches, Mr. Presley turned off most parents while turning on a whole generation of children to a new, hard-driving sound that influence the more "refined" artists of song who followed.[153]

---

[149]*Los Angeles Sentinel,* August 25, 1977; *Baltimore African-American,* August 27, 1977; *Afro-American,* August 27, 1977. Similar takes in *Los Angeles Times,* August 17, 1977; *Boston Globe,* August 17, 1977; *Chicago Tribune,* August 17, 1977.
[150]*Los Angeles Sentinel,* August 25, 1977.
[151]*Boston Globe,* August 18, 1977.
[152]*New York Times,* August 17, 1977.
[153]*Chicago Tribune,* August 18, 1977.

Some also took Elvis as a poignant symbol of the darker sides of the so-called American Dream. *Time* depicted his life as the "parody of an American success story," in which Elvis "burnt himself out" and became "absorbed in the lavish trappings of his own celebrity."[154] The singer's consumerist excesses and private isolation featured prominently in such interpretations. The *Washington Post* compared Elvis to "the reclusive character in 'Citizen Kane'; handing out jewels and Cadillacs to friends and even casual acquaintances ... ensconced in his Graceland Mansion behind locked gates," while *Newsweek* postulated in graphic terms how "Elvis, bloated by the American ambrosias – peanut butter, Pepsi, pills and success – died in the midst of his own private lonely crowd."[155] In the *LA Times,* the pugnacious columnist Mike Royko used Elvis's death for a comprehensive, if half-ironic, onslaught on American popular culture. "Musical taste is not what this country is about," he proclaimed;

Success is ... Success is what the whole game was about, and if it took a con, that was part of it, too. Elvis pulled off a marvelous con. And the best part of it was whom he pulled it on. There he was, a depression-born, unread hillbilly. And he managed to convince the highly educated, privileged postwar generation that he was a monumental figure in our cultural development.[156]

Traits of such cultural pessimism and critical takes on US identity constructions were also prevalent outside the United States. Particularly in Western Europe, there was a tendency to focus the coverage of Elvis's death on the issues of marketing and commercial exploitation that had become so intimately associated with his legacy. The British newspaper *The Guardian,* for example, mused that Elvis would always embody "not only rock and roll but the sudden explosion of young white affluence which created it," and that his legacy would also be shaped by his "bland, commercial films which celebrated the wholesome, girl-loving, patriotic decency of young America."[157] In West Germany, the *Frankfurter Allgemeine Zeitung* described Elvis as somebody who had "lived the American Dream in its most vulgar form – the uninhibited satisfaction of even the most infantile wishes"; *Der Spiegel* claimed that Elvis should be remembered not least for "the total commercialization of his talent."[158] It also offered a lengthy report on Elvis's funeral, which it denounced it as a "pilgrimage to the pandemonium" and an "American-style fun fair with coke and ice-cream booths, as well as street

---

[154]*Time Magazine*, August 29, 1977.

[155]*Washington Post*, August 17, 1977; *Newsweek*, August 29, 1977.

[156]*Los Angeles Times*, August 19, 1977.

[157]*The Guardian*, August 17, 1977.

[158]*Frankfurter Allgemeine Zeitung*, August 18, 1977; *Der Spiegel* 35/1977.

vendors selling Elvis memorial T-shirts." It even mused pejoratively that the three fans killed by the drunk driver outside Graceland might have died "with a feeling of happiness because they were now close to their idol even in death."[159] The Soviet Union's *Pravda* offered its own particular take on Elvis. "How Capitalism Exploits Talent," it proclaimed in its obituary, depicting Elvis as the hapless victim of the brutality of the US "show business" and an "advertising-permeated 'consumer society'." "Elvis Presley died of cardiac arrhythmia at the age of 42," it concluded, "[b]ut life will give its own, more tragic diagnosis."[160]

# Conclusions

The "long" 1970s from Elvis's 1968 comeback special to his tragic death in August 1977 form an integral and indispensable part of Elvis's image and legacy. Although Elvis remained inextricably intertwined with his 1950s legacy, his elevation into a larger-than-life American folk hero would not have been possible without his comeback. Through his artistic reinvention and return to live performances, Elvis resurrected himself as a major generational reference point precisely at a time when nostalgic and highly idealized cultural fragments of the 1950s came to occupy a central place in public memory. No longer confined solely to his rock 'n' roll or Hollywood persona, Elvis thus became an American icon whose legacy eventually came to overshadow his artistry. As the singer's artistic output diminished and personal problems became more evident, he also came to serve as a pop-cultural symbol of the general confusion and solipsism in the United States in the mid-1970s. The coverage surrounding Elvis's passing, then, merely rehashed some of the most central questions of American identity that had been negotiated through Elvis's public image since his rise to fame in the 1950s.

---

[159]*Der Spiegel*, 35/1977.
[160]*Pravda*, August 26, 1977, as translated and quoted in: *Current Digest of the Russian Press*, Vol. 29 No. 34 (September 21, 1977), 4.

# EPILOGUE

In August 1991, the city of Moscow was held hostage by a coup d'état, as key members of the Soviet government tried to take power from General Secretary Mikhail Gorbachev. With Gorbachev being held in Crimea, it fell on the Russian President Boris Yeltsin to organize an effective resistance movement. During the final hours of the coup, the exhausted Yeltsin hid away in his office, trying to find some escape in music. He switched on the record player and played his favorite Elvis song: "Are You Lonesome Tonight?"[1]

While the Yeltsin anecdote has often been taken as anecdotal evidence of the supposedly all-encompassing power of American popular culture, Elvis Presley's relationship with the Cold War was more complex and much more ambivalent. It certainly does not provide for any sort of triumphalist account; but neither is it simply a cliché-laden tale of the decadence of US mass consumerism and the corruption of the American Dream. Rather, Elvis's image constituted a unique pop-cultural platform through which bigger constructions of American identity were articulated in multifaceted and often contradictory ways, and one whose meanings changed massively at a time of unprecedented political, social, and cultural transition. Taken together, the debates over Elvis's relationship with the United States during the Cold War therefore do not only offer a rich panorama of the singer's changing public image and its underlying historical transformations, but they also show how popular culture came to shape everyday perceptions of the United States and common understandings of the East–West conflict.[2]

Even within the United States, Elvis's relationship with bigger notions of American identity was ambivalent and heavily contested from the very beginning. In the mid-1950s, Elvis's rise to fame exposed the cracks and

---

[1] *The Guardian*, August 26, 1991.

[2] For historical approaches to "nation branding" and popular understandings of the Cold War, see as starting points Carolin Viktorin, Jessica Gienow-Hecht, Annika Estner, and Marcel Will, "Beyond Marketing and Diplomacy: Exploring the Historical Origins of Nation Branding," in Carolin Viktorin, Jessica Gienow-Hecht, Annika Estner and Marcel Will (eds.), *Nation Branding in Modern History* (Oxford: Berghahn, 2018), 1–26; Annette Vowinckel, Marcus Payk and Thomas Lindenberger, "European Cold War Culture(s)? An Introduction," in Annette Vowinckel, Marcus Payk and Thomas Lindenberger (eds.), *Cold War Cultures: Perspectives on Eastern and Western European Societies* (Oxford: Berghahn, 2014), 1–20.

hypocrisy inherent in the fragile Cold War consensus of Eisenhower's America. Yet, while opponents denounced Elvis as a threat to American values, his fans endorsed him precisely because he was seen as a challenge to the prevailing social and moral order of the day. Ultimately, these tensions inherent in Elvis's image became submerged in a powerful American Dream narrative that transfigured Elvis into a rags-to-riches story of upward mobility and capitalist advance while sidelining or ignoring the more contentious issues at the heart of his appeal. Elvis thus both embodied and challenged the fragile Cold War consensus of 1950s America, and in so doing shows how much bigger tensions between social liberalism and conservatism were negotiated through his image.

Outside the United States too, Elvis's impact was debated controversially not least because his rise to fame was intimately tied to the US' unprecedented political, economic, and cultural expansion after 1945. Although Elvis became a major icon of a burgeoning and highly transnational youth culture, his image thus remained inextricably intertwined with the United States throughout his lifetime.[3] In Western Europe in particular, large parts of the establishment rejected the new singer as a seeming sign of an alleged American cultural infiltration, whereas a new generation of teenagers embraced him precisely because he stood for the excitement and vitality they associated with the postwar United States. In the Soviet Union and the Eastern bloc, Elvis became even more directly politicized, in terms of both state-driven propaganda and the political persecution of some of his fans. At the height of the Cold War, then, Elvis came to symbolize the many alleged vices and virtues of American cultural influences in the wider struggle between East and West, even if such arguments ultimately reflected much more general debates over the rise of mass consumerism, global capitalism, and modernity after 1945.[4]

Such pop-cultural constructions of Elvis Presley as an American icon were never static; they constantly changed their meaning and altered massively over time. In so doing, they reflected changes in the singer's career as well as the much wider historical transformations between the mid-1950s and the late 1970s. The singer's military service, for example, was pivotal in transforming his erstwhile rebel image into an all-American boy doing his patriotic duty; it also helped him gain acceptance outside the United States. His subsequent 1960s Hollywood and 1970s Las Vegas careers then transfigured Elvis into a shining example of the so-called American Dream; but yet again, such meanings were contested heavily. While some saw his 1960s movies as shining examples of American-style modernity,

---

[3]For recent takes on the transnationalism inherent in 1950s youth culture, see Mrozek, *Jugend—Pop—Kultur*, 28–33, 717–46; Hüser, "Transnationale Populärkultur," 7–14.
[4]Kroes, *Europeans and American Mass Culture*, x–xii.

for example, others depicted them as anachronistic relics that completely ignored the harsh realities of the decade. And while the 1970s comeback canonized Elvis as a quintessential American folk hero, his evident personal decline during the final years of his career tied neatly into much longer-term stereotypes about the alleged decadence of US mass culture and unabashed consumerism.

As the book has shown, then, most of the popular images and narratives we commonly associate with Elvis today already emerged during the singer's lifetime. They were the product of a complex web of interactions between Elvis himself, his management, producers, journalists, entrepreneurs, fans, and the wider public; and they also reflected the much wider historical transformations during the singer's career. And yet, while many of such tropes and narratives still resonate heavily in Elvis's contemporary image, a key thing has changed: Elvis himself is no longer there. While his image had always been shaped by a myriad of agents, Elvis could never be left out of the equation entirely; in one way or the other, the debates surrounding him always linked back in some form to his life, career, and art. Today, however, the countless cultural fragments of Elvis tend to float around freely and seemingly at random in our postmodern world. It remains elusive, for example, why Madame Tussauds thought it appropriate to celebrate the unveiling of its first-ever Elvis wax figure with a fried peanut butter and banana sandwich eating contest.

Nonetheless, there are some general trends and patterns in Elvis's posthumous reception that can be discerned. First, it is important to stress the extent to which Elvis's reputation took a massive nosedive immediately after his death, and that it stayed low for much of the 1980s and 1990s. The gossip surrounding his troubled final years was part of the reason. Just prior to Elvis's passing, a group of former friends and bodyguards had published a highly sensationalized memoir of their lives with Elvis, revealing the singer's erratic private behavior and escalating prescription drug abuse.[5] The book became a bestseller in the immediate aftermath of Elvis's death, and popularized many of the most unflattering stereotypes and clichés that are associated with Elvis's image today. In 1981, it was followed up by Albert Goldman's even more controversial biography of the singer.[6] Not hiding his personal resentment, Goldman refuted Elvis's musical talent and cultural contributions entirely, depicting him as a cultural appropriator and puppet of the mass entertainment industry. He also dwelt at length on sensationalist stories about Elvis's overeating and allegedly perverse sexual preferences. While the book succeeded in destroying Elvis's reputation for much of the decade, it was already contested at the time of its release. Greil Marcus

---

[5]Red West, Sonny West, Dave Hebler and Steve Dunleavy, *Elvis, What Happened?* (New York, NY: Ballentine Books, 1977).
[6]Albert H. Goldman, *Elvis* (New York, NY: McGraw-Hill Book Company, 1981).

wrote a damning review in *Village Voice*, which claimed that Goldman's sole purpose had been "to entirely discredit Elvis Presley, the culture that produced him, and the culture he helped create"; an attempt to "exclude Elvis Presley, and the culture of the white working-class South ... from any serious consideration of American culture."[7] Taken together, the debates surrounding both books are excellent examples of how the class contempt and cultural snobbism, as well as misleading dichotomies between "high" and "low" culture, had survived Elvis's death, and were now being rehashed in fights over the singer's historical legacy.

Since the early 1980s, there have been many attempts to reinstate Elvis's historical importance. The singer's estate was quickly transformed into Elvis Presley Enterprises (EPE) by his former wife Priscilla, who helped turn it into a colossal marketing machine and developed his Graceland mansion into a major tourist attraction. Today, Graceland still attracts over half a million visitors a year, and has recently been developed into a full-scale entertainment complex that boasts several thematic exhibits, two diners, a cinema, and a newly built 450-room hotel. While Elvis's daughter Lisa Marie retains ownership of the mansion as well as a 15 percent stake in EPE, the Authentic Brands Group acquired the rights to the licensing and merchandising of Elvis's name and image for $145 million in 2013.[8] Perhaps even more important was the fostering of the singer's legacy by music specialists, collectors, and devoted fans. In the 1990s, Peter Guralnick's two-volume biography of Elvis finally offered a sophisticated and comprehensive treatment of the singer's life and times; it constitutes an excellent complement to Ernst Jorgensen's meticulous study of Elvis's musical recordings that was published around the same time.[9] Elvis's record company, now owned by Sony Music Entertainment, has also taken some efforts to present Elvis's significant musical oeuvre adequately, as the release of many legacy box sets and the founding of the collectors' label Follow That Dream (FTD) demonstrate. Yet it is the dedication and activism of fans that has been the most significant factor behind Elvis's posthumous popularity, and the incredibly rich amount of highly specialized knowledge in countless books, websites, and online forums often rivals the knowledge of even the very best experts in the field.

While Elvis still holds enormous cultural significance today, there have been signs of a gradual waning of interest in the singer's music and legacy. Part of it has to do with demographics. According to the Authentic Brands Group, almost 80 percent of Elvis's fans are over thirty-five years old, and only 1.6 percent under eighteen. These trends have become reflected in

---

[7]As reprinted in Marcus, *Dead Elvis*, 47–59.
[8]"Can Elvis Rise Again?," *Rolling Stone*, www.rollingstone.com/music/music-features/elvis-presley-business-revenue-953324/ [last accessed April 28, 2020].
[9]Guralnick, *Last Train*; Guralnick, *Careless Love*; Jorgensen, *A Life in Music*.

the singer's posthumous income: the sale figures of Elvis memorabilia, for example, have fallen from around $4 million in 2017 to merely $1.5 million two years later, and the Presley estate's annual revenue has declined by 30 percent over the past decade. In light of these figures, the Authentic Brands Group has launched an extensive campaign trying to make Elvis relevant to a younger age group: it includes an Elvis filter on Snapchat, videos of his favorite animals on Dodo, and the animated Netflix series *Agent King* that features the singer as an undercover agent.[10]

Above all, however, the new marketing strategy is to once again portray Elvis by transfiguring him into a larger-than-life American Dream story that alludes powerfully to much bigger narratives of American identity. "He's the guy who was 18 and straight out of a not-great high school, trying to make something of himself," a representative of the Authentic Brands Group recently told the *Rolling Stone*. "That's all that Drake and Justin Bieber wanted. You don't present him as a rocker. You present him as this iconic American story."[11] Graceland already frames Elvis's life and career largely in such a way. The most popular exhibition, for example, is an enormous hall that displays Elvis's countless luxury cars, not least the famous pink Cadillac of the 1950s. It is accompanied by a huge sign on the wall, which presents one of Elvis's most popular quips: "Ambition is a dream with a v8 engine."

And yet, such popular constructions of Elvis as the quintessential American folk hero remain hotly contested to this day. In the recent film documentary *The King* (2017), Eugene Jarecki actually took one of Elvis's cars to travel around the United States and quiz celebrities as well as random by-passers about the singer.[12] He then used the countless images, clichés, and stereotypes surrounding Elvis in public memory to present his own impressionistic take on the United States in the early twenty-first century. "America seemed like a new sensation for a time, even if built upon the backs of an exploited repressed class," one film critic aptly summarized the film's provocative thesis. "Now we're in a drugged-out haze in a dopey white jumpsuit, fat and bloated and depressed. Donald Trump is our president and we're about to drop dead in the bathroom."[13] More than forty years after his passing, Elvis remains a powerful articulation point for much bigger questions of American culture and identity.

---

[10]"Can Elvis Rise Again?," *Rolling* Stone, www.rollingstone.com/music/music-features/elvis-presley-business-revenue-953324/ [last accessed April 28, 2020].
[11]Ibid.
[12]Interestingly, not a Cadillac but a 1963 Rolls Royce Phantom V.
[13]*The Guardian*, May 20, 2017.

# Bibliography

## Unpublished Sources

Academy of Motion Picture Arts and Sciences, Margaret Herrick Library, Los Angeles, CA (United States)
- Hal Wallis Papers
- Hedda Hopper Papers

Cinematic Arts Library, University of Southern California, Los Angeles, CA (United States)
- David Weisbart Collection
- Frankie and Johnny Files
- Philip Dunne Collection

Eisenhower Presidential Library, Abilene, KS (United States)
- White House Central Files, Alphabetical File, Box 2496, Presley, Elvis.

Georgetown University, Both Family Center for Special Collections, Washington, DC (United States)
- Department of Defense Film Collection, Box 22: G.I. Blues

Lee County Library, Tupelo, MS (United States)
- Elaine Dundy Collection

National Archives and Records Administration, College Park, MD (United States)
- Record Group 306: Records of the United States Information Agency (USIA)
- Record Group 407: Records of the Adjutant General's office, 1917–

Roosevelt Institute for American Studies, Middelburg (Netherlands)
- Records of the U.S. Information Agency (USIA), Part 1: Cold War Era Special Reports, Series A: 1953–1963
- Records of the U.S. Information Agency (USIA), Part 1: Cold War Era Special Reports, Series B: 1964–1982
- Records of the U.S. Information Agency (USIA), Part 3: Cold War Era Research Reports, Series A: 1960–1963

# Published Primary Sources

## Print

Carter, Jimmy. "Death of Elvis Presley: Statement by the President." In *Public Papers of the Presidents of the United States: Jimmy Carter, 1977*. Washington, DC, 1977.

Congressional Record. "4 March 1960," *Congressional Record: Proceedings of Congress and General Congressional Publications*, 85th Congress, 2nd Season, 106/4. Washington, DC, 1960, 4151–2.

## Websites

"Can Elvis Rise Again?," *Rolling Stone*, www.rollingstone.com/music/music-features/elvis-presley-business-revenue-953324/ [last accessed April 28, 2020].

"Discurso Pronunciado por El Commandante Fidel Castro Ruz, Primer Ministro del Gobierno revolucionario de Cuba, en la Clausura del acto para Commemorar el vi aniversario del as alto al Palacio Presidencial, celebrado en la escalinata de la Universidad de la Habana, el 13 de Marzo de 1963," www.cuba.cu/gobierno/discursos/1963/esp/f130363e.html [last accessed December 22, 2019].

"Elvis Aaron Presley—Elvis' Middle Name, Is It Aron or Aaron?," *Elvis Australia*, www.elvis.com.au/presley/news/article-aron-or-aaron.shtml [last accessed November 7, 2019].

"Elvis Presley | Jacksonville, FL," *Elvis Presley Photos*, www.elvispresleymusic.com.au/pictures/1956-florida-state-theater-august-10-11.html [last accessed December 12, 2019].

"Elvis Presley Meets the Beatles," *Elvis Australia*, www.elvis.com.au/presley/elvis-meets-the-beatles.shtml [last accessed November 21, 2019].

"Elvis Presley's GOLD Cadillac Tour of AUSTRALASIA 1968-69 (book review)," www.elvisinfonet.com/bookreview_goldcaddy_2011edition.htm [last accessed May 3, 2020.]

"Interview with Colonel Frank Athanason," *Foreign Affairs Oral History Collection of the Association for Diplomatic Studies and Training, Library of Congress, Washington, DC* www.loc.gov/item/mfdipbib001678/ [last accessed May 3, 2019].

"Medal of Freedom," *The White House*, www.whitehouse.gov/medaloffreedom/ [last accessed February 12, 2019].

"Transcript of Elvis' 1972 Madison Square Garden Press Conference," *Elvis Australia*, www.elvis.com.au/presley/interview-with-elvis-presley-the-1972-press-conference.shtml [last accessed August 25, 2019].

"When Elvis Met Nixon," *Online Exhibition by the U.S. National Archives*, www.archives.gov/exhibits/nixon-met/elvis [last accessed August 22, 2019].

British Broadcasting Cooperation. "Press Releases: General Colin Powell on Elvis Presley the soldier and patriot," www.bbc.co.uk/pressoffice/pressreleases/stories/2007/08_august/21/elvis.shtml [last accessed September 4, 2019].

Deelen, Arjan. "Interview with Jerry Scheff," *Elvis Australia*, www.elvis.com.au/presley/interview-jerryscheff.shtml [last accessed August 21, 2019].

Ebert, Roger. "Speedway," June 28, 1968. www.rogerebert.com/reviews/speedway-1968 [last accessed December 31, 2019].

English, David and Troedson, David. "Elvis Presley | U.S. Jaycees | Ten Outstanding Young Men 1970," https://www.elvispresleyphotos.com/1971-january-16-jaycees-award.html [last accessed January 21, 2020].

Werner, Michael and Weber, Bianca. "Aloha from Hawaii via Satellite: Fact&Fancy," *Elvis Australia*. www.elvis.com.au/presley/aloha-from-hawaii-via-satellite-fact-fancy.shtml [last accessed May 13, 2019].

### Newspapers and Magazines

*Abendzeitung, Aberdeen Evening Express, Afro-American, Arizona Republic, Atlanta Daily World, Baltimore African-American, Baltimore Sun, Berliner Zeitung, Billboard, Biloxi Daily Herald, BRAVO, Breckenridge American, Boston Globe, Charlotte Observer, Chicago Daily News, Chicago Tribune, Commercial Appeal, The Christian Science Monitor, Corpus Christi Caller Times, Cosmopolitan, Daily Mail, Daily Mirror, Daily Telegraph, Dallas Morning News, Dallas Morning Star, Der Spiegel, Detroit News, Disc, Elvis Monthly, Evening Times Glasgow, The Florence Times, Frankfurter Allgemeine Zeitung, Guardian, The Great Speckled Bird, Hartford Currant, Hollywood Reporter, Junge Welt, Kansas City Times, Lakeland Ledger, Life Magazine, Long Beach Independent, Los Angeles Sentinel, Los Angeles Times, Lubbock Evening Avalanche Journal, Manchester Guardian, Melody Maker, Memphis Press-Scimitar, Minnesota Star Tribune, New Musical Express, New York Herald Tribune, New York Journal, New York Mag, New York Magazine, New York Times, New Yorker, Newsweek, Nevada State Journal, Oakland Tribune, Orlando Sentinel, Picturegoer, Pravda, The Post Standard, Rolling Stone, San Antonio Express and News, San Diego Evening News, The Sioux City Journal, St. Louis Post-Dispatch, St. Petersburg Times, Tampa Daily Times, Tribune, Stanford Daily, The Times, The Times Herald, This Week, Time Magazine, Tucson Daily Citizen, Tulsa Daily World, Village Voice, Wall Street Journal, Washington Post, Weidener Nachrichten*

## Secondary Works

Alden, Ginger. *Elvis and Ginger: Elvis Presley's Fiancée and Last Love Finally Tells Her Story*. New York, NY: Ace Books, 2014.

Altschuler, Glenn D. *All Shook Up: How Rock 'n' Roll Changed America*. Oxford: Oxford University Press, 2003.

Aquila, Richard. *Let's Rock! How 1950s America created Elvis and the Rock & Roll craze*. Lanham, MD: Rowan & Littlefield, 2017.

Bailey, Beth and Farber, David. "Introduction." In *America in the Seventies*, edited by Beth Bailey and David Farber, 1–8. Lawrence, KS: University Press of Kansas, 2004.

Balzer, Jens. *Das Entfesselte Jahrzehnt: Sound und Geist der 70er*. Berlin: Rowohlt, 2019.

Becker, Tobias. "Rückkehr der Geschichte? Die „Nostalgie-Welle" in den 1970er und 1980er Jahren." In *Zeitenwandel: Transformationen geschichtlicher Zeitlichkeit nach dem Boom*, edited by Fernando Esposito, 93–117. Göttingen: Vandenhoeck & Ruprecht, 2017.

Becker, Tobias. "The Meanings of Nostalgia: Genealogy and Critique." In *History and Theory* 57/2 (2018), 234–50.

Belmonte, Laura A. *Selling the American Way: U.S. Propaganda and the Cold War.* Philadelphia, PA: University of Pennsylvania Press, 2008.

Bertrand, Michael T. *Race, Rock, and Elvis.* Chicago, IL: University of Illinois Press, 2004.

Bertrand, Michael T. "'A Tradition-Conscious Cotton City': (East) Tupelo, Mississippi, Birthplace of Elvis Presley." In *Destination Dixie: Tourism & Southern History*, edited by Karen L. Cox, 87–112. Gainesville, FL: University Press of Florida, 2012.

Binder, Steve. *Comeback '68 / Elvis: The Story of the Elvis Special.* Los Angeles, CA: Meteor 17 Books, 2018.

Blaszczyk, Regina Lee. *American Consumer Society, 1865–2005: From Hearth to HDTV.* Hoboken, NJ: John Wiley & Sons, 2008.

Bloemeke, Rüdiger. *Roll over Beethoven: Wie der Rock 'n' Roll nach Deutschland kam.* St. Andrä-Wördern: Hannibal Verlag, 1996.

Bösch, Frank. *Mediengeschichte: Vom asiatischen Buchdruck zum Computer.* Frankfurt and New York, NY: Campus, 2019.

Boucher, David. *Dylan and Cohen: Poets of Rock and Roll.* London: Bloomsbury, 2004.

Bradley, Dick. *Understanding Rock 'n' Roll: Popular Music in Britain, 1955–1964.* Buckingham: Open University Press, 1992.

Briggs, Jonathyne. *Sounds French: Globalization, Cultural Communities, and Pop Music in France, 1958–1980.* Oxford: Oxford University Press, 2015.

Brode, Douglas. *Elvis Cinema and Popular Culture.* Jefferson, NC: McFarland & Company, 2006.

Browder, Dewey A. "Appendix: Population Statistics for U.S. Military in Germany, 1945-2000." In *GIs in Germany: The Social, Economic, Cultural, and Political History of the American Military Presence*, edited by Thomas W. Maulucci Jr. and Detlef Junker, 347–52. Cambridge: Cambridge University Press, 2013.

Buckley, David. *Strange Fascination—David Bowie: The Definitive Story.* London: Virgin, 2005.

Burzik, Monika. "Von singenden Seemännern und Musikern vom Sirius. Die Musik der fünfziger Jahre." In *Die Kultur der Fünfziger Jahre*, edited by Werner Faulstich, 249–62. Munich: Wilhelm Fink Verlag, 2007.

Cahn, Susan K. *Sexual Reckonings: Southern Girls in a Troubling Age.* Cambridge, MA: Harvard University Press, 2012.

Cantor, Louis. *Dewey and Elvis: The Life and Times of a Rock 'n' Deejay.* Chicago, IL: University of Illinois Press, 2005.

Capozzola, Cristopher. "'It Makes You Want to Believe in the Country': Celebrating the Bicentennial in an Age of Limits." In *America in the Seventies*, edited by Beth Baily and David Farber, 29–49. Lawrence, KS: University Press of Kansas, 2004.

Caute, David. *The Dancer Defects: The Struggle for Cultural Supremacy During the Cold War.* Oxford: Oxford University Press, 2003.

Chadwick, Vernon (ed.). *In Search of Elvis: Music, Race, Art, Religion.* New York, NY and London: Routledge, 1997.

Clayton, David. "The Consumption of Radio Broadcast Technologies in Hong Kong, c. 1930–1960." In *The Economic History Review* 57/4 (2004), 691–726.

Cohen, Lizbeth. *A Consumers' Republic: The Politics of Mass Consumption in Postwar America*. New York NY: Vintage Books, 2004.

Connolly, Ray. *Being Elvis. A Lonely Life*. London: Weidenfeld & Nicholson, 2016.

Cross, Gary S. *Machines of Youth: America's Car Obsession*. Chicago, IL: University of Chicago Press, 2018.

Davenport, Lisa E. *Jazz Diplomacy: Promoting America in the Cold War Era*. Jackson, MI: University Press of Mississippi, 2009.

Dawson, Jim. *Rock Around the Clock: The Record That Started The Rock Revolution!* San Francisco, CA: Backbeat Books, 2005.

Dick, Bernard F. *Hal Wallis: Producer to the Stars*. Lexington, KY: University Press of Kentucky, 2004.

Doll, Susan. *Understanding Elvis: Southern Roots vs. Star Image*. London and New York, NY: Routledge, 1998 [2016].

Doss, Erika Lee. *Elvis Culture: Fans, Faith & Image*. Lawrence, KA: University Press of Kansas, 1999.

Duffett, Mark. *Counting Down Elvis: His 100 Finest Songs*. Lanham, MD: Rowman & Littlefield, 2018.

Duffett, Mark. *Elvis: Roots, Image, Comeback, Phenomenon*. Sheffield: Equinox Publishing Limited, 2020.

Duffett, Mark. *Understanding Fandom: An Introduction to the Study of Media Fan Culture*. London: Bloomsbury, 2013.

Dundy, Elaine. *Elvis and Gladys: The Genesis of the King*. New York, NY: Macmillan, 1985.

Dussel, Konrad. "The Triumph of English-Language Pop Music: West German Radio Programming." In *Between Marx and Coca-Cola: Youth Cultures in Changing European Societies, 1960-1980*, edited by Axel Schildt and Detlef Siegfried, 127–48. New York, NY and Oxford: Berghahn Books, 2006.

Dwyer, Michael D. *Back to the Fifties: Nostalgia, Hollywood Film, and Popular Music of the Seventies and Eighties*. New York, NY and Oxford: Oxford University Press, 2015.

Eschen, Penny von. *Satchmo Blows Up the World: Jazz Ambassadors Play the Cold War*. Cambridge, MA: Harvard University Press, 2006.

Esposito, Joe. *Good Rockin' Tonight: Twenty Years on the Road and on the Town with Elvis*. New York, NY: Simon & Schuster, 1994.

Fenemore, Mark. *Sex, Thugs and Rock 'n' Roll: Teenage Rebels in Cold-War East Germany*. New York, NY and Oxford: Berghahn Books, 2007.

Ferguson, Niall et al. (eds.). *The Shock of the Global: The 1970s in Perspective*. Cambridge, MA and London: Harvard University Press, 2010.

Field, Douglas (ed.). *American Cold War Culture*. Edinburgh: Edinburgh University Press, 2005.

Fischer, Michael. "Musik, Stars, Medien: Peter Kraus als Beispiel einer domestizierten Amerikanisierung der deutschen Musikkultur." In *Amerika-Euphorie—Amerika-Hysterie: Populäre Musik made in USA in der Wahrnehmung der Deutschen 1914-2014*, edited by Michael Fischer and Christofer Jost, 211–26. Münster: Waxmann, 2017.

Flynn, George Q. *The Draft, 1940–1973*. Lawrence, KS: University Press of Kansas, 1993.

Forsberg, Aaron. *America and the Japanese Miracle: The Cold War Context of Japan's Postwar Economic Revival, 1950–1960*. Chapel Hill, NC: University of North Carolina Press, 2014.

Fosler-Lussier, Danielle. *Music in America's Cold War Diplomacy*. Oakland, CA: University of California Press, 2015.

Friedlander, Paul. *Rock and Roll: A Social History*. Boulder, CO: Westview Press, 1996.

Fuchs. "Rock 'n' Roll in the German Democratic Republic, 1949–1961." In "*Here, There and Everywhere*": *The Foreign Politics of American Popular Culture*, edited by Reinhold Wagnleitner and Elaine Tyler May, 192–206. Hanover, NH: University of New England Press, 2000.

Fürst, Juliane. *Stalin's Last Generation: Soviet Post-war Youth and the Emergence of Mature Socialism*. Oxford: Oxford University Press, 2010.

Geller, Larry and Spector, Joel. *If I Can Dream*. New York, NY: Simon and Schuster, 1989.

Gienow-Hecht, Jessica. *Transmission Impossible: American Journalism as Cultural Diplomacy in Postwar Germany 1945–1955*. Baton Rouge, LA: Louisiana State University Press, 1999.

Gienow-Hecht, Jessica. "Culture and the Cold War in Europe". In *The Cambridge History of the Cold War, Vol. I: Origins*, edited by Melvyn P. Leffler and Odd A. Westad, 398–419. Cambridge: Cambridge University Press, 2010.

Gilbert, James. *A Cycle of Outrage: America's Reaction to the Juvenile Delinquent in the 1950s*. New York, NY and Oxford: Oxford University Press, 1986.

Goldman, Albert H. *Elvis*. New York, NY: McGraw-Hill Book Company, 1981.

Goltz, Anna von der and Waldschmidt-Nelson, Britta (eds.). *Inventing the Silent Majority in Western Europe and the United States: Conservatism in the 1960s and 1970s*. Cambridge: Cambridge University Press, 2017.

Gordon, Robert. *It Came From Memphis*. Boston, MA and London: Faber and Faber, 1995.

Goto, Zoey. *Elvis Style: From Zoot Suits to Jump Suits*. Faringdon: Redshank Books, 2016.

Gould, Jonathan. *Can't Buy Me Love: The Beatles, Britain, and America*. New York, NY: Harmony Books, 2007.

de Grazia, Victoria. *Irresistible Empire. America's Advance Through Twentieth-Century Europe*. Cambridge, MA: Belknap Press, 2005.

Gray, Michael. *The Bob Dylan Encyclopedia*. New York, NY and London: continuum, 2006.

Greiner, Florian and Röger, Maren. "Den Kalten Krieg Spielen: Brett- und Computerspiele in der Systemkonfrontation." In *Zeithistorische Forschung / Studies in Contemporary History* 16/1 (2019), 46–73.

Grotum, Thomas. *Die Halbstarken: Zur Geschichte einer Jugendkultur der 50er Jahre*. Frankfurt am Main: Campus, 1994.

Guralnick, Peter. *Careless Love: The Unmaking of Elvis Presley*. London: Abacus, 2000.

Guralnick, Peter. *Last Train to Memphis: The Rise of Elvis Presley*. London: Abacus, 1995.

Guralnick, Peter. *Lost Highway: Journeys & Arrivals of American Musicians*. Edinburgh: Canongate, 1979 [2002].

Guralnick, Peter. *Sam Phillips: The Man Who Invented Rock 'n' Roll*. London: Weidenfeld & Nicolson, 2015.

Guralnick, Peter and Jorgensen, Ernst. *Elvis Day by Day: The Definitive Record of His Life and Music*. New York, NY: Ballantine Books, 1999.

Hamm, Charles. *Putting Popular Music in its Place*. Cambridge: Cambridge University Press, 1995 [2006].

Harrison, Ted. *The Death and Resurrection of Elvis Presley*. London: Reaktion Books, 2016.

Heigl, Peter. *Sergeant Elvis Presley in Grafenwöhr*. Amberg: Buch & Kunstverlag Oberpfalz, 2007.

Hilgert, Christoph. *Die unerhörte Generation: Jugend im westdeutschen und britischen Hörfunk 1945–1963*. Göttingen: Wallstein, 2015.

Hilgert, Christoph. "Der junge Hörer, das unbekannte Wesen: Programmangebote für Jugendliche im westdeutschen Hörfunk in der Mitte des 20. Jahrhunderts." In *Let's Historize It! Jugendmedien im 20. Jahrhundert*, edited by Aline Maldener and Clemens Zimmermann, 131–56. Köln: Böhlau, 2018.

Hitchcock, William. *The Age of Eisenhower: America and the World in the 1950s*. New York, NY and London: Simon & Schuster, 2018.

Hixon, Walter. *Parting the Curtain: Propaganda, Culture, and the Cold War, 1945–1961*. Basingstoke: Macmillan, 1997.

Hodge, Charlie. *Me 'n Elvis*. Memphis, TN: Castle Books, 1984.

Hoeres, Peter. *Außenpolitik und Öffentlichkeit: Massenmedien, Meinungsforschung und Arkanpolitik in den deutsch-amerikanischen Beziehungen von Erhard bis Brandt*. Munich: Oldenbourg, 2013.

Höhn, Maria. *GIs and Fräuleins: The German-American Encounter in 1950s West Germany*. Chapel Hill, NC and London: The University of North Carolina Press, 2002.

Hopkins, Jerry. *Elvis: A Biography*. New York, NY: Simon & Schuster, 1971.

Horn, Adrian. *Juke Box Britain: Americanisation and Youth Culture, 1945–60*. Manchester: Manchester University Press, 2009.

Hüser, Dietmar. "Einleitung: Transnationale Populärkultur im Europa der langen 1960er Jahre: Forschungsstand und Forschungspisten." In *Populärkultur Transnational: Lesen, Hören, Sehen, Erleben im Europa der langen 1960er Jahre*, edited by Dietmar Hüser, 7–14. Bielefeld: transcript, 2017.

Hüser, Dietmar. "'Rock Around the Clock'. Überlegungen zu amerikanischer Populärkultur in der französischen und westdeutschen Gesellschaft der 1950er und 1960er Jahre." In *Deutschland – Frankreich – Nordamerika: Transfers, Imaginationen, Beziehungen*, edited by Chantal Metzger and Hartmut Kaelble, 189–208. Munich: Franz Steiner Verlag, 2006.

Ilson, Bernie. *Sundays with Sullivan: How the Ed Sullivan Show Brought Elvis, The Beatles, and Culture to America*. Lanham, MD: Taylor Trade Publishing, 2009.

James, David E. *Rock 'N' Film: Cinema's Dance with Popular Music*. New York, NY and Oxford: Oxford University Press, 2016.

James, David E. "Rock 'n' Film: Generic Permutations in Three Feature Films from 1964." *Grey Room* 49 (2012), 6–31.

Janssen, Wiebke. *Halbstarke in der DDR: Verfolgung und Kriminalisierung Einer Jugendkultur*. Berlin: Ch. Links Verlag, 2010.

Jeansonne, Glen, Luhrssen, David and Sokolovic, Dan. *Elvis Presley, Reluctant Rebel: His Life and Our Times*. Santa Barbara, CA: Praeger, 2011.

Jehle Anna. *Welle der Konsumgesellschaft: Radio Luxembourg in Frankreich 1945–1975*. Göttingen: Wallstein, 2018.

John, Elton. *Me*. London: Macmillan, 2019.

Johnstone, Nick. *Melody Maker History of 20th Century Popular Music*. London: Bloomsbury, 1999.

Jorgensen, Ernst. *Elvis Presley: A Life In Music*. New York, NY: St. Martin's Press, 1998.

Juanico, June. *Elvis: In the Twilight of Memory*. New York, NY: Arcade, 1997.

Judt, Tony. *Postwar: A History of Europe since 1945*. London: Vintage, 2005 [2010].

Kan, Alex and Hayes, Nick. "Big Beat in Poland." In *Rocking the State: Rock Music and Politics in Eastern Europe and Russia*, edited by Sabrina P. Ramet, 41–53. Boulder, CO: Westview Press, 1994.

King, B.B. *Blues All Around Me: The Autobiography of B.B. King*. New York, NY: Avon Books, 1996.

Kitamura, Hiroshi. *Screening Enlightenment: Hollywood and the Cultural Reconstruction of Defeated Japan*. Ithaca, NY: Cornell University Press, 2010.

Klautke, Egbert. "Die 'britische Invasion': britische Pop- und Rockmusik in den USA." In *Populärkultur—transnational: Sehen, Hören, Lesen, Erleben im Europa der langen 1960er Jahre*, edited by Dietmar Hüser, 107–25. Bielefeld: Transcript, 2017.

Klein, George. *Elvis: My Best Man*. New York, NY: Three Rivers Press, 2011.

Krenn, Michael L. *The History of United States Cultural Diplomacy: 1770 to the Present Day*. London: Bloomsbury, 2017.

Kroes, Rob. "American Mass Culture and European Youth Culture." In *Between Marx and Coca-Cola: Youth Cultures in Changing European Societies, 1960–1980*, edited by Axel Schildt and Detlef Siegfried, 82–108. New York, NY and Oxford: Berghahn, 2006.

Kroes, Rob. *If You've Seen One, You've Seen the Mall: Europeans and American Mass Culture*. Urbana and Chicago, IL: University of Illinois Press, 1996.

Krough, Egil. *The Day Elvis Met Nixon*. Bellevue, WA: Pejama Press, 1994.

Larsen, Charlotte Rørdam. "'Above all, it's because he's English …' Tommy Steele and the Notion of "Englishness" as Mediator of Wild Rock 'n' Roll". In *Britain and Denmark: Political, Economic and Cultural Relations in the 19th and 20th Centuries*, edited by Jørgen Sevaldsen, Bo Bjørke and Claus Bjørn, 493–510. Copenhagen: Museum Tusculanum Press, 2003.

Leiber, Jerry and Stoller, Mike. *Hound Dog: The Leiber and Stoller Autobiography*. New York, NY: Simon&Schuster, 2009.

Leigh, Spencer. *Elvis Presley: Caught in a Trap*. Carmarthen: McNidder & Grace, 2017.

Leuerer, Thomas. "U.S. Army Military Communities in Germany." In *GIs in Germany: The Social, Economic, Cultural, and Political History of the American Military Presence*, edited by Thomas W. Maulucci Jr. and Detlef Junker, 121–41. Cambridge: Cambridge University Press, 2013.

Levine, Lawrence W. *Highbrow/Lowbrow: The Emergence of Cultural Hierarchy in America* Cambridge, MA: Harvard University Press, 1990.

Levy, Alan. *Operation Elvis*. London: André Deutsch Limited, 1960.

Liew, Kai Khiun. "Rock 'n' Roll and the Restringing and Resounding of the Singapore story." In *Singapore. Negotiating State and Society, 1965-2015*, edited by Jason Lim and Terence Lee, 187–200. London and New York, NY: Routledge, 2016.

Linn, Brian McAllister. *Elvis's Army: Cold War GIs and the Atomic Battlefield.* Cambridge, MA: Harvard University Press, 2016.

Lucas, Scott. *Freedom's War: The U.S. Crusade against the Soviet Union, 1945–1956.* New York, NY: New York University Press, 1999.

Lüdtke, Alf, Marßolek, Inge and Saldern, Adelheid von. "Amerikanisierung: Traum und Alptraum im Deutschland des 20. Jahrhunderts." In *Amerikanisierung: Traum und Alptraum im Deutschland des 20. Jahrhunderts*, edited by Alf Lüdtke, Inge Marßolek, Adelheid von Saldern, 7–36. Stuttgart: Steiner Verlag, 1996.

Lundestad, Geir. "Empire by Invitation? The United States and Western Europe, 1945–1952." In *Journal of Peace Research* 23/3 (1986), 263–77.

Maase, Kaspar. *BRAVO Amerika: Erkundungen zur Jugendkultur der Bundesrepublik in den fünfziger Jahren.* Hamburg: Junius, 1992.

Maase, Kaspar. "Establishing Cultural Democracy: Youth, "Americanization," and the Irresistible Rise of Popular Culture." In *The Miracle Years: A Cultural History of West Germany, 1949–1968*, edited by Hanna Schissler, 528–50. Princeton, NJ: Princeton University Press, 2001.

Magnúsdóttir, Rosa. *Enemy Number One: The United States of America in Soviet Ideology and Propaganda, 1945–1959.* Oxford: Oxford University Press, 2019.

Maldener, Aline and Zimmermann, Clemens (eds.). *Let's Historize It! Jugendmedien im 20. Jahrhundert.* Köln: Böhlau, 2018.

Maldener, Aline. "Fabulous consumerism? Mediale Repräsentationen jugendlicher Konsumkultur in westdeutschen, britischen und französischen Jugendzeitschriften der 1960er und 1970er Jahre." In *Populärkultur Transnational: Lesen, Hören, Sehen, Erleben im Europa der langen 1960er Jahre*, edited by Dietmar Hüser, 199–224. Bielefeld: transcript, 2017.

Mansfield, Rex and Mansfield, Elisabeth. *Elvis the Soldier.* Bamberg: Collectors Service, 1983.

Marcus, Daniel. *Happy Days and Wonder Years: The Fifties and the Sixties in Contemporary Cultural Politics.* Piscataway, NJ: Rutgers University Press, 2004.

Marcus, Greil. *Dead Elvis: A Chronicle of a Cultural Obsession.* New York, NY: Doubleday, 1991.

Marcus, Greil. *Mystery Train: Images of America in Rock 'n' Roll Music.* New York, NY: E.P. Dutton & Co., Inc., 1975.

Marcus, Sharon. *The Drama of Celebrity.* Princeton, NJ: Princeton University Press, 2019.

Marsh, Dave. *Elvis.* New York, NY: Times Books, 1982.

Maulucci, Thomas W. Jr. "Introduction." In *GIs in Germany: The Social, Economic, Cultural, and Political History of the American Military Presence*, edited by Thomas W. Maulucci Jr. and Detlef Junker, 1–36. Cambridge: Cambridge University Press, 2013.

Maulucci, Thomas W. Jr. and Junker, Detlef (eds.). *GIs in Germany: The Social, Economic, Cultural, and Political History of the American Military Presence.* Cambridge: Cambridge University Press, 2013.

Martin, Linda and Segrave, Kerry. *Anti-Rock: The Opposition to Rock 'n' Roll.* Hamden, CT: Archon Books, 1988.

Marwick, Arthur. *The Sixties: Cultural Revolution in Britain, France, Italy, and the United States, c. 1958–c.1974.* Oxford: Oxford University Press, 1998.

Marwick, Arthur. "Youth Culture and the Cultural Revolution of the Long Sixties." In *Between Marx and Coca-Cola: Youth Cultures in Changing European Societies, 1960–1980*, edited by Axel Schildt and Detlef Siegfried, 39–58. New York, NY and Oxford: Berghahn, 2006.

Maulucci, Thomas W. Jr and Junker, Detlef (eds.). *GIs in Germany: The Social, Economic, Cultural, and Political History of the American Military Presence.* Cambridge: Cambridge University Press, 2013.

May, Elaine Tyler. *Homeward Bound: American Families in the Cold War Era.* New York, NY: Basic Books 1988 [1999].

McGovern, Charles F. *Sold American: Consumption and Citizenship, 1890–1945.* Chapel Hill, NC: University of North Carolina Press, 2006.

Medovoi, Leerom. *Rebels: Youth and the Cold War Origins of Identity.* Durham, NC and London: Duke University Press, 2005.

Meeuf, Russell and Raphael, Raphael. "Introduction." In *Transnational Stardom: International Celebrity in Film and Popular Culture*, edited by Russell Meeuf and Raphael Raphael, 1–16. New York, NY: Palgrave Macmillan, 2013.

Meyerowitz, Joanne. "The Liberal 1950s? Reinterpreting Postwar U.S. Sexual Culture." In *Gender and the Long Postwar: Reconsiderations of the United States and the Two Germanys, 1945-1989*, edited by Karen Hagemann and Sonya Michel, 297–319. Baltimore, MD: Johns Hopkins University Press, 2014.

Miller, Jennifer M. *Cold War Democracy: The United States and Japan.* Harvard, MA: University Press, 2019.

Miller-Davenport, Sarah. *Gateway State: Hawai'i and the Cultural Transformation of American Empire.* Lawrenceville, NJ: Princeton University Press, 2019.

Mitchell, Gillian A. M. *Adult Responses to Popular Music and Intergenerational Relations in Britain, c. 1955–1975.* London and New York, NY: Anthem Press, 2019.

Mitchell, Gillian A. M. *The British National Daily Press and Popular Music, c. 1956–1975.* London and New York, NY: Anthem Press, 2019.

Mitchell, Gillian A. M. "A Very "British" Introduction to Rock 'n Roll: Tommy Steele and the Advent of Rock 'n' Roll Music in Britain, 1956–1960." In *Contemporary British History* 25/2 (2011), 205–25.

Mitchell, Gillian A. M. "Reassessing 'the Generation Gap': Bill Haley's 1957 Tour of Britain, Inter-Generational Relations and Attitudes to Rock 'n' Roll in the late 1950s." In *Twentieth Century British History* 24/4 (2013), 573–605.

Morgner, Christian. "Zeitlichkeiten globaler Medienereignisse: Am Beispiel der Ermordung John F. Kennedys." In *Medienereignisse der Moderne*, edited by Friedrich Lenger and Ansgar Nünning, 130–49. Darmstadt: Wissenschaftliche Buchgesellschaft, 2008.

Mrozek, Bodo. *Jugend—Pop—Kultur: Eine transnationale Geschichte.* Berlin 2019.

Nash, Alanna. *The Colonel: The Extraordinary Story of Colonel Tom Parker and Elvis Presley.* London: Aurum Press, 2003.

Nash, Alanna. *Elvis Aaron Presley: Revelations from the Memphis Mafia.* New York; NY: HarperCollins, 1995.

Nathaus, Klaus. "Nationale Produktionssysteme im transatlantischen Kulturtransfer. Zur „Amerikanisierung" populärer Musik in Westdeutschland und Großbritannien im Vergleich, 1950–1980." In *Kulturen der Weltwirtschaft*, edited by Werner Abelshauser, David A. Gilgen and Andreas Leutzsch, 202–27. Göttingen: Vandenhoeck & Ruprecht, 2012.

Neibaur, James L. *The Elvis Movies*. London: Rowman & Littlefield, 2014.

Nekrasov, Viktor. *Both Sides of the Ocean: A Russian Writer's Travels in Italy and the United States*. New York: Holt, Rinehart and Winston, 1964.

Nolan, Mary. *The Transatlantic Century. Europe and America, 1890–2010*. Cambridge: Cambridge University Press, 2012.

Notaker, Hallvard, Scott-Smith, Giles and Snyder, David J. "Introduction: Reasserting America in the 1970s." In *Reasserting America in the 1970s: U.S. Public Diplomacy and the Rebuilding of America's Image Abroad*, edited by Hallvard Notaker, Giles Scott-Smith and David J. Snyder, 1–8. Manchester: University Press, 2016.

Nygaard, Bertel. "The High Priest of Rock and Roll: The Reception of Elvis Presley in Denmark, 1956–1960." In *Popular Music and Society* 42/3 (2019), 330–47.

Oakley, J. Ronald. *God's Country: America in the Fifties*. New York, NY: W. W. Norton, 1986.

Osborne, Jerry. *Elvis: Word for Word*. New York, NY: Harmony Books, 2000.

Osgerby, Bill. *Youth in Britain since 1945*. Oxford: Blackwell, 1998.

Osgerby, Bill. *Youth Media*. London: Routledge, 2004.

Osgood, Kenneth. *Total Cold War: Eisenhower's Secret Propaganda Battle at Home and Abroad*. Lawrence, KS: University Press of Kansas, 2006.

Pakes, Bob. *The EPE Catalog: A Comprehensive A to Z Guide of Vintage Elvis Presley Enterprises memorabilia*. Oslo: KJ Consulting, 2017.

Palmer, Landon. "'And Introducing Elvis Presley': Industrial Convergence and Transmedia Stardom in the Rock 'n' Roll Movie." In *Music, Sound & the Moving Image* 9/2 (2015), 177–90.

Palmer, Landon. "King Creole: Michael Curtiz and the Great Elvis Presley Industry." In *The Many Cinemas of Michael Curtiz*, edited by Barton Palmer and Murray Pomerance, 171–84. Austin, TX: University of Texas Press, 2018.

Pells, Richard. *Not Like Us: How Europeans Have Loved, Hated, and Transformed American Culture since World War II*. New York, NY: Basic Books, 1997.

Pérez, Louis A. Jr. *On Becoming Cuban: Identity, Nationality, and Culture*. Chapel Hill, NC: The University of North Carolina Press, 1999.

Peters, Christian and Reiche, Jürgen. *Elvis in Deutschland*. Bonn: Haus der Geschichte der Bundesrepublik Deutschland, 2004.

Peterson, Richard A. "Why 1955? Explaining the Advent of Rock Music." In *Popular Music* 9/1 (1990), 97–116.

Pleasants, Henry. *The Great American Popular Singers*. London: Simon & Schuster, 1974.

Poiger, Uta. *Jazz, Rock and Rebels: Cold War Politics and American Culture in a Divided Germany*. Berkeley, CA: University of California Press, 2000.

Poiger, Uta. "Rock 'n' Roll, Female Sexuality, and the Cold War Battle over German Identities." In *The Journal of Modern History* 68/3 (September 1996), 577–616.

Poiger, Uta. "Rock 'n' Roll, Female Sexuality, and the Cold War Battle over German Identities." In *West Germany under Construction: Politics, Society, and Culture in the Adenauer Era*, edited by Robert G. Moeller, 373–412. Ann Arbor, MI: The University of Michigan Press, 1997.

Pratt, Linda Ray. "Elvis, or the Ironies of a Southern Identity." In *The Elvis Reader*, edited by Kevin Quain, 93–103. New York: St. Martin's Press, 1992.

Presley, Priscilla. *Elvis and Me*. New York, NY: G. P. Putnam's Sons, 1985.

Ramet, Sabrina P. "Rock Music in Czechoslovakia." In *Rocking the State: Rock Music and Politics in Eastern Europe and Russia*, edited by Sabrina Ramet, 55–72. Boulder, CO: Westview Press, 1994.

Ramet, Sabrina P. and Crnković, Gordana P. (eds.). *Kazaam! Splat! Ploof! The American Impact on European Popular Culture since 1945*. Lanham, MA: Rowman & Littlefield, 2003.

Rauhut, Michael. *Beat in der Grauzone: DDR-Rock 1964 bis 1972*. Berlin: BasisDruck, 1993.

Reynolds, David. *Rich Relations: The American Occupation of Britain, 1942–1945*. New York, NY: Random House, 1995.

Reynolds, David. "A 'Special' Relationship? America, Britain and the International Order since the Second World War." In *International Affairs* 62/1 (1985), 1–20.

Risch, William J. "Introduction." In *Youth Cultures, Music, and the State in Russia and Eastern Europe*, edited by William J. Risch, 1–24. Lanham, MA: Lexington Books, 2015.

Rodman, Gilbert B. *Elvis after Elvis: The Posthumous Career of a Living Legend*. London and New York, NY: Routledge, 1996.

Romero, Federico. "Cold War Historiography at the Crossroads." In *Cold War History* 14/4 (2014), 685–703.

Rosenberg, Emily S. *Spreading the American Dream: American Economic and Cultural Expansion, 1890–1945*. New York, NY: Hill and Wang, 1982.

Roth, Andreas. *The Ultimate Elvis in Munich Book*. Munich: Self-published, 2004.

Rumpf, Wolfgang. *Pop & Kritik: Medien und Popkultur*. Münster: Lit Verlag, 2004.

Rushing, Wanda. *Memphis and the Paradox of Place: Globalization in the American South*. Chapel Hill, NC: University of North Carolina Press, 2009.

Ryback, Timothy W. *Rock around the Bloc: A History of Rock Music in Eastern Europe and the Soviet Union*. New York, NY and Oxford: Oxford University Press, 1990.

Salisbury, Harrison E. *The Shook-Up Generation*. New York, NY: Harper, 1958.

Saunders, Frances S. *Who Paid the Piper? The CIA and the Cultural Cold War*. London: Granta Books, 1999.

Saunders, Thomas J. *Hollywood in Berlin: American Cinema and Weimar Germany*. Berkeley, CA: University of California Press, 1994.

Schäfers, Anja. *Mehr als Rock 'n' roll: der Radiosender AFN bis Mitte der sechziger Jahre*. Stuttgart: Steiner, 2014.

Scheff, Jerry. *Way Down: Playing Bass with Elvis, Dylan, The Doors, and More*. Milwaukee, WI: Backbeat Books, 2012.

Schildt, Axel. *Moderne Zeiten: Freizeit, Massenmedien und "Zeitgeist" in der Bundesrepublik der 50er Jahre*. Hamburg: Christians Verlag, 1995.

Schildt, Axel and Siegfried, Detlef. "Youth, Consumption, and Politics in the Age of Radical Change." In *Between Marx and Coca-Cola: Youth Cultures in Changing European Societies, 1960-1980*, edited by Axel Schildt and Detlef Siegfried, 1–38. New York, NY and Oxford: Berghahn Books, 2006.

Schilling, Jerry. *Me and A Guy Named Elvis: My Lifelong Friendship with Elvis Presley*. London: Gotham Books, 2006 [2007].

Schulman, Bruce J. *The Seventies: The Great Shift in American Culture, Society, and Politics*. New York: The Free Press, 2001.

Schulman, Bruce J. and Zelizer, Julian E. (eds.). *Rightward Bound: Making America Conservative in the 1970s*. Cambridge, MA: Harvard University Press, 2008.

Schwarz, Hans-Peter. "The Division of Germany, 1945–1949." In *The Cambridge History of the Cold War, Vol. I: Origins*, edited by Melvyn P. Leffler and Odd A. Westad, 133–53. Cambridge: Cambridge University Press, 2010.

Schwarzkopf, Stefan. "Transatlantic Invasions or Common Culture? Modes of Cultural and Economic Exchange between the American and the British Advertising Industries, 1945–2000." In *Anglo-American Media Interactions, 1850–2000*, edited by Joel H. Wiener and Mark Hampton, 254–74. Basingstoke: Palgrave Macmillan, 2007.

Sewlall, Harry. "Elvis Presley in the South African Musical Imaginary." In *Acta Academica* 47/2 (2015), 54–71.

Sewlall, Harry. "'Image Music, Text': Elvis Presley as a Postmodern Semiotic Construct." In *Journal of Literary Studies* 26/2 (2010), 44–57.

Shaw, Tony. *Hollywood's Cold War*. Edinburgh: Edinburgh University Press, 2007.

Shaw, Tony and Youngblood, Denise J. *Cinematic Cold War: The American and Soviet Struggle for Hearts and Minds*. Lawrence, KS: University Press of Kansas, 2010.

Shumway, David. *Rock Star: The Making of Musical Icons from Elvis to Springsteen*. Baltimore, MD: Johns Hopkins University Press, 2005.

Siefert, Marsha. "From Cold War to Wary Peace: American Culture in the USSR and Russia." In *The Americanization of Europe: Culture, Diplomacy, and Anti-Americanism after 1945*, edited by Alexander Stephan, 185–217. New York, NY and Oxford: Berghahn, 2006.

Siegfried, Detlef. *Time Is on My Side: Konsum und Politik in der westdeutschen Jugendkultur der 60er Jahre*. Göttingen: Wallstein, 2006.

Silverman, Jonathan. "A 'Dove with Claws'? Johnny Cash as Radical." In *Journal for the Study of Radicalism* 1/2 (2007), 91–106.

Simpson, Paul. *Elvis Films FAQ: All That's Left to Know about the King of Rock 'n' Roll in Hollywood*. New York, NY: Applause, 2014.

Simpson, Paul. *The Rough Guide to Elvis*. London: Rough Guides, 2002.

Sneeringer, Julia. *A Social History of Early Rock 'n' Roll in Germany: Hamburg from Burlesque to The Beatles, 1956–79*. London: Bloomsbury 2018.

Stabursvik, Sigbjorn and Engvold, Hans Otto. *How RCA Brought Elvis to Europe: The Nordic Elvis Presley Discography 1956–1977*. Oslo: KJ Consulting, 2016.

Tamagne, Florence. "La Nuit de la Nation. Jugendkultur, Rock 'n' Roll und moral panics im Frankreich der sechziger Jahre." In *Popgeschichte, Band 2: Historische Fallstudien 1958–1988*, edited by Bodo Mrozek, Alexa Geisthövel and Jürgen Danyel, 41–54. Bielefeld: transcript Verlag, 2014.

Taylor, William J. Jr. *Elvis in the Army. The King of Rock 'n' Roll as seen by an Officer Who Served with him*. Novato, CA: Presido Press, 1995.

Thompson, Linda. *A Little Thing Called Life: On Loving Elvis Presley, Bruce Jenner, and Songs in Between*. New York; NY: Dey St., 2016.

Toivonen, Timo and Laiho, Antero. "'You Don't Like Crazy Music': The Reception of Elvis Presley in Finland." In *Popular Music and Society* 13 (1989), 1–22.

Tsipursky, Gleb. *Socialist Fun: Youth, Consumption, and State-Sponsored Popular Culture in the Soviet Union*. Pittsburgh, PA: University of Pittsburgh Press, 2016.

Upton, Bryan. *Hollywood and the End of the Cold War: Signs of Cinematic Change*. Lanham, MD: Rowan & Littlefield, 2014.

Viktorin, Carolin, Gienow-Hecht, Jessica, Estner, Annika, and Will, Marcel. "Beyond Marketing and Diplomacy: Exploring the Historical Origins of Nation Branding." In *Nation Branding in Modern History*, edited by Carolin Viktorin, Jessica Gienow-Hecht, Annika Estner, and Marcel Will, 1–26. Oxford: Berghahn, 2018.

Vowinckel, Annette, Payk, Marcus, and Lindenberger, Thomas. "European Cold War Culture(s)? An Introduction." In *Cold War Cultures: Perspectives on Eastern and Western European Societies*, edited by Annette Vowinckel, Marcus Payk, and Thomas Lindenberger, 1–20. Oxford: Berghahn, 2014.

Vuletic, Dean. "Swinging between East and West: Yugoslav Communism and the Dilemmas of Popular Music." In *Youth and Rock in the Soviet Bloc: Youth Culture, Music, and the State in Russia and Eastern Europe*, edited by William Jay Risch, 25–42. Lanham: Lexington Books, 2015.

Wagnleitner Reinhold and May, Elaine Tyler (eds.). *"Here, There and Everywhere": The Foreign Politics of American Popular Culture*. Hanover, NH: University Press of New England, 2000.

Wallis, Hal and Higham, Charles. *Starmaker: The Autobiography of Hal Wallis*. New York: Macmillan, 1980.

Ward, Brian. *Just My Soul Responding: Rhythm and Blues, Black Consciousness, and Race Relations*. Berkeley, CA: University of California Press, 1998.

Weingarten, Marc. *Station to Station: The Secret History of Rock 'n' Roll on Television*. New York, NY: Pocket Books, 2000.

Weinstein, Deena. *Rock'n America: A Social and Cultural History*. Toronto: University of Toronto Press, 2015.

Wensierski, Hans-Jürgen von. "„Die anderen nannten uns Halbstarke" – Jugendsubkultur in den 50er Jahren." In *„Die Elvis-Tolle, die hatte ich mir unauffällig wachsen lassen": Lebensgeschichte und Jugendliche Alltagskultur in den fünfziger Jahren*, edited by Heinz-Hermann Krüger, 103–28. Opladen: Leske und Budrich, 1985.

West, Red, West, Sonny, Hebler, Dave, and Dunleavy, Steve. *Elvis, What Happened?* New York, NY: Ballentine Books, 1977.

Westad, Odd. A. "The Cold War and the International History of the twentieth century." In *The Cambridge History of the Cold War, Vol. I: Origins*, edited by Melvyn P. Leffler and Odd A. Westad, 1–19. Cambridge: Cambridge University Press, 2010.

Whitfield, Stephen J. *The Culture of the Cold War*. Baltimore, MD: Johns Hopkins University Press, 1991.

Wiener, Allen J. *Channeling Elvis: How Television Saved the King of Rock 'n' Roll*. Potomac, MD: Beats & Measures Press, 2014.

Wiener, Jon. *How We Forget the Cold War: A Historical Journey across America*. Berkeley, CA: University of California Press, 2012.

Wilentz, Sean. *Bob Dylan in America*. New York, NY: Anchor Books, 2010 [2011].

Williamson, Joel. *Elvis Presley: A Southern Life*. New York, NY and Oxford: Oxford University Press, 2014.

Wipplinger, Jonathan O. *The Jazz Republic: Music, Race, and American Culture in Weimar Germany*. Ann Arbor, MI: University of Michigan Press, 2017.

Wolle, Stefan. *Der große Plan. Alltag und Herrschaft in der DDR 1949–1961*. Berlin: Ch. Links, 2013.

Wright, Julie Lobalzo. *Crossover Stardom: Popular Male Music Stars in American Cinema*. London: Bloomsbury, 2017.

Zeiler, Thomas W. "Historical Setting: The Age of Fear, Uncertainty, and Doubt." In *Reasserting America in the 1970s: U.S. Public Diplomacy and the Rebuilding of America's Image Abroad*, edited by Hallvard Notaker, Giles Scott-Smith, and David J. Snyder, 9–24. Manchester: University Press, 2016.

Zhuk, Sergei I. *Rock and Roll in the Rocket City: The West, Identity, and Ideology in Soviet Dniepropetrovsk, 1960–1985*. Baltimore: Johns Hopkins University Press, 2010.

Zoglin, Richard. *Elvis in Vegas: How the King Reinvented the Las Vegas Show*. New York, NY: Simon & Schuster, 2019.

Zolov, Eric. *Refried Elvis: The Rise of the Mexican Counterculture*. Berkeley, CA: University of California Press, 1999.

# INDEX